TRANSFORMERS G.I. JOE

FIRST STRIKE

CHAMPIONS

G.I. JOE

MASK
MOBILE ARMORED STRIKE KOMMAND

ROM

MICRONAUTS

TRANSFORMERS

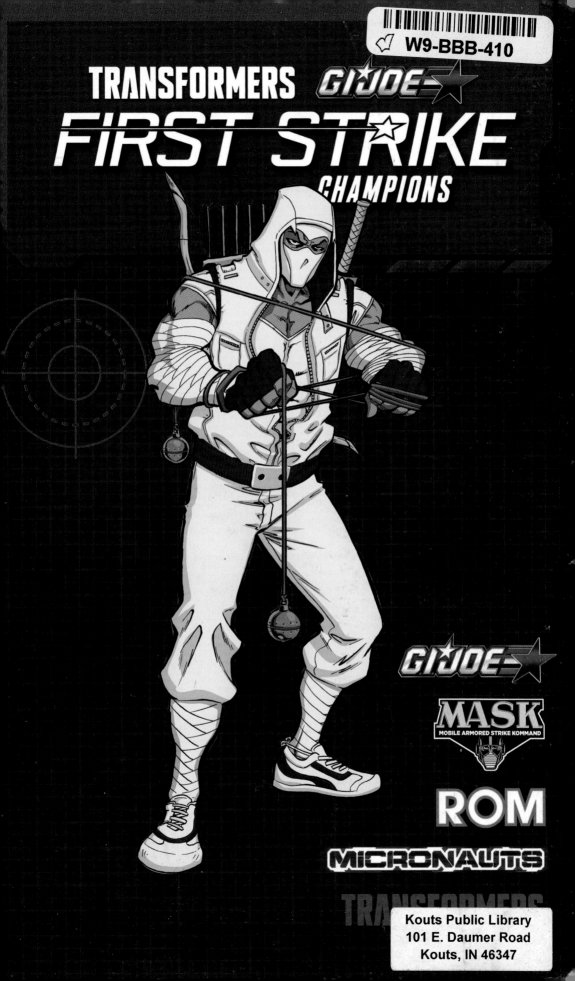

Become our fan on Facebook **facebook.com/idwpublishing**
Follow us on Twitter **@idwpublishing**
Subscribe to us on YouTube **youtube.com/idwpublishing**
See what's new on Tumblr **tumblr.idwpublishing.com**
Check us out on Instagram **instagram.com/idwpublishing**

COVER ART BY
SARA PITRE-DUROCHER

COLLECTION EDITS BY
JUSTIN EISINGER
AND ALONZO SIMON

COLLECTION DESIGN BY
GILBERTO LAZCANO

PUBLISHER
GREG GOLDSTEIN

Licensed By:

Special thanks to
Ben Montano, David Erwin,
Josh Feldman, Ed Lane,
Beth Artale, Derryl DePriest,
and Michael Kelly for their
invaluable assistance.

ISBN: 978-1-68405-123-6   21 20 19 18   1 2 3 4

Originally published as G.I. JOE FIRST STRIKE, M.A.S.K. FIRST STRIKE, MICRONAUTS FIRST STRIKE, OPTIMUS PRIME FIRST STRIKE, ROM FIRST STRIKE, and TRANSFORMERS FIRST STRIKE.

Greg Goldstein, President & Publisher
Robbie Robbins, EVP/Sr. Graphic Artist
Chris Ryall, Chief Creative Officer & Editor-in-Chief
David Hedgecock, Associate Publisher
Laurie Windrow, Sr. VP of Sales & Marketing
Matthew Ruzicka, CPA, Chief Financial Officer
Lorelei Bunjes, VP of Digital Services
Eric Moss, Sr. Director, Licensing & Business Development
Ted Adams, Founder & CEO of IDW Media Holdings

For international rights, please contact
licensing@idwpublishing.com

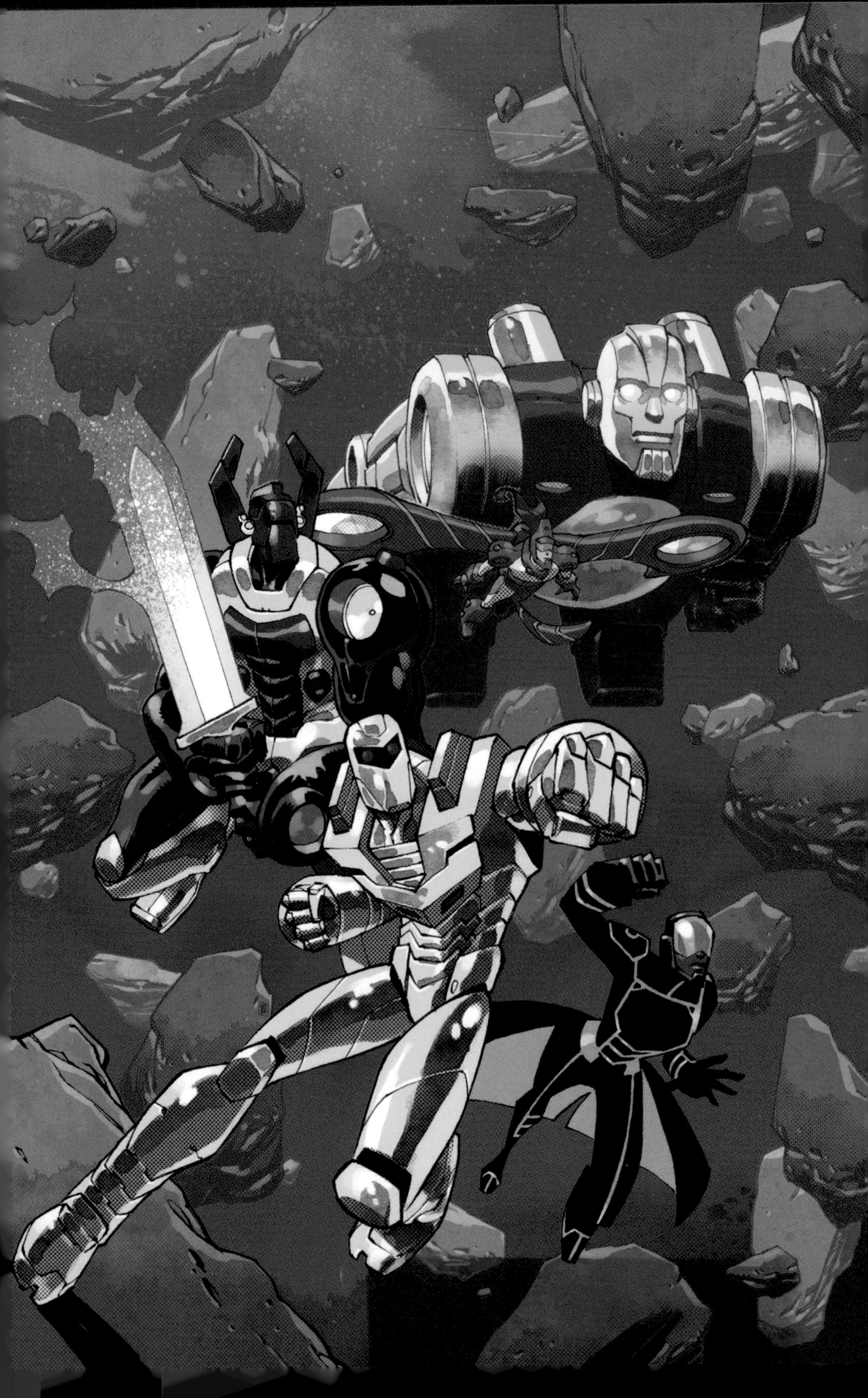

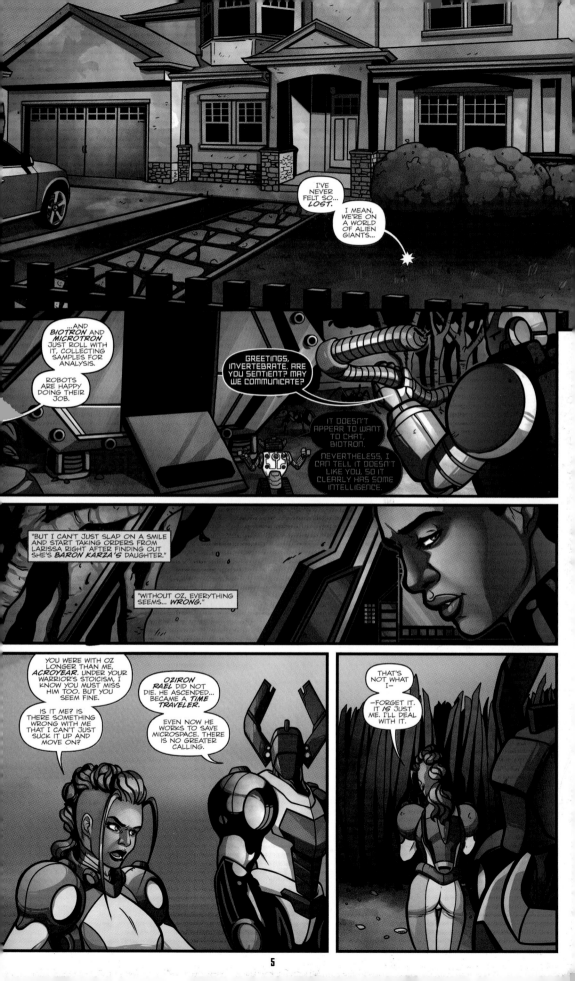

I'VE NEVER FELT SO... *LOST.*

I MEAN, WE'RE ON A WORLD OF ALIEN GIANTS...

...AND *BIOTRON* AND *MICROTRON* JUST ROLL WITH IT, COLLECTING SAMPLES FOR ANALYSIS.

ROBOTS ARE HAPPY DOING THEIR JOB.

GREETINGS, INVERTEBRATE. ARE YOU SENTIENT? MAY WE COMMUNICATE?

IT DOESN'T APPEAR TO WANT TO CHAT, BIOTRON.

NEVERTHELESS, I CAN TELL IT DOESN'T LIKE YOU, SO IT CLEARLY HAS SOME INTELLIGENCE.

"BUT I CAN'T JUST SLAP ON A SMILE AND START TAKING ORDERS FROM LARISSA RIGHT AFTER FINDING OUT SHE'S *BARON KARZA'S* DAUGHTER."

"WITHOUT OZ, EVERYTHING SEEMS... *WRONG.*"

YOU WERE WITH OZ LONGER THAN ME, *ACROYEAR.* UNDER YOUR WARRIOR'S STOICISM, I KNOW YOU MUST MISS HIM TOO. BUT YOU SEEM FINE.

IS IT ME? IS THERE SOMETHING WRONG WITH ME THAT I CAN'T JUST SUCK IT UP AND MOVE ON?

OZIRON RAEL DID NOT DIE. HE ASCENDED... BECAME A *TIME TRAVELER.*

EVEN NOW HE WORKS TO SAVE MICROSPACE. THERE IS NO GREATER CALLING.

THAT'S NOT WHAT I—

—FORGET IT. IT *IS* JUST ME. I'LL DEAL WITH IT.

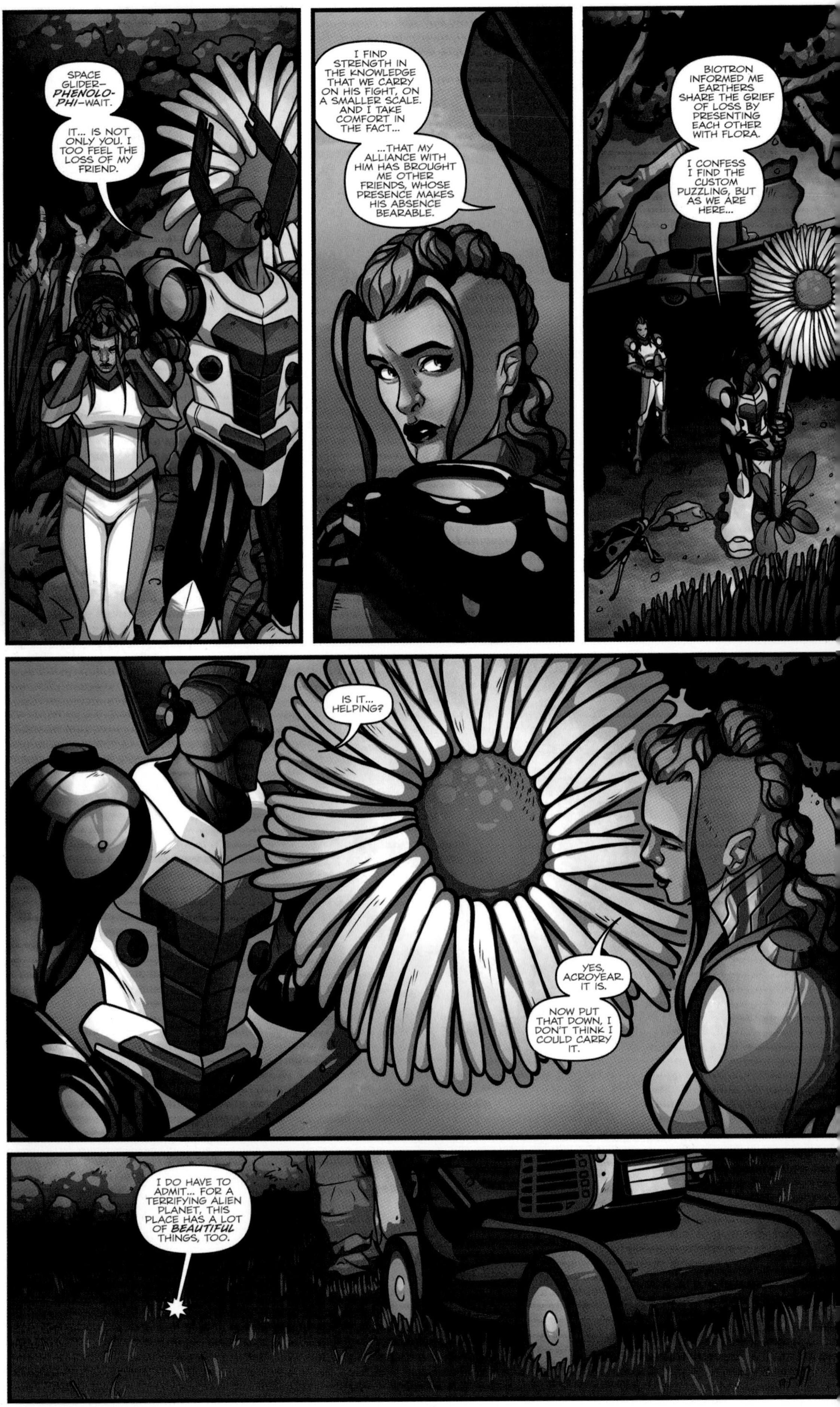
SPACE GLIDER-*PHENOLO-PHI*-WAIT.
IT... IS NOT ONLY YOU. I TOO FEEL THE LOSS OF MY FRIEND.
I FIND STRENGTH IN THE KNOWLEDGE THAT WE CARRY ON HIS FIGHT, ON A SMALLER SCALE. AND I TAKE COMFORT IN THE FACT...
...THAT MY ALLIANCE WITH HIM HAS BROUGHT ME OTHER FRIENDS, WHOSE PRESENCE MAKES HIS ABSENCE BEARABLE.
BIOTRON INFORMED ME EARTHERS SHARE THE GRIEF OF LOSS BY PRESENTING EACH OTHER WITH FLORA.
I CONFESS I FIND THE CUSTOM PUZZLING, BUT AS WE ARE HERE...
IS IT... HELPING?
YES, ACROYEAR. IT IS.
NOW PUT THAT DOWN, I DON'T THINK I COULD CARRY IT.
I DO HAVE TO ADMIT... FOR A TERRIFYING ALIEN PLANET, THIS PLACE HAS A LOT OF *BEAUTIFUL* THINGS, TOO.

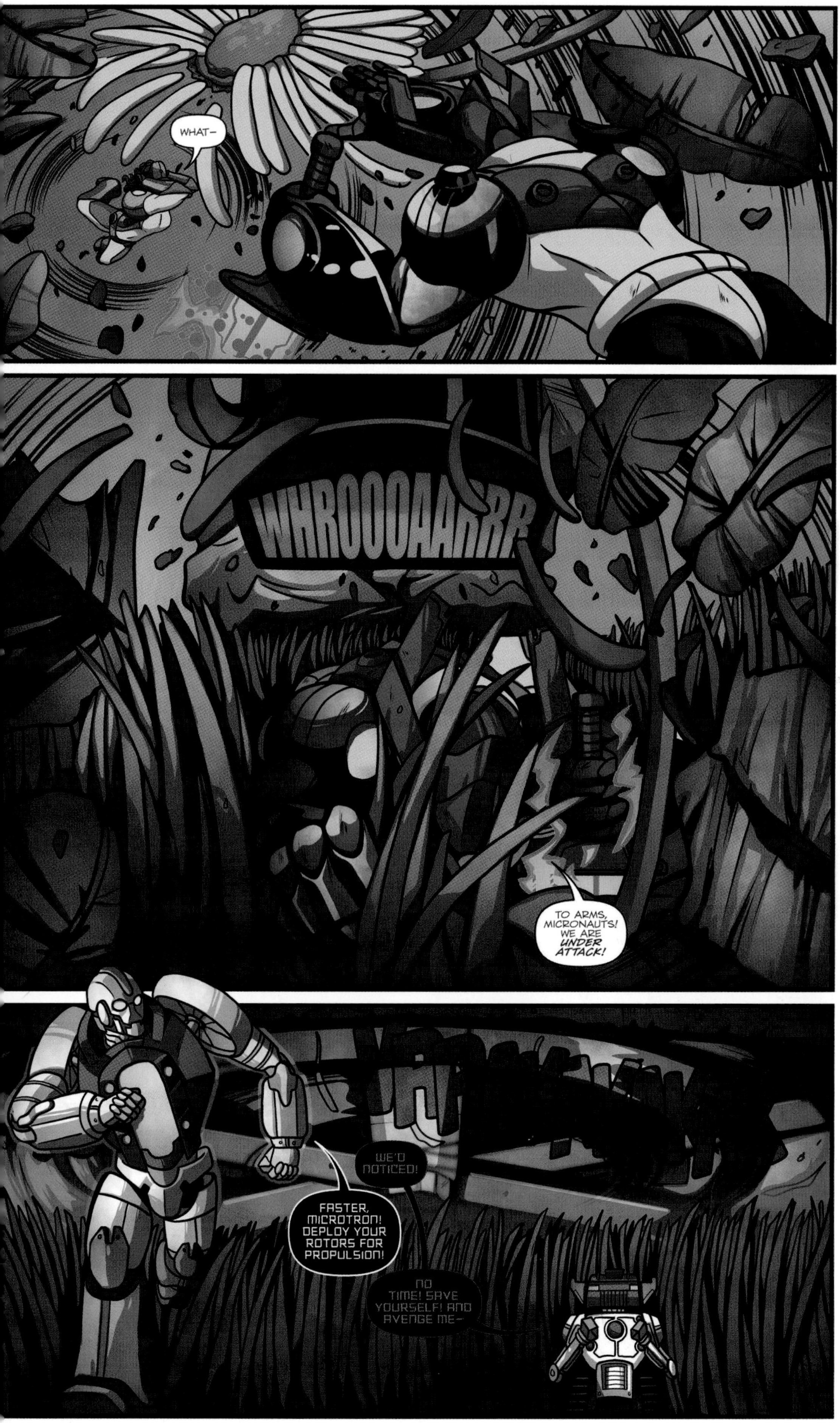
WHAT–
WHROOOAARRR
TO ARMS, MICRONAUTS! WE ARE UNDER ATTACK!
WE'D NOTICED!
FASTER, MICROTRON! DEPLOY YOUR ROTORS FOR PROPULSION!
NO TIME! SAVE YOURSELF! AND AVENGE ME–

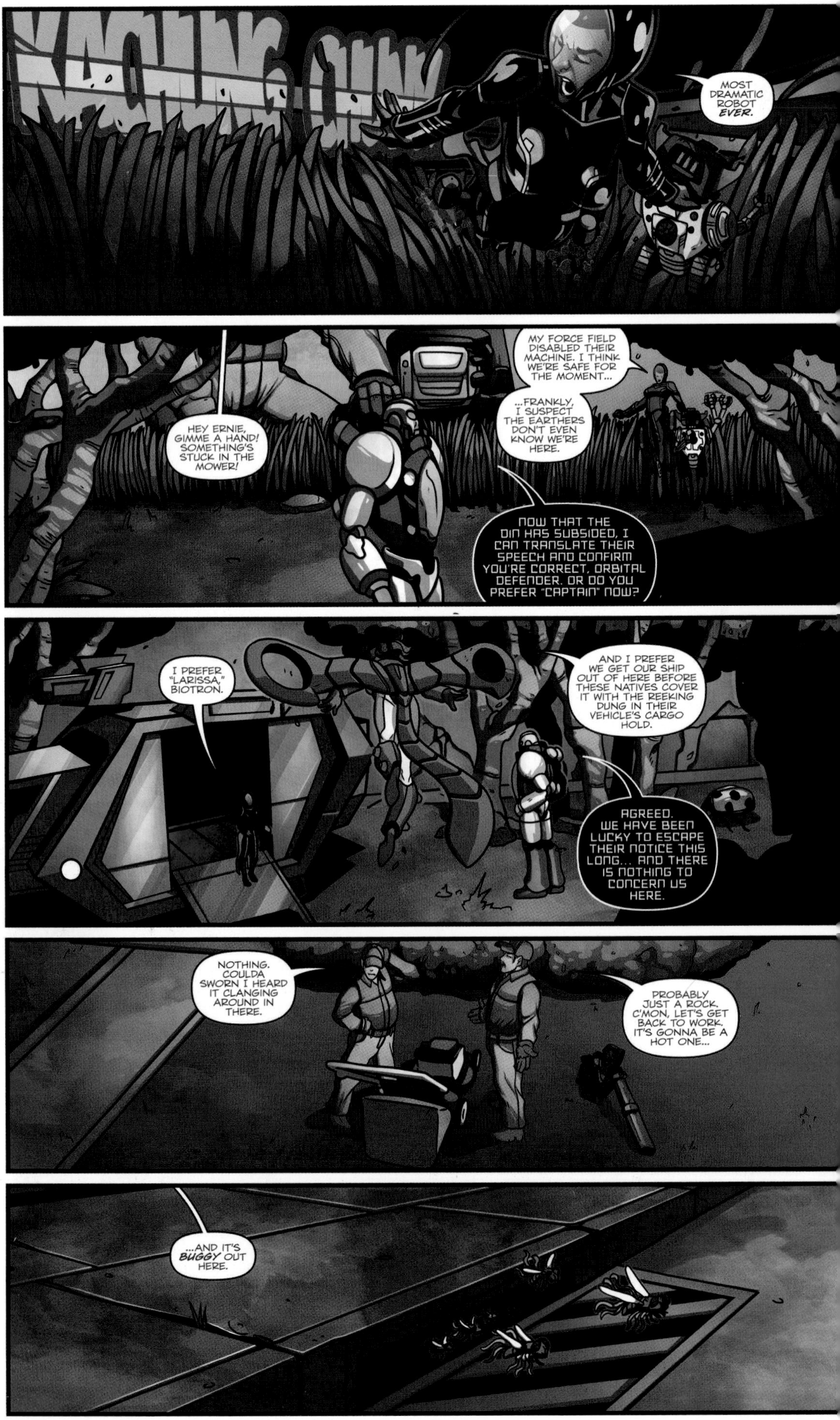
MOST DRAMATIC ROBOT *EVER.*
HEY ERNIE, GIMME A HAND! SOMETHING'S STUCK IN THE MOWER!
MY FORCE FIELD DISABLED THEIR MACHINE. I THINK WE'RE SAFE FOR THE MOMENT...
...FRANKLY, I SUSPECT THE EARTHERS DON'T EVEN KNOW WE'RE HERE.
NOW THAT THE DIN HAS SUBSIDED, I CAN TRANSLATE THEIR SPEECH AND CONFIRM YOU'RE CORRECT, ORBITAL DEFENDER. OR DO YOU PREFER "CAPTAIN" NOW?
I PREFER "LARISSA," BIOTRON.
AND I PREFER WE GET OUR SHIP OUT OF HERE BEFORE THESE NATIVES COVER IT WITH THE REEKING DUNG IN THEIR VEHICLE'S CARGO HOLD.
AGREED. WE HAVE BEEN LUCKY TO ESCAPE THEIR NOTICE THIS LONG... AND THERE IS NOTHING TO CONCERN US HERE.
NOTHING. COULDA SWORN I HEARD IT CLANGING AROUND IN THERE.
PROBABLY JUST A ROCK. C'MON, LET'S GET BACK TO WORK. IT'S GONNA BE A HOT ONE...
...AND IT'S *BUGGY* OUT HERE.

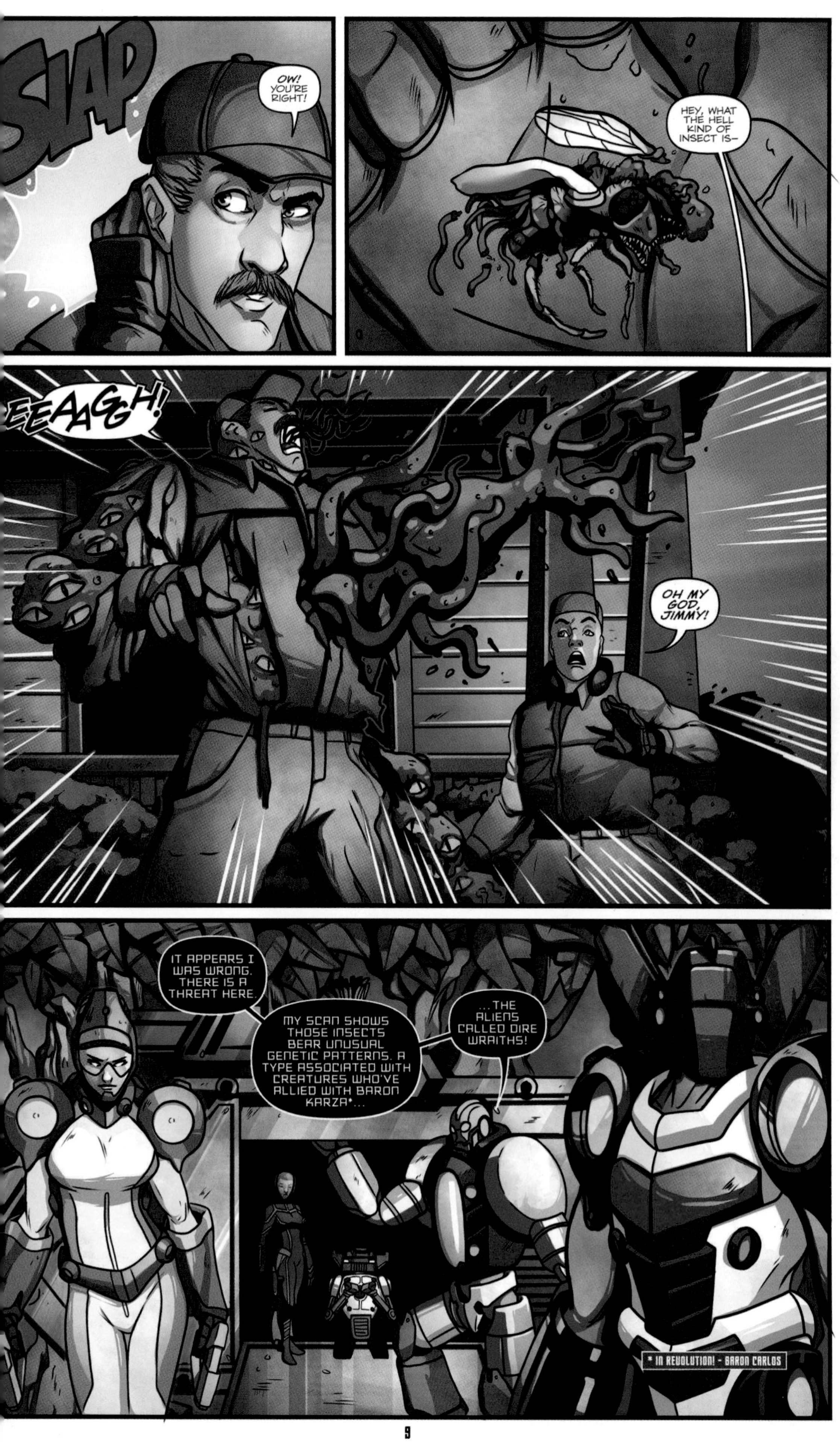
SLAP
OW! YOU'RE RIGHT!
HEY, WHAT THE HELL KIND OF INSECT IS—
EEAAAGGH!
OH MY GOD, JIMMY!
IT APPEARS I WAS WRONG. THERE IS A THREAT HERE.
MY SCAN SHOWS THOSE INSECTS BEAR UNUSUAL GENETIC PATTERNS. A TYPE ASSOCIATED WITH CREATURES WHO'VE ALLIED WITH BARON KARZA*...
...THE ALIENS CALLED DIRE WRAITHS!
* IN REVOLUTION! - BARON CARLOS

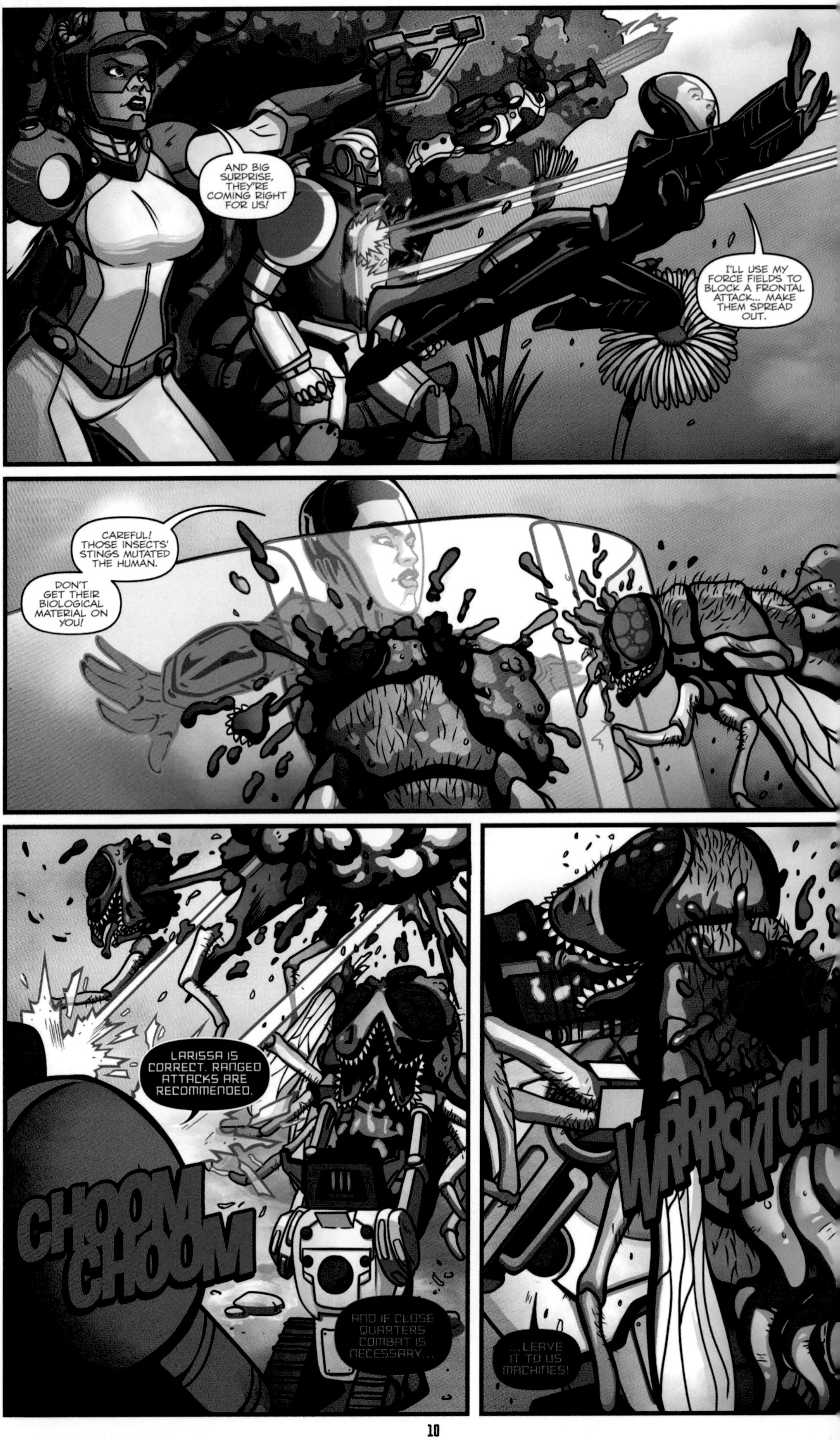
AND BIG SURPRISE, THEY'RE COMING RIGHT FOR US!
I'LL USE MY FORCE FIELDS TO BLOCK A FRONTAL ATTACK... MAKE THEM SPREAD OUT.
CAREFUL! THOSE INSECTS' STINGS MUTATED THE HUMAN.
DON'T GET THEIR BIOLOGICAL MATERIAL ON YOU!
LARISSA IS CORRECT. RANGED ATTACKS ARE RECOMMENDED.
CHOOM CHOOM
AND IF CLOSE QUARTERS COMBAT IS NECESSARY...
WRRRSKTCH
...LEAVE IT TO US MACHINES!

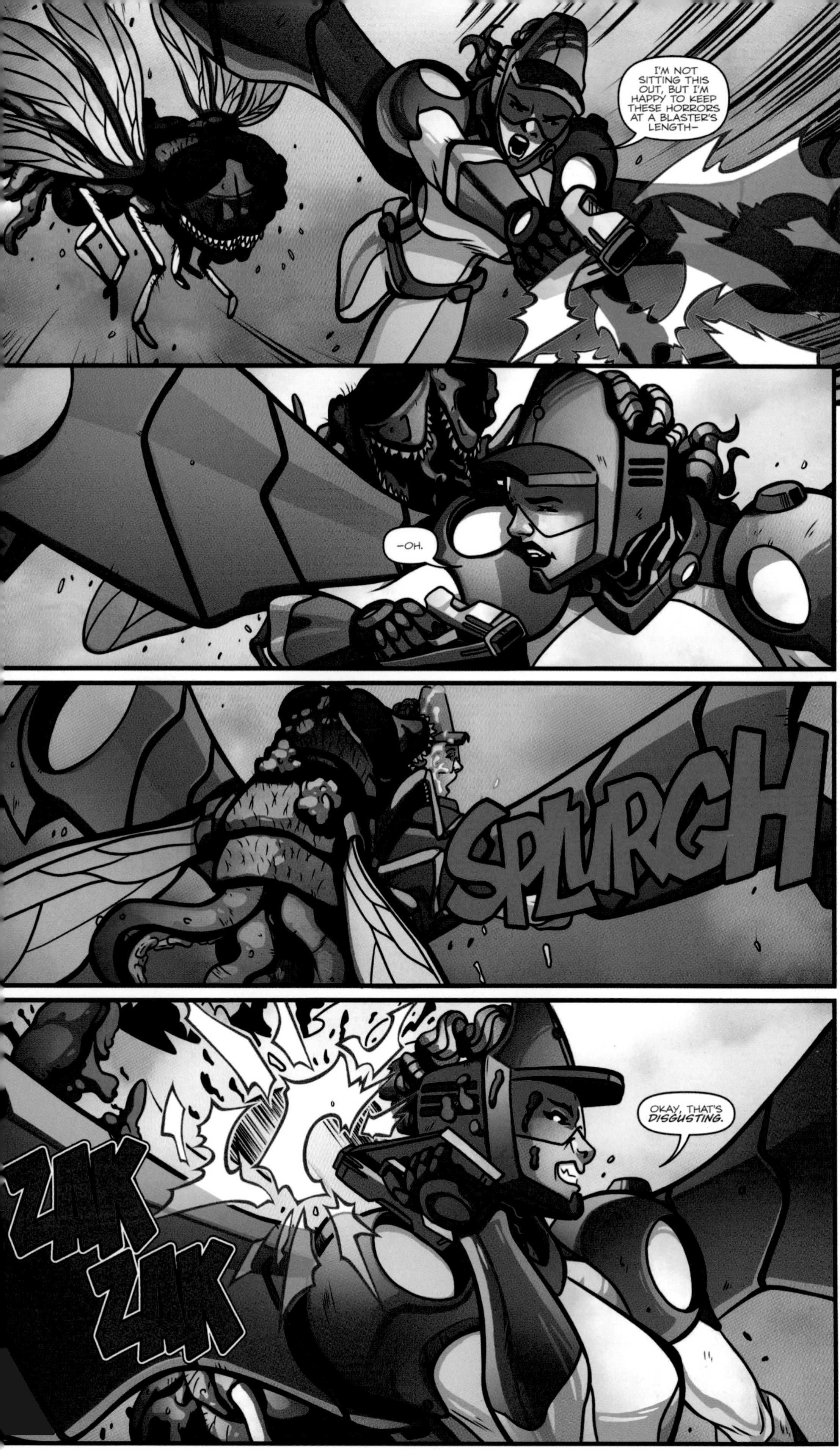
I'M NOT SITTING THIS OUT, BUT I'M HAPPY TO KEEP THESE HORRORS AT A BLASTER'S LENGTH–
–OH.
SPLURGH
OKAY, THAT'S *DISGUSTING.*
ZAK ZAK

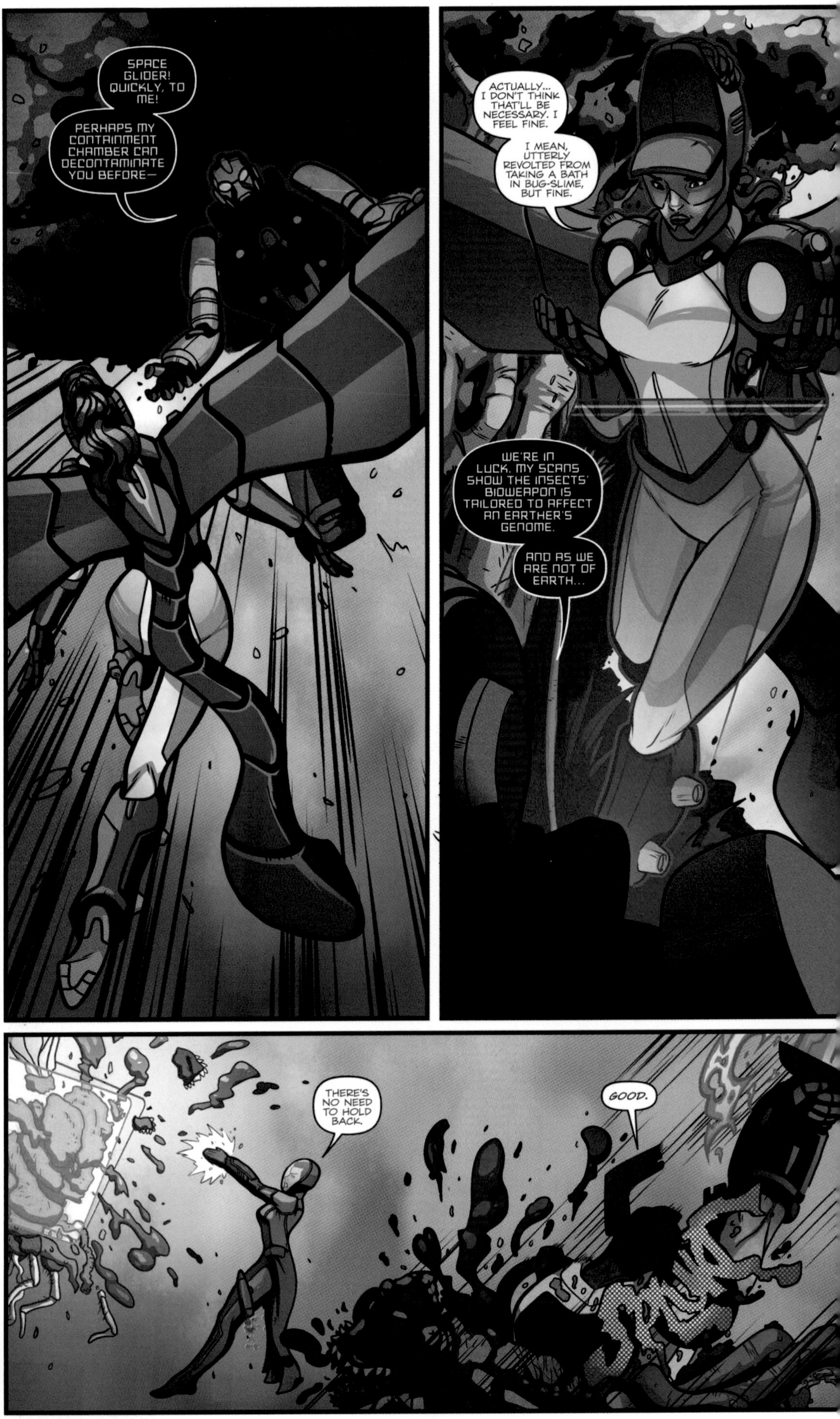
SPACE GLIDER! QUICKLY, TO ME!
PERHAPS MY CONTAINMENT CHAMBER CAN DECONTAMINATE YOU BEFORE—
ACTUALLY... I DON'T THINK THAT'LL BE NECESSARY. I FEEL FINE.
I MEAN, UTTERLY REVOLTED FROM TAKING A BATH IN BUG-SLIME, BUT FINE.
WE'RE IN LUCK. MY SCANS SHOW THE INSECTS' BIOWEAPON IS TAILORED TO AFFECT AN EARTHER'S GENOME.
AND AS WE ARE NOT OF EARTH...
THERE'S NO NEED TO HOLD BACK.
GOOD.

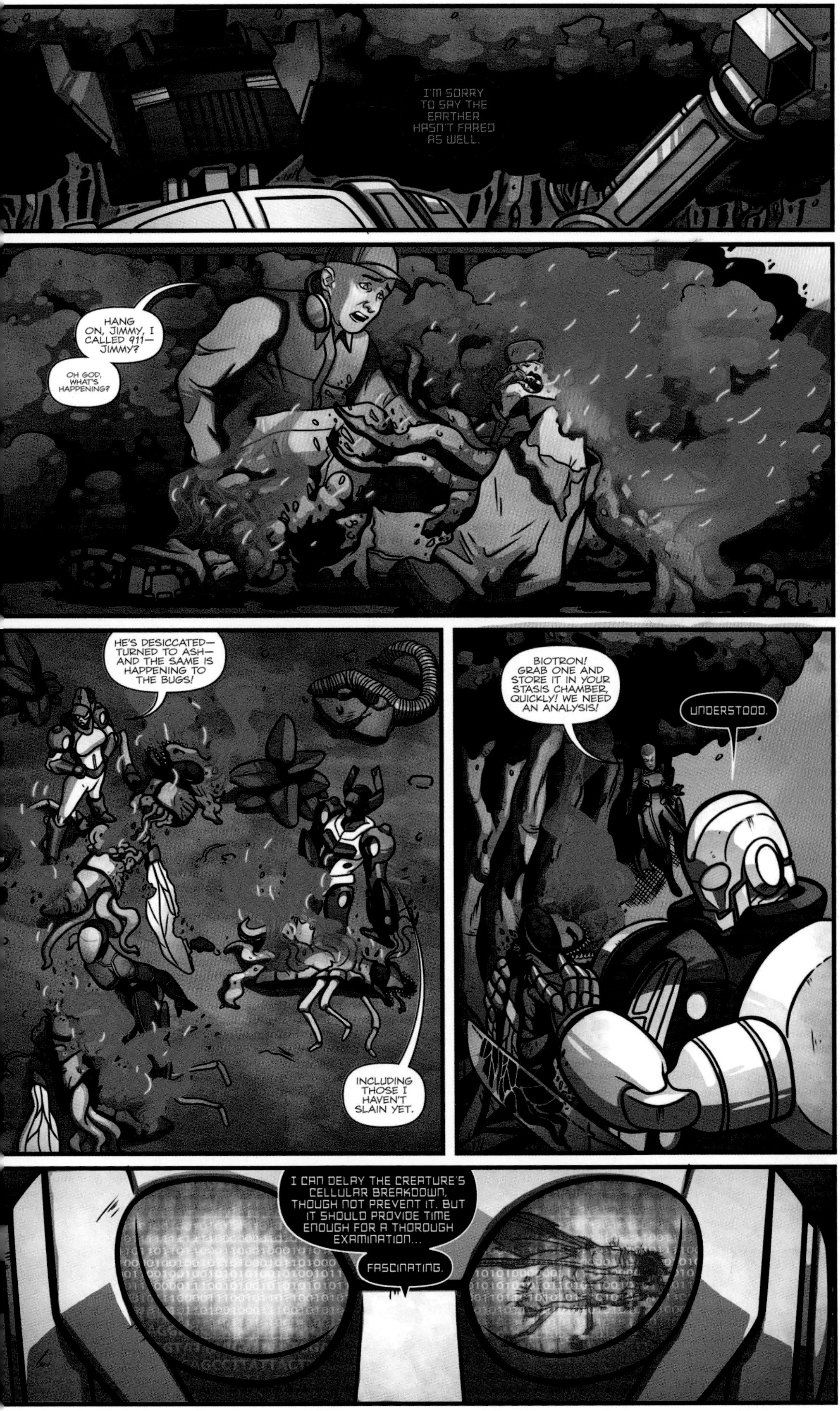
I'M SORRY TO SAY THE EARTHER HASN'T FARED AS WELL.
HANG ON, JIMMY, I CALLED 911— JIMMY?
OH GOD, WHAT'S HAPPENING?
HE'S DESICCATED— TURNED TO ASH— AND THE SAME IS HAPPENING TO THE BUGS!
INCLUDING THOSE I HAVEN'T SLAIN YET.
BIOTRON! GRAB ONE AND STORE IT IN YOUR STASIS CHAMBER, QUICKLY! WE NEED AN ANALYSIS!
UNDERSTOOD.
I CAN DELAY THE CREATURE'S CELLULAR BREAKDOWN, THOUGH NOT PREVENT IT. BUT IT SHOULD PROVIDE TIME ENOUGH FOR A THOROUGH EXAMINATION...
FASCINATING.

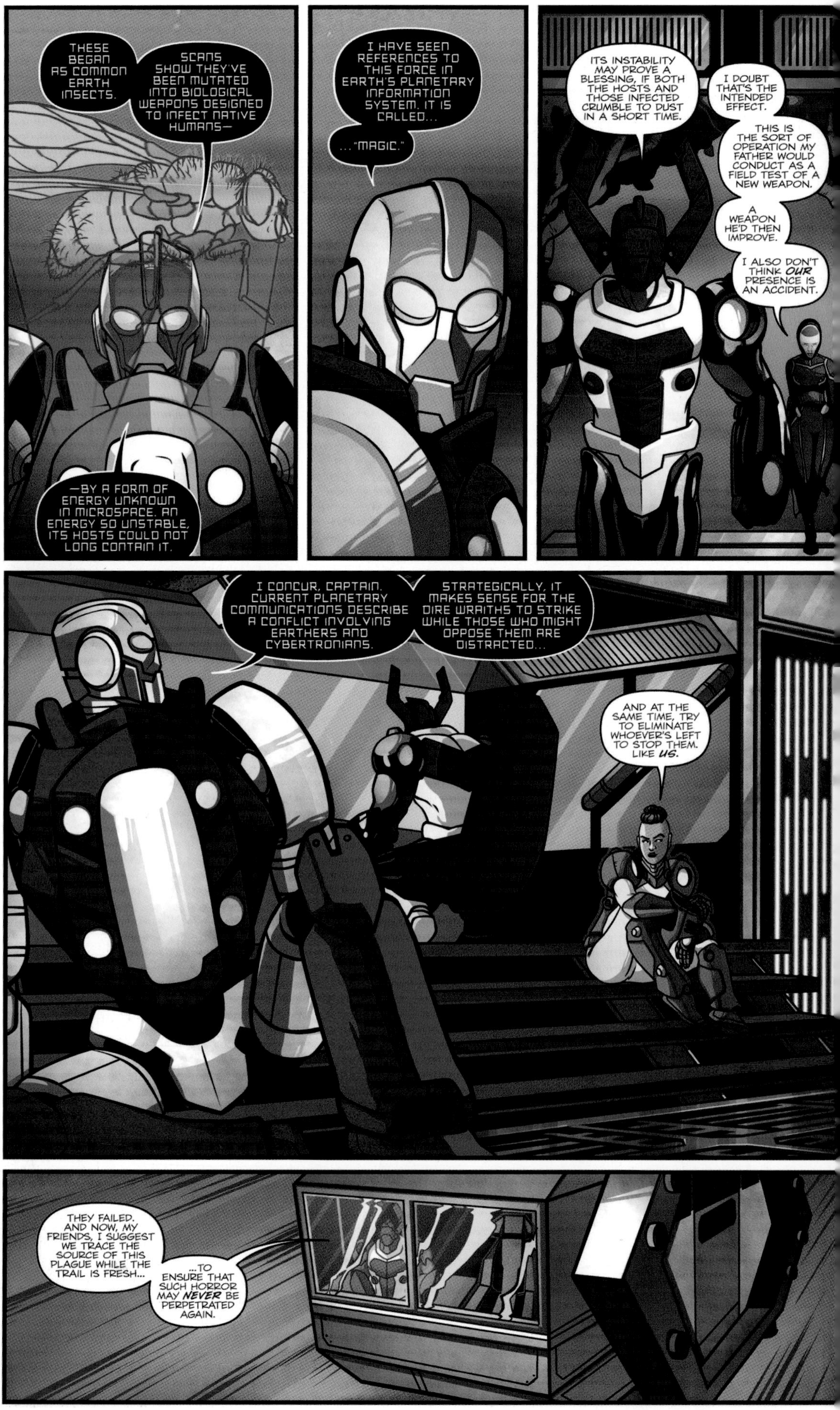
THESE BEGAN AS COMMON EARTH INSECTS.
SCANS SHOW THEY'VE BEEN MUTATED INTO BIOLOGICAL WEAPONS DESIGNED TO INFECT NATIVE HUMANS—
—BY A FORM OF ENERGY UNKNOWN IN MICROSPACE. AN ENERGY SO UNSTABLE, ITS HOSTS COULD NOT LONG CONTAIN IT.
I HAVE SEEN REFERENCES TO THIS FORCE IN EARTH'S PLANETARY INFORMATION SYSTEM. IT IS CALLED...
..."MAGIC."
ITS INSTABILITY MAY PROVE A BLESSING, IF BOTH THE HOSTS AND THOSE INFECTED CRUMBLE TO DUST IN A SHORT TIME.
I DOUBT THAT'S THE INTENDED EFFECT.
THIS IS THE SORT OF OPERATION MY FATHER WOULD CONDUCT AS A FIELD TEST OF A NEW WEAPON.
A WEAPON HE'D THEN IMPROVE.
I ALSO DON'T THINK *OUR* PRESENCE IS AN ACCIDENT.
I CONCUR, CAPTAIN. CURRENT PLANETARY COMMUNICATIONS DESCRIBE A CONFLICT INVOLVING EARTHERS AND CYBERTRONIANS.
STRATEGICALLY, IT MAKES SENSE FOR THE DIRE WRAITHS TO STRIKE WHILE THOSE WHO MIGHT OPPOSE THEM ARE DISTRACTED...
AND AT THE SAME TIME, TRY TO ELIMINATE WHOEVER'S LEFT TO STOP THEM. LIKE *US*.
THEY FAILED. AND NOW, MY FRIENDS, I SUGGEST WE TRACE THE SOURCE OF THIS PLAGUE WHILE THE TRAIL IS FRESH...
...TO ENSURE THAT SUCH HORROR MAY *NEVER* BE PERPETRATED AGAIN.

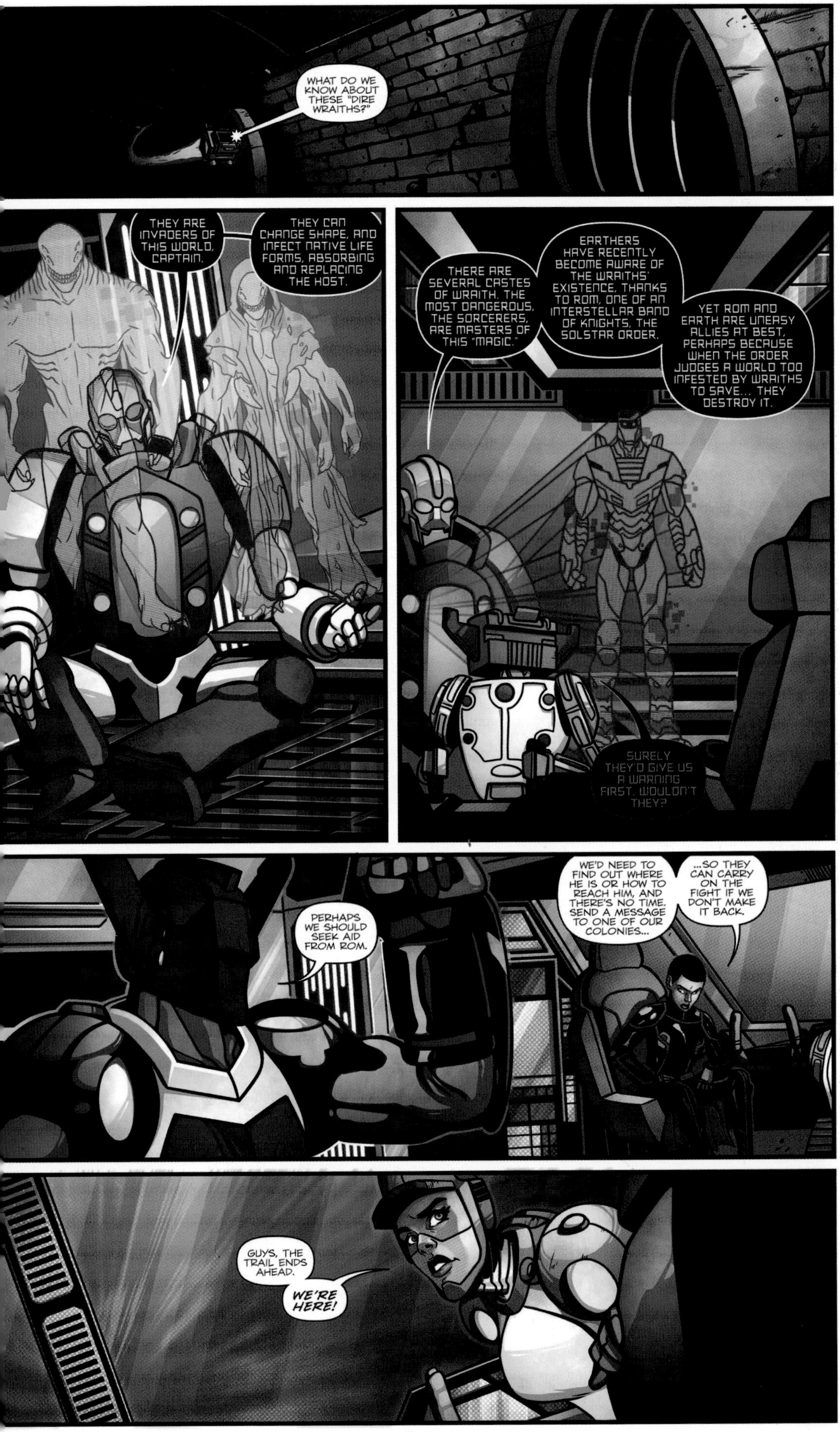
WHAT DO WE KNOW ABOUT THESE "DIRE WRAITHS?"
THEY ARE INVADERS OF THIS WORLD, CAPTAIN.
THEY CAN CHANGE SHAPE, AND INFECT NATIVE LIFE FORMS, ABSORBING AND REPLACING THE HOST.
THERE ARE SEVERAL CASTES OF WRAITH. THE MOST DANGEROUS, THE SORCERERS, ARE MASTERS OF THIS "MAGIC."
EARTHERS HAVE RECENTLY BECOME AWARE OF THE WRAITHS' EXISTENCE, THANKS TO ROM, ONE OF AN INTERSTELLAR BAND OF KNIGHTS, THE SOLSTAR ORDER.
YET ROM AND EARTH ARE UNEASY ALLIES AT BEST, PERHAPS BECAUSE WHEN THE ORDER JUDGES A WORLD TOO INFESTED BY WRAITHS TO SAVE... THEY DESTROY IT.
SURELY THEY'D GIVE US A WARNING FIRST. WOULDN'T THEY?
PERHAPS WE SHOULD SEEK AID FROM ROM.
WE'D NEED TO FIND OUT WHERE HE IS OR HOW TO REACH HIM, AND THERE'S NO TIME. SEND A MESSAGE TO ONE OF OUR COLONIES...
...SO THEY CAN CARRY ON THE FIGHT IF WE DON'T MAKE IT BACK.
GUYS, THE TRAIL ENDS AHEAD.
WE'RE HERE!

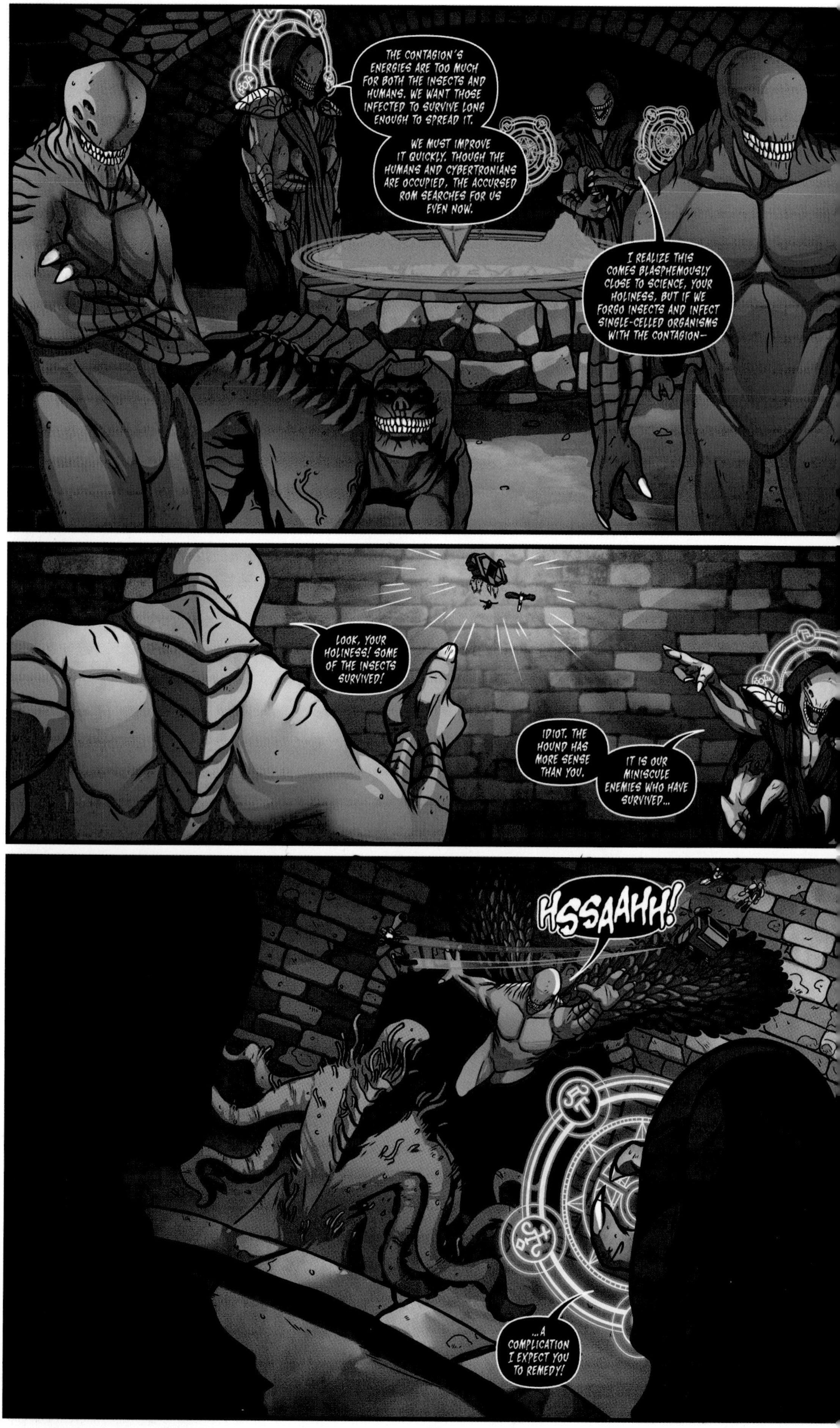
THE CONTAGION'S ENERGIES ARE TOO MUCH FOR BOTH THE INSECTS AND HUMANS. WE WANT THOSE INFECTED TO SURVIVE LONG ENOUGH TO SPREAD IT.
WE MUST IMPROVE IT QUICKLY. THOUGH THE HUMANS AND CYBERTRONIANS ARE OCCUPIED, THE ACCURSED ROM SEARCHES FOR US EVEN NOW.
I REALIZE THIS COMES BLASPHEMOUSLY CLOSE TO SCIENCE, YOUR HOLINESS, BUT IF WE FORGO INSECTS AND INFECT SINGLE-CELLED ORGANISMS WITH THE CONTAGION—
LOOK, YOUR HOLINESS! SOME OF THE INSECTS SURVIVED!
IDIOT. THE HOUND HAS MORE SENSE THAN YOU.
IT IS OUR MINISCULE ENEMIES WHO HAVE SURVIVED...
HSSAAHH!
...A COMPLICATION I EXPECT YOU TO REMEDY!

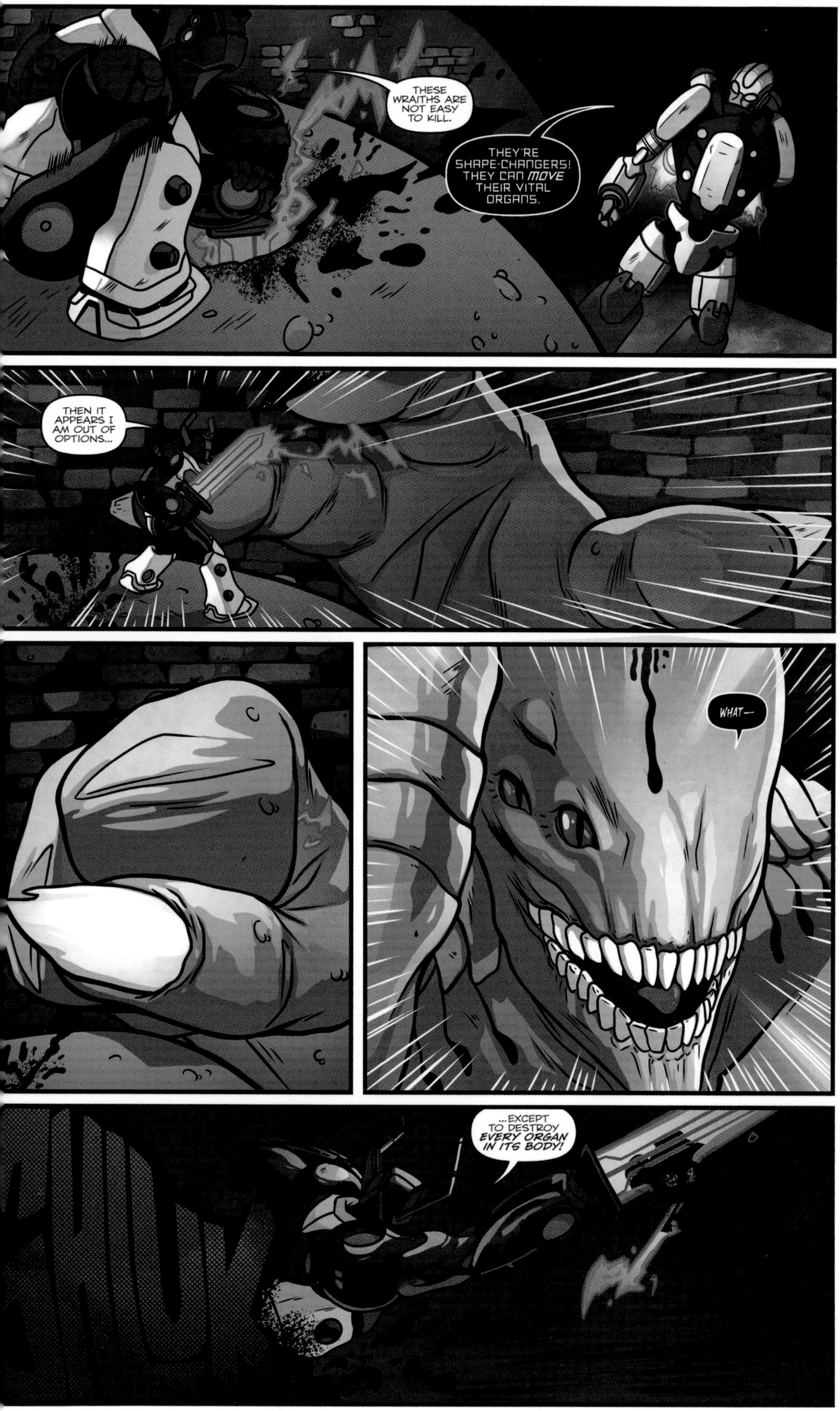
THESE WRAITHS ARE NOT EASY TO KILL.
THEY'RE SHAPE-CHANGERS! THEY CAN MOVE THEIR VITAL ORGANS.
THEN IT APPEARS I AM OUT OF OPTIONS...
WHAT—
...EXCEPT TO DESTROY EVERY ORGAN IN ITS BODY!

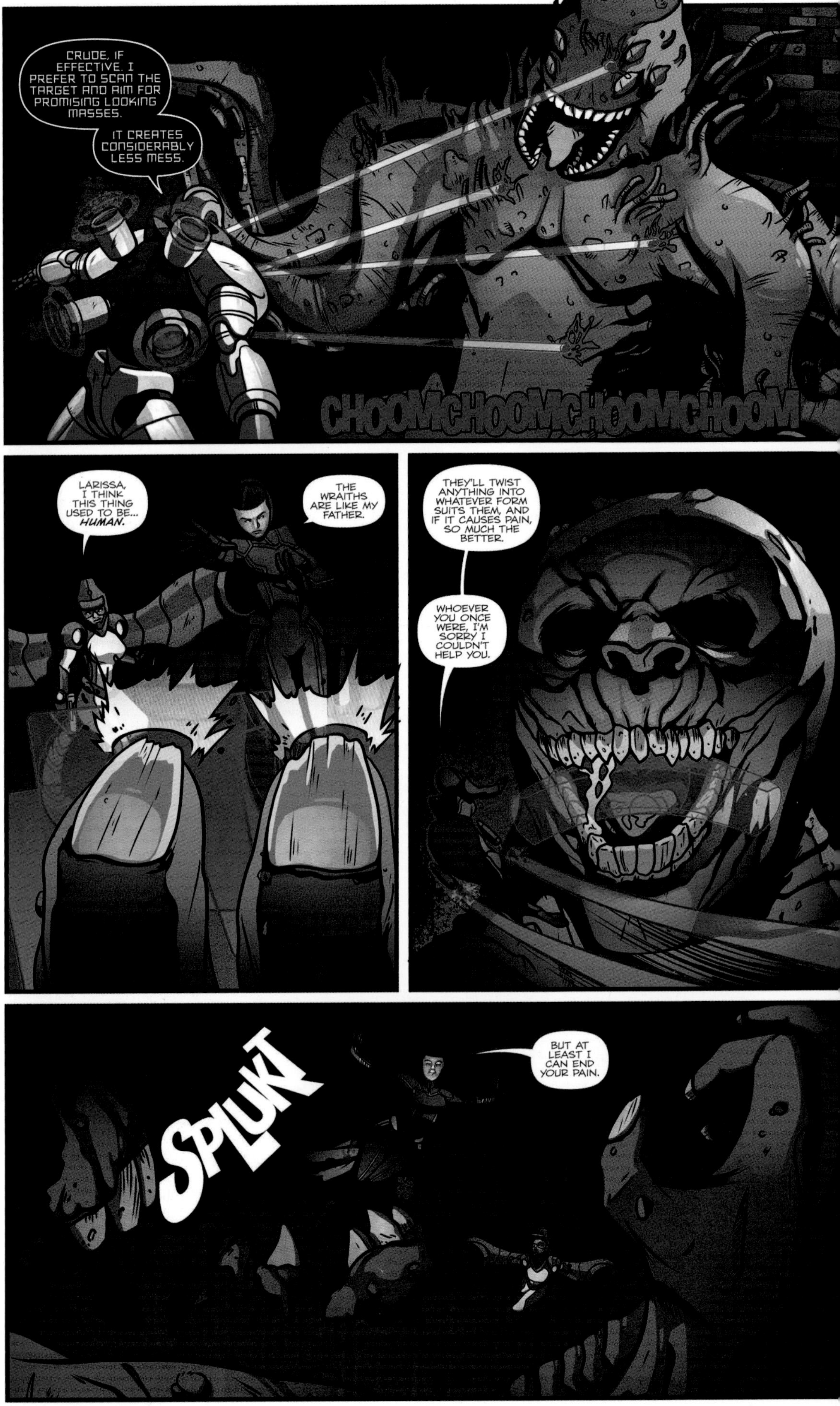
CRUDE, IF EFFECTIVE. I PREFER TO SCAN THE TARGET AND AIM FOR PROMISING LOOKING MASSES.
IT CREATES CONSIDERABLY LESS MESS.
CHOOMCHOOMCHOOMCHOOM
LARISSA, I THINK THIS THING USED TO BE... HUMAN.
THE WRAITHS ARE LIKE MY FATHER.
THEY'LL TWIST ANYTHING INTO WHATEVER FORM SUITS THEM, AND IF IT CAUSES PAIN, SO MUCH THE BETTER.
WHOEVER YOU ONCE WERE, I'M SORRY I COULDN'T HELP YOU.
SPLUKT
BUT AT LEAST I CAN END YOUR PAIN.

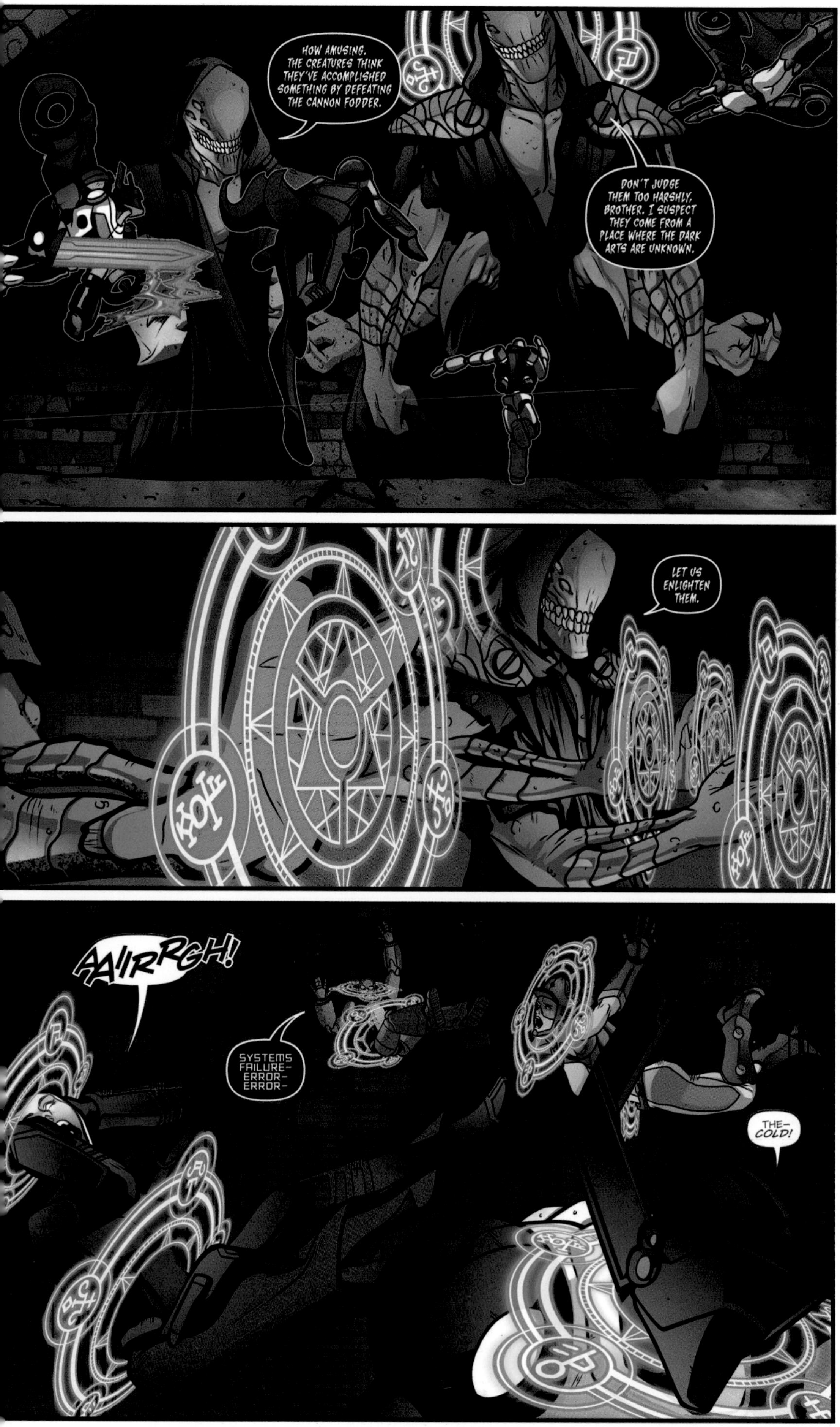
HOW AMUSING. THE CREATURES THINK THEY'VE ACCOMPLISHED SOMETHING BY DEFEATING THE CANNON FODDER.
DON'T JUDGE THEM TOO HARSHLY, BROTHER. I SUSPECT THEY COME FROM A PLACE WHERE THE DARK ARTS ARE UNKNOWN.
LET US ENLIGHTEN THEM.
AAIIRRGH!
SYSTEMS FAILURE- ERROR- ERROR-
THE- COLD!

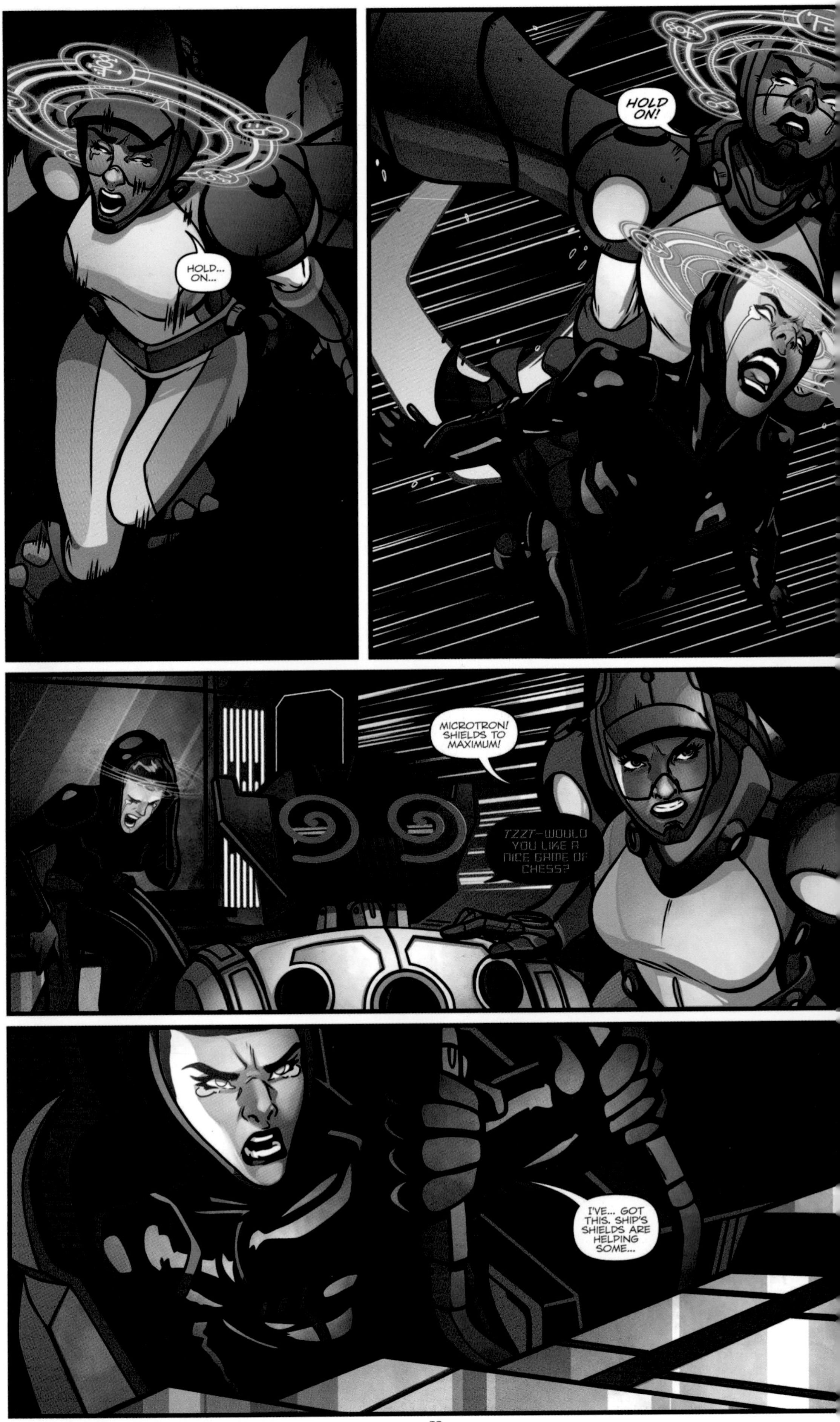
HOLD... ON...
HOLD ON!
MICROTRON! SHIELDS TO MAXIMUM!
TZZT—WOULD YOU LIKE A NICE GAME OF CHESS?
I'VE... GOT THIS. SHIP'S SHIELDS ARE HELPING SOME...

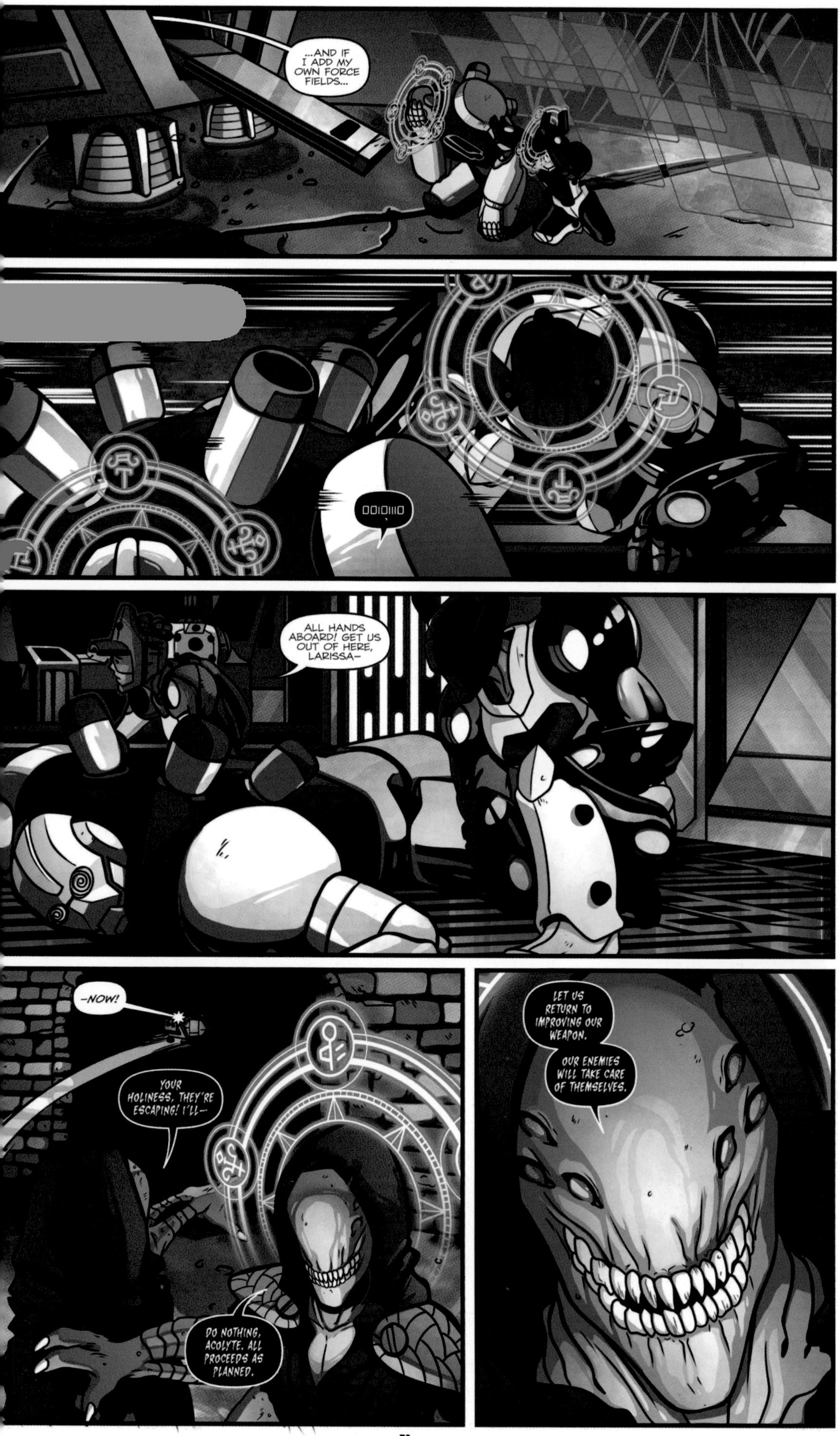
...AND IF I ADD MY OWN FORCE FIELDS...
00101110
ALL HANDS ABOARD! GET US OUT OF HERE, LARISSA-
-NOW!
YOUR HOLINESS, THEY'RE ESCAPING! I'LL-
DO NOTHING, ACOLYTE. ALL PROCEEDS AS PLANNED.
LET US RETURN TO IMPROVING OUR WEAPON.
OUR ENEMIES WILL TAKE CARE OF THEMSELVES.

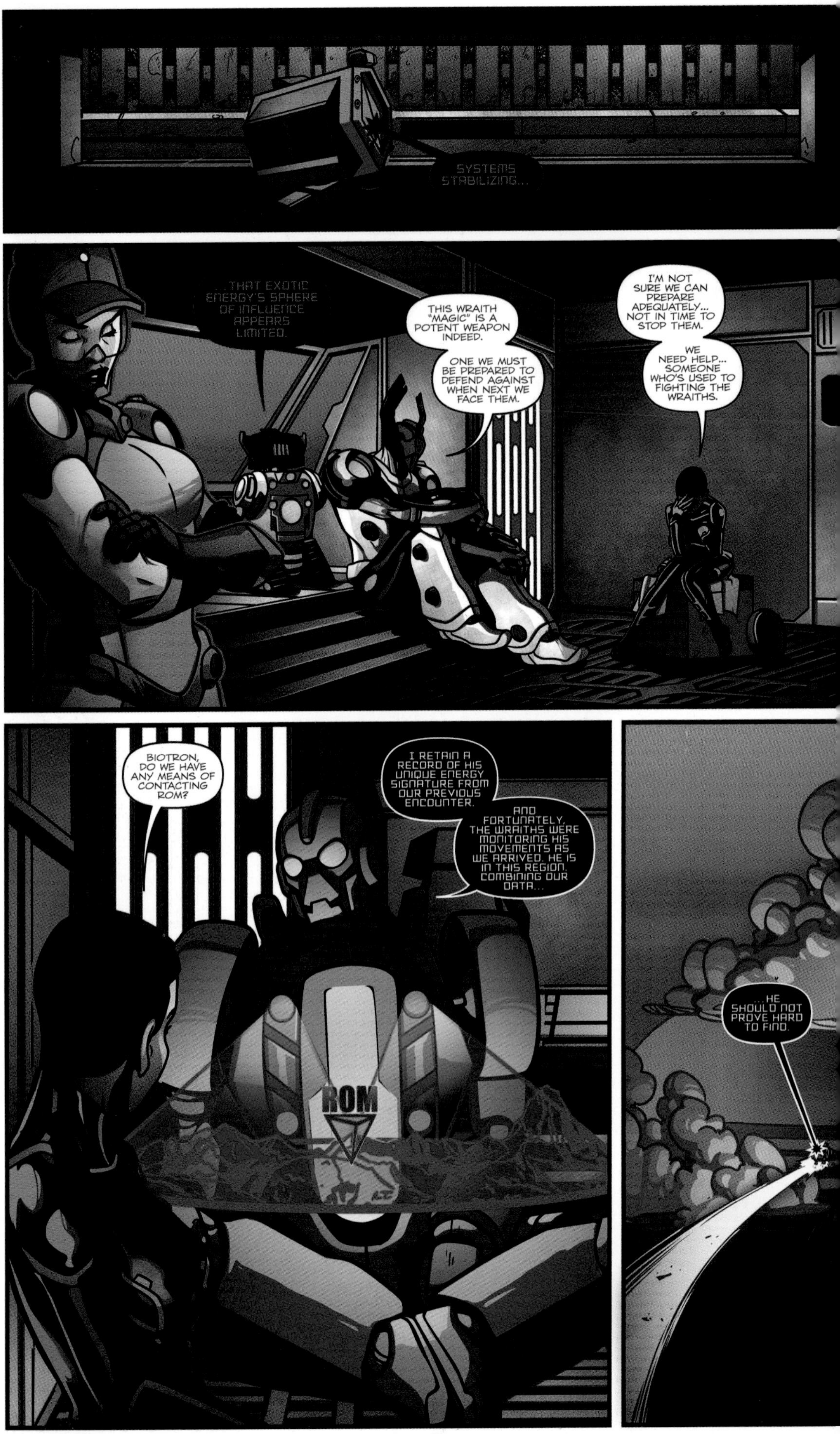

SYSTEMS STABILIZING...
...THAT EXOTIC ENERGY'S SPHERE OF INFLUENCE APPEARS LIMITED.
THIS WRAITH "MAGIC" IS A POTENT WEAPON INDEED.
ONE WE MUST BE PREPARED TO DEFEND AGAINST WHEN NEXT WE FACE THEM.
I'M NOT SURE WE CAN PREPARE ADEQUATELY... NOT IN TIME TO STOP THEM.
WE NEED HELP... SOMEONE WHO'S USED TO FIGHTING THE WRAITHS.
BIOTRON, DO WE HAVE ANY MEANS OF CONTACTING ROM?
I RETAIN A RECORD OF HIS UNIQUE ENERGY SIGNATURE FROM OUR PREVIOUS ENCOUNTER.
AND FORTUNATELY, THE WRAITHS WERE MONITORING HIS MOVEMENTS AS WE ARRIVED. HE IS IN THIS REGION. COMBINING OUR DATA...
ROM
...HE SHOULD NOT PROVE HARD TO FIND.

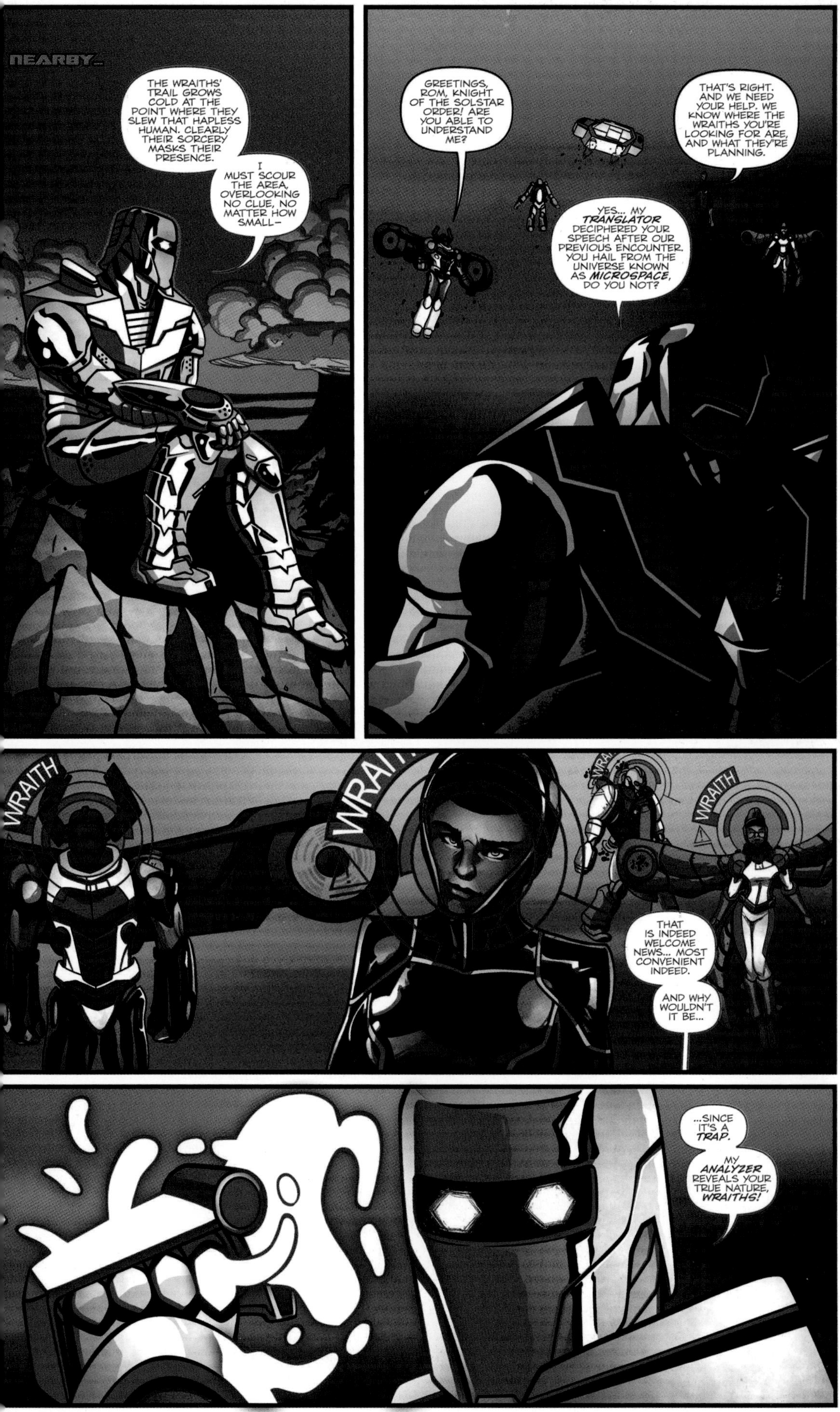
NEARBY...
THE WRAITHS' TRAIL GROWS COLD AT THE POINT WHERE THEY SLEW THAT HAPLESS HUMAN. CLEARLY THEIR SORCERY MASKS THEIR PRESENCE.
I MUST SCOUR THE AREA, OVERLOOKING NO CLUE, NO MATTER HOW SMALL–
GREETINGS, ROM, KNIGHT OF THE SOLSTAR ORDER! ARE YOU ABLE TO UNDERSTAND ME?
YES... MY TRANSLATOR DECIPHERED YOUR SPEECH AFTER OUR PREVIOUS ENCOUNTER. YOU HAIL FROM THE UNIVERSE KNOWN AS MICROSPACE, DO YOU NOT?
THAT'S RIGHT. AND WE NEED YOUR HELP. WE KNOW WHERE THE WRAITHS YOU'RE LOOKING FOR ARE, AND WHAT THEY'RE PLANNING.
WRAITH
WRAITH
WRAITH
WRAITH
THAT IS INDEED WELCOME NEWS... MOST CONVENIENT INDEED.
AND WHY WOULDN'T IT BE...
...SINCE IT'S A TRAP.
MY ANALYZER REVEALS YOUR TRUE NATURE, WRAITHS!

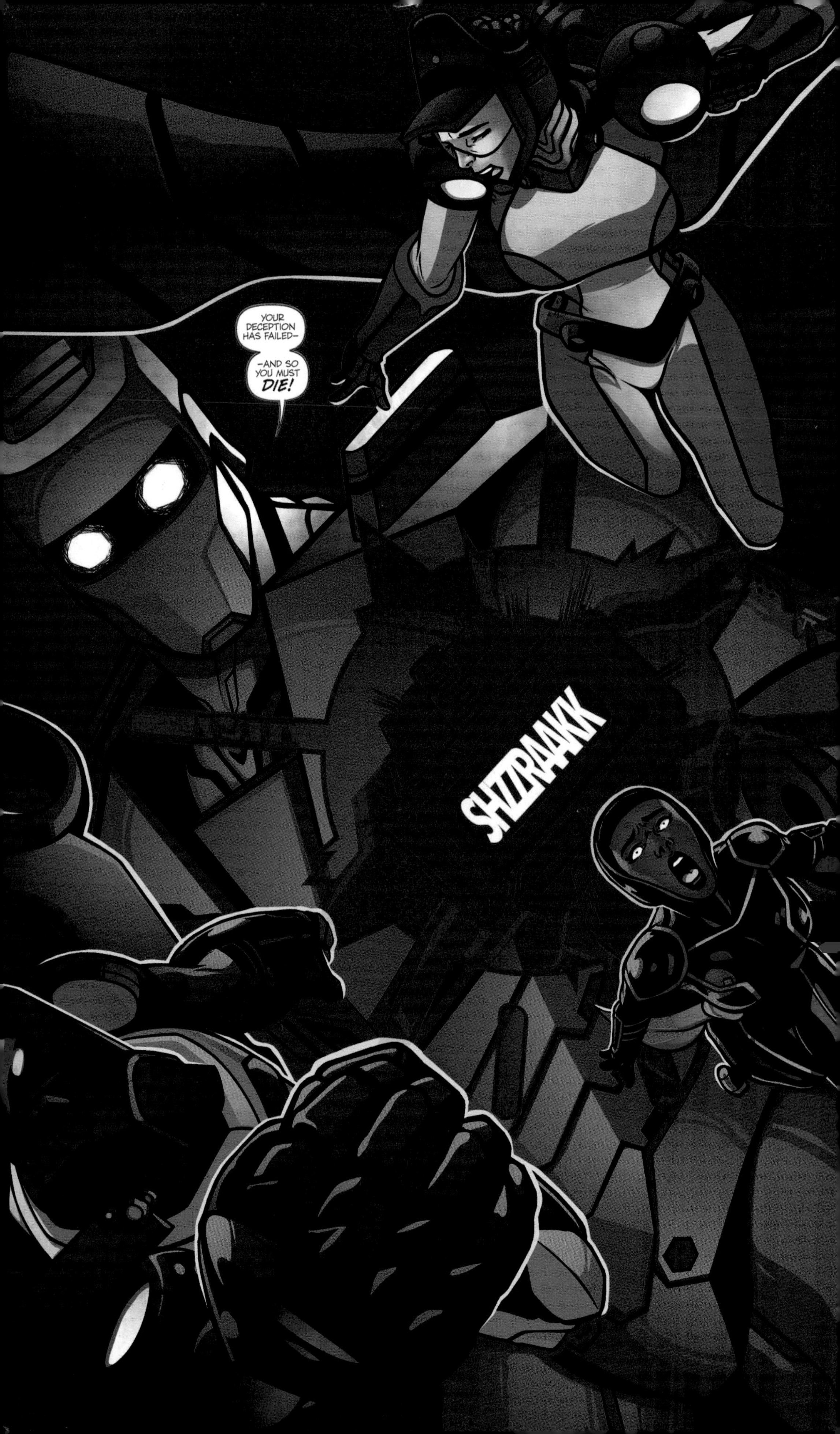
YOUR DECEPTION HAS FAILED—
—AND SO YOU MUST DIE!
SHZZRAAKK

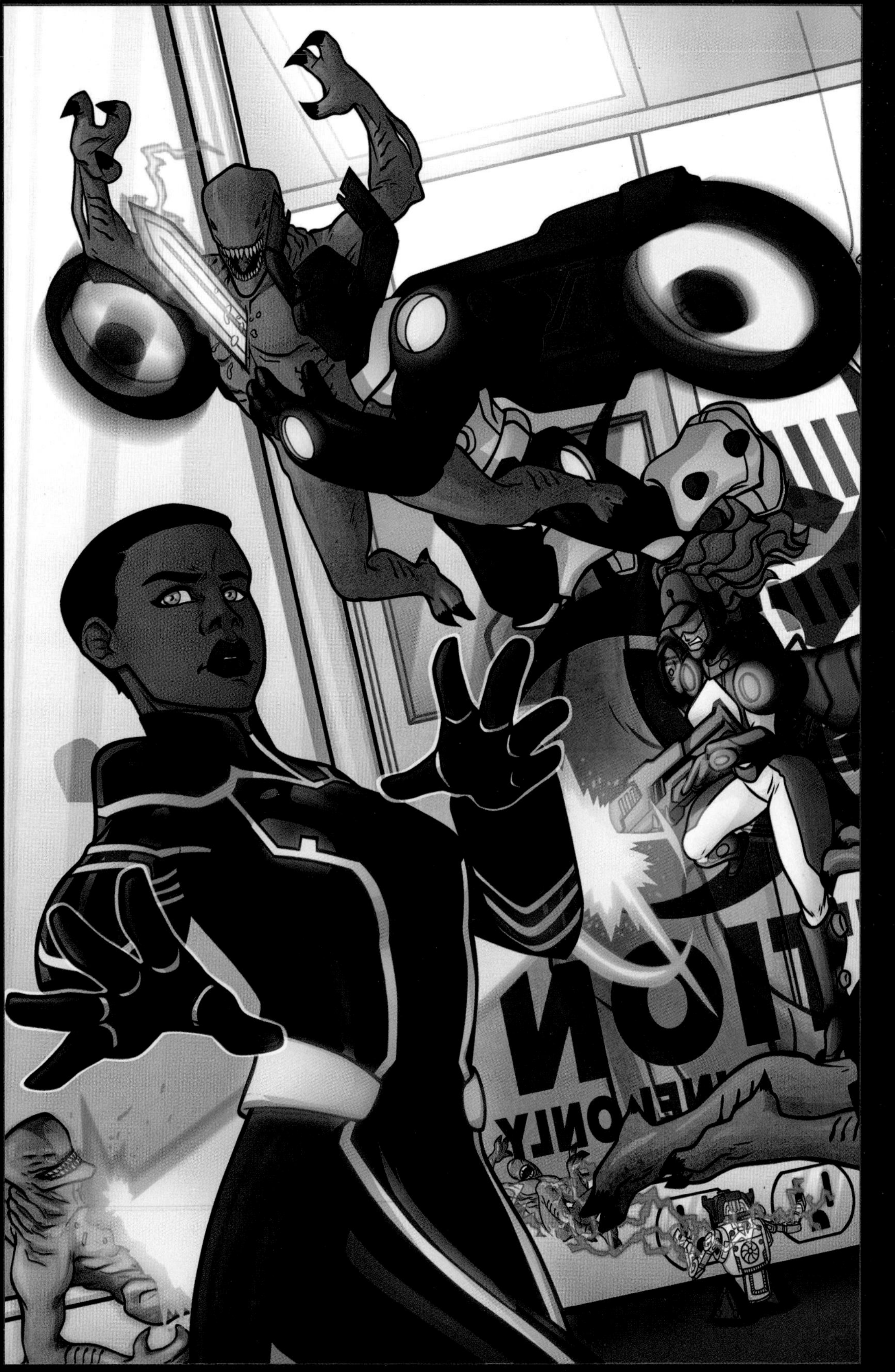

// art by Chris "Panda" Mercier

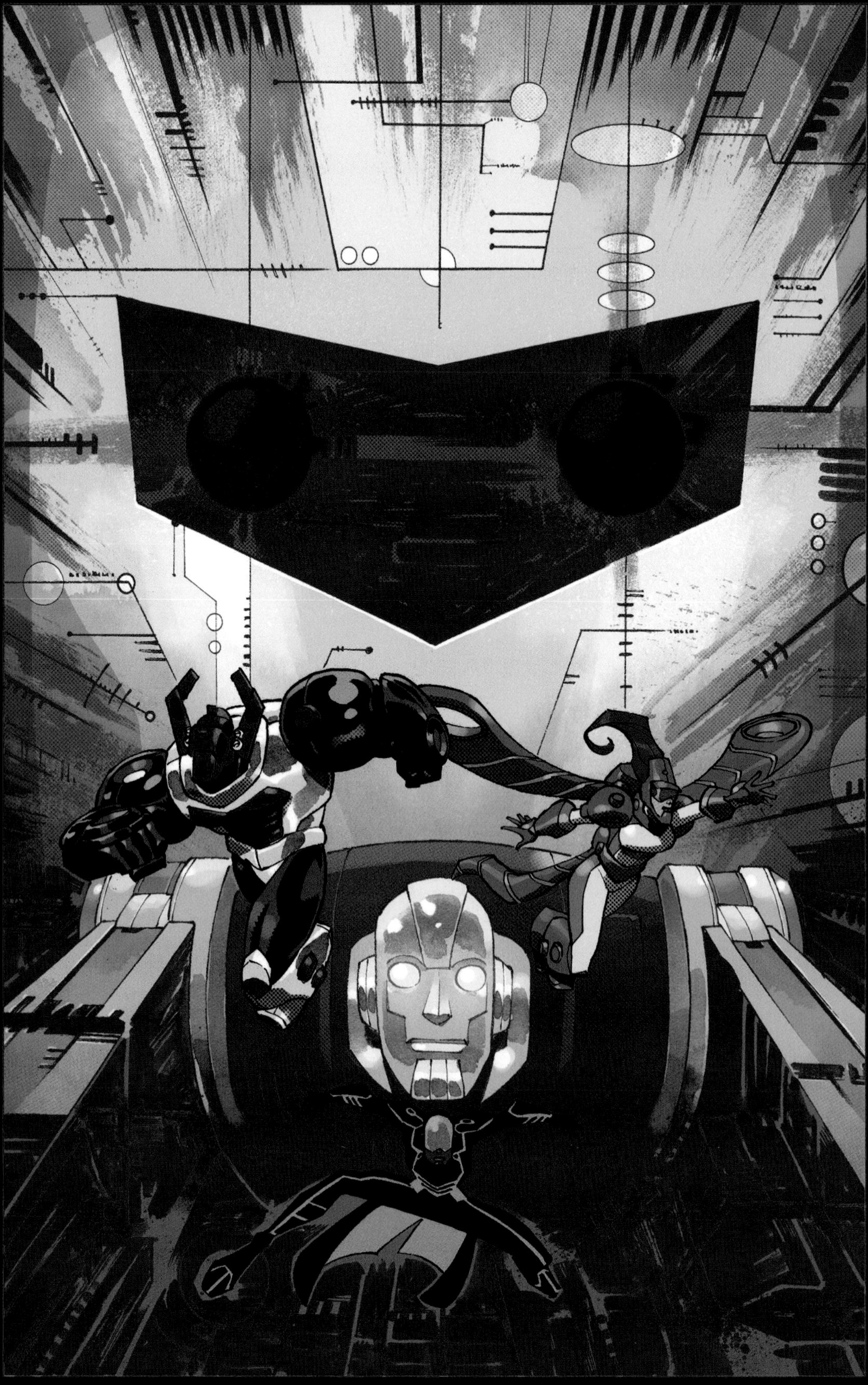

// art by Nelson Daniel

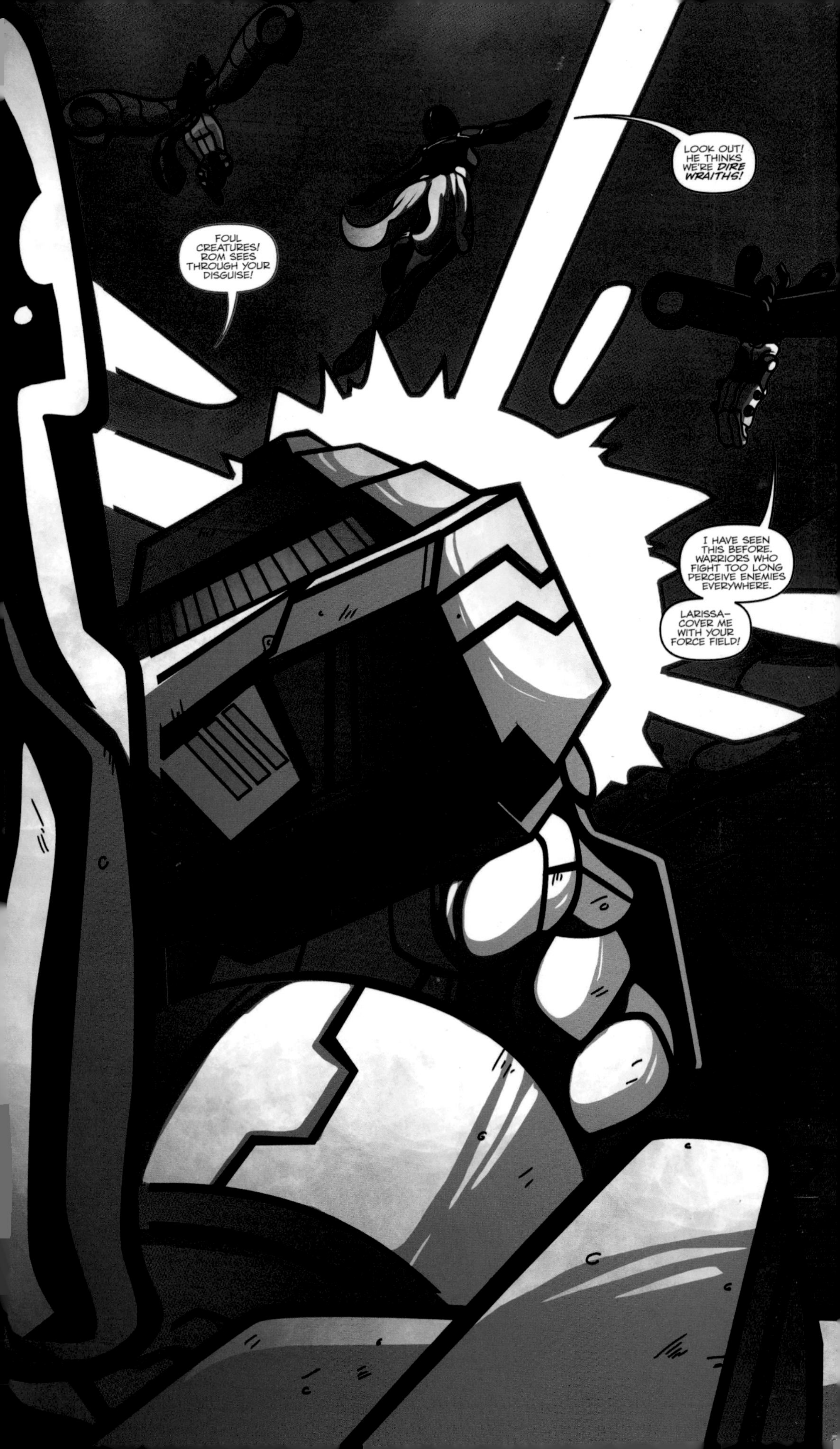

LOOK OUT! HE THINKS WE'RE *DIRE WRAITHS!*
FOUL CREATURES! ROM SEES THROUGH YOUR DISGUISE!
I HAVE SEEN THIS BEFORE. WARRIORS WHO FIGHT TOO LONG PERCEIVE ENEMIES EVERYWHERE.
LARISSA--COVER ME WITH YOUR FORCE FIELD!

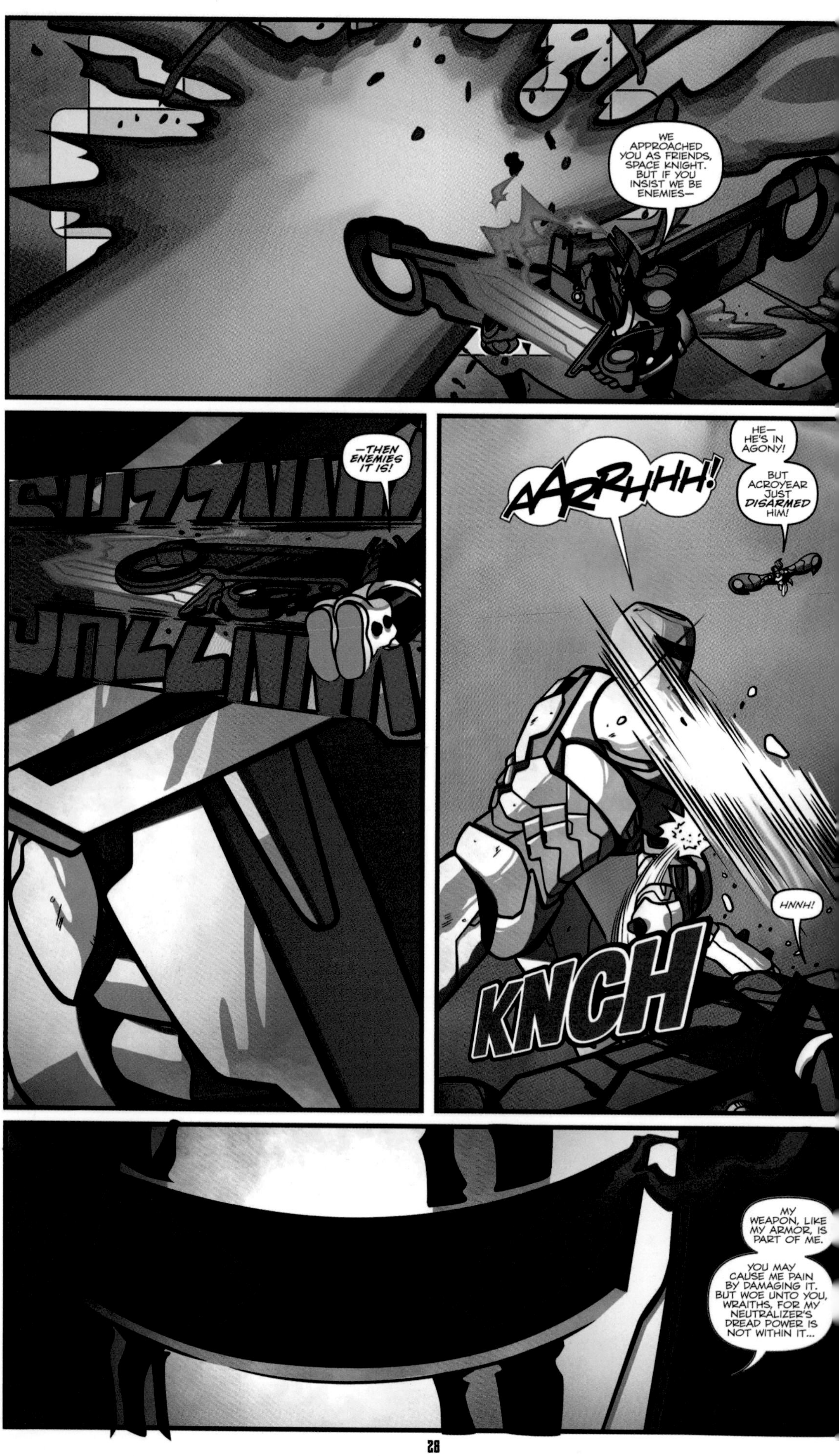
WE APPROACHED YOU AS FRIENDS, SPACE KNIGHT. BUT IF YOU INSIST WE BE ENEMIES—
—THEN ENEMIES IT IS!
AARRHHH!
HE— HE'S IN AGONY!
BUT ACROYEAR JUST DISARMED HIM!
HNNH!
KNCH
MY WEAPON, LIKE MY ARMOR, IS PART OF ME.
YOU MAY CAUSE ME PAIN BY DAMAGING IT. BUT WOE UNTO YOU, WRAITHS, FOR MY NEUTRALIZER'S DREAD POWER IS NOT WITHIN IT...

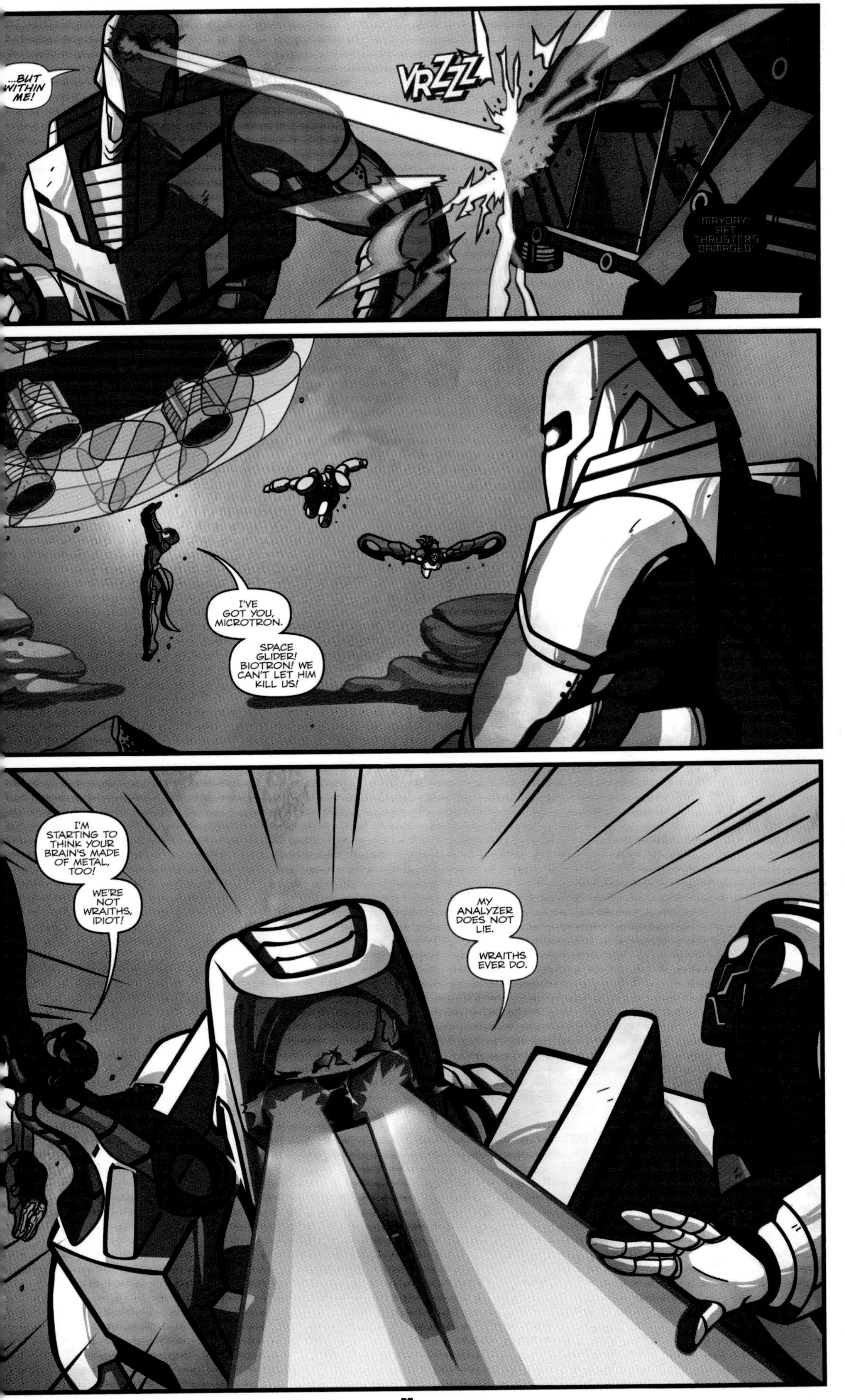
...BUT WITHIN ME!
VRZZZ
MAYDAY! AFT THRUSTERS DAMAGED!
I'VE GOT YOU, MICROTRON.
SPACE GLIDER! BIOTRON! WE CAN'T LET HIM KILL US!
I'M STARTING TO THINK YOUR BRAIN'S MADE OF METAL, TOO!
WE'RE NOT WRAITHS, IDIOT!
MY ANALYZER DOES NOT LIE.
WRAITHS EVER DO.

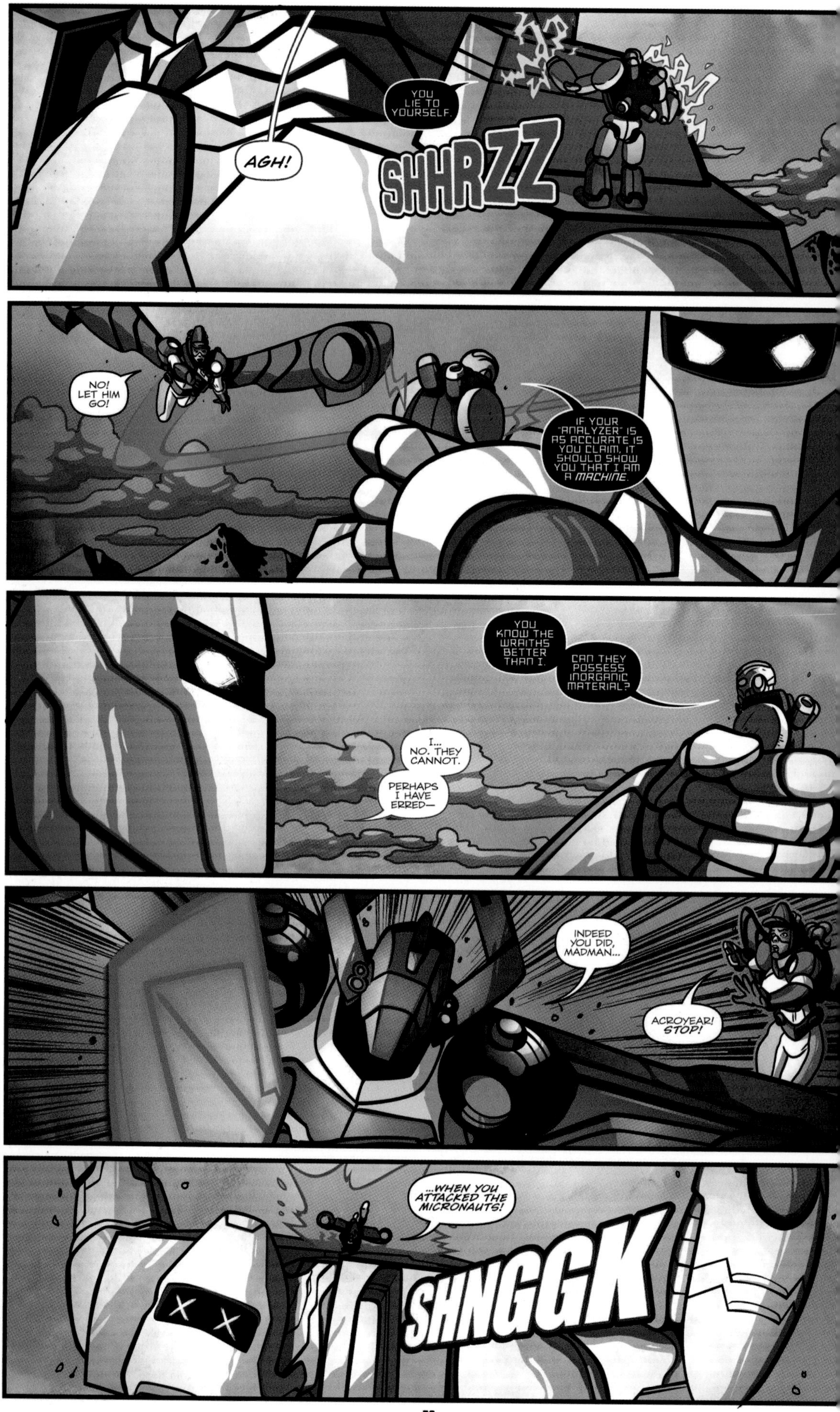

YOU LIE TO YOURSELF.
AGH!
SHHRZZ
NO! LET HIM GO!
IF YOUR "ANALYZER" IS AS ACCURATE IS YOU CLAIM, IT SHOULD SHOW YOU THAT I AM A *MACHINE*.
YOU KNOW THE WRAITHS BETTER THAN I.
CAN THEY POSSESS INORGANIC MATERIAL?
I... NO. THEY CANNOT.
PERHAPS I HAVE ERRED—
INDEED YOU DID, MADMAN...
ACROYEAR! *STOP!*
...WHEN YOU ATTACKED THE MICRONAUTS!
SHNGGK

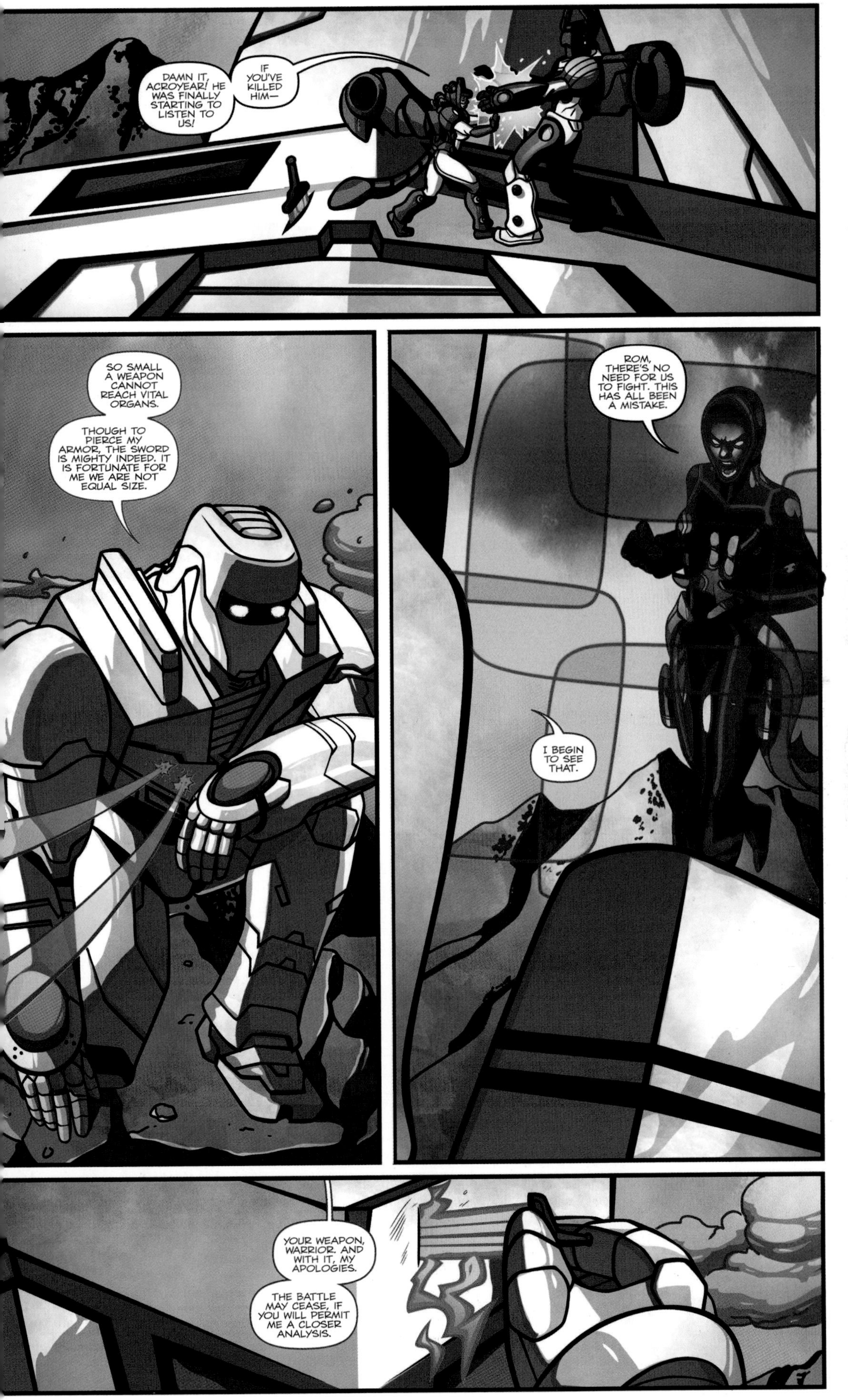
DAMN IT, ACROYEAR! HE WAS FINALLY STARTING TO LISTEN TO US!
IF YOU'VE KILLED HIM—
SO SMALL A WEAPON CANNOT REACH VITAL ORGANS.
THOUGH TO PIERCE MY ARMOR, THE SWORD IS MIGHTY INDEED. IT IS FORTUNATE FOR ME WE ARE NOT EQUAL SIZE.
ROM, THERE'S NO NEED FOR US TO FIGHT. THIS HAS ALL BEEN A MISTAKE.
I BEGIN TO SEE THAT.
YOUR WEAPON, WARRIOR. AND WITH IT, MY APOLOGIES.
THE BATTLE MAY CEASE, IF YOU WILL PERMIT ME A CLOSER ANALYSIS.

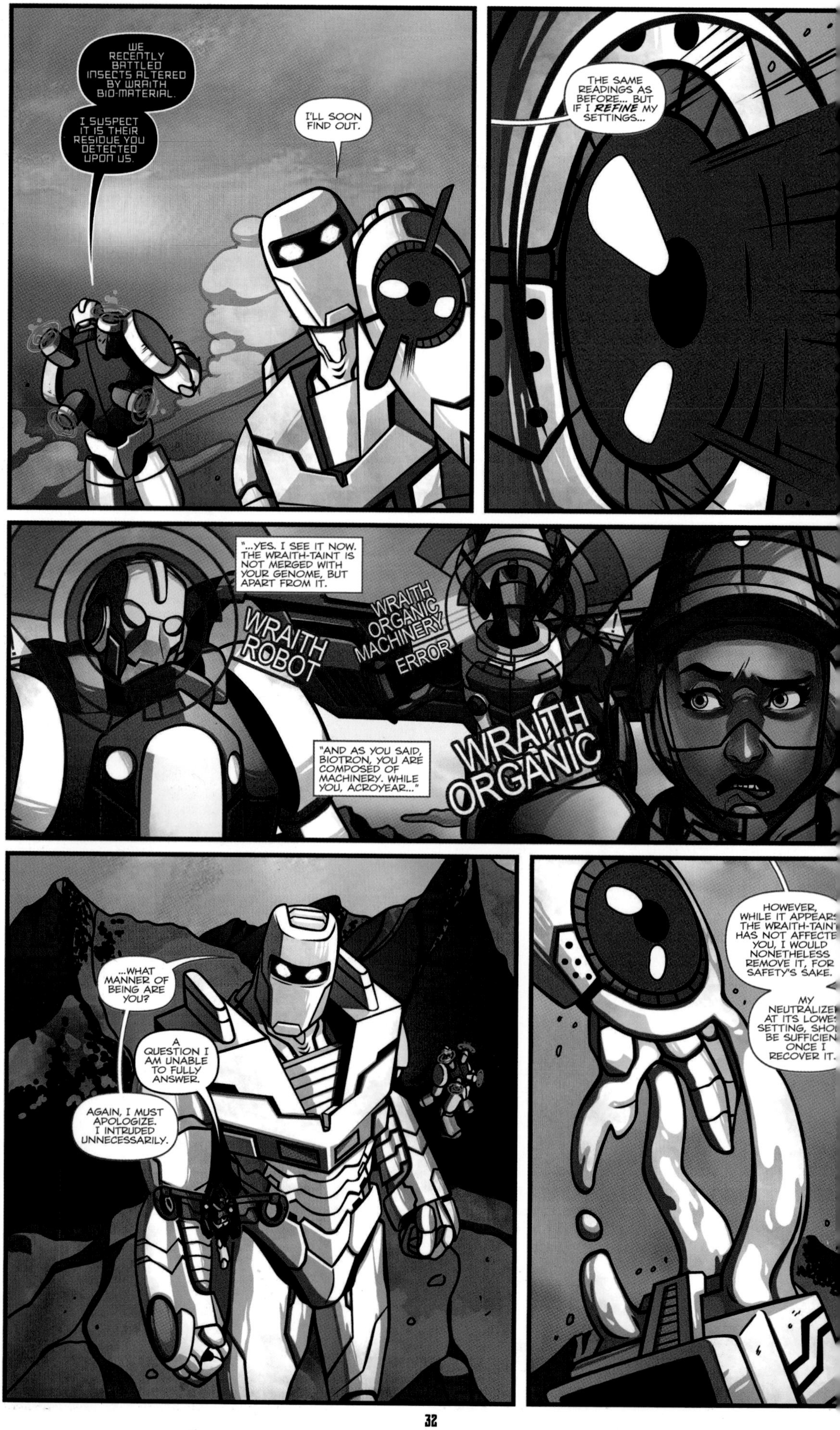
WE RECENTLY BATTLED INSECTS ALTERED BY WRAITH BIO-MATERIAL.
I SUSPECT IT IS THEIR RESIDUE YOU DETECTED UPON US.
I'LL SOON FIND OUT.
THE SAME READINGS AS BEFORE... BUT IF I REFINE MY SETTINGS...
"...YES. I SEE IT NOW. THE WRAITH-TAINT IS NOT MERGED WITH YOUR GENOME, BUT APART FROM IT.
WRAITH ROBOT
WRAITH ORGANIC MACHINERY
ERROR
"AND AS YOU SAID, BIOTRON, YOU ARE COMPOSED OF MACHINERY. WHILE YOU, ACROYEAR..."
WRAITH ORGANIC
...WHAT MANNER OF BEING ARE YOU?
A QUESTION I AM UNABLE TO FULLY ANSWER.
AGAIN, I MUST APOLOGIZE. I INTRUDED UNNECESSARILY.
HOWEVER, WHILE IT APPEAR THE WRAITH-TAIN HAS NOT AFFECTE YOU, I WOULD NONETHELESS REMOVE IT, FOR SAFETY'S SAKE.
MY NEUTRALIZE AT ITS LOWE SETTING, SHO BE SUFFICIEN ONCE I RECOVER IT.

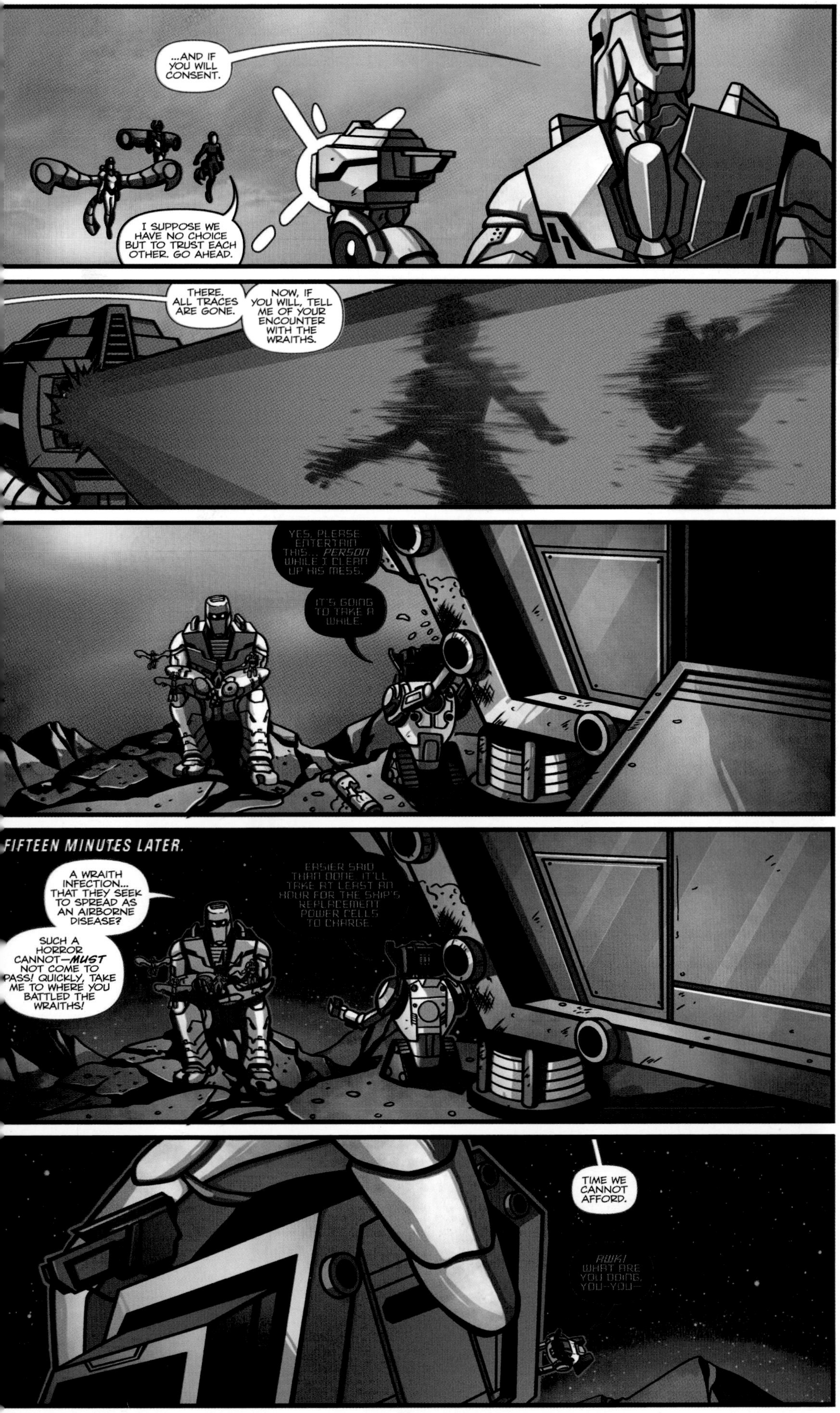

...AND IF YOU WILL CONSENT.
I SUPPOSE WE HAVE NO CHOICE BUT TO TRUST EACH OTHER. GO AHEAD.
THERE. ALL TRACES ARE GONE.
NOW, IF YOU WILL, TELL ME OF YOUR ENCOUNTER WITH THE WRAITHS.
YES, PLEASE. ENTERTAIN THIS... *PERSON* WHILE I CLEAN UP HIS MESS.
IT'S GOING TO TAKE A WHILE.
FIFTEEN MINUTES LATER.
A WRAITH INFECTION... THAT THEY SEEK TO SPREAD AS AN AIRBORNE DISEASE?
SUCH A HORROR CANNOT—*MUST* NOT COME TO PASS! QUICKLY, TAKE ME TO WHERE YOU BATTLED THE WRAITHS!
EASIER SAID THAN DONE. IT'LL TAKE AT LEAST AN HOUR FOR THE SHIP'S REPLACEMENT POWER CELLS TO CHARGE.
TIME WE CANNOT AFFORD.
AWK! WHAT ARE YOU DOING, YOU--YOU—

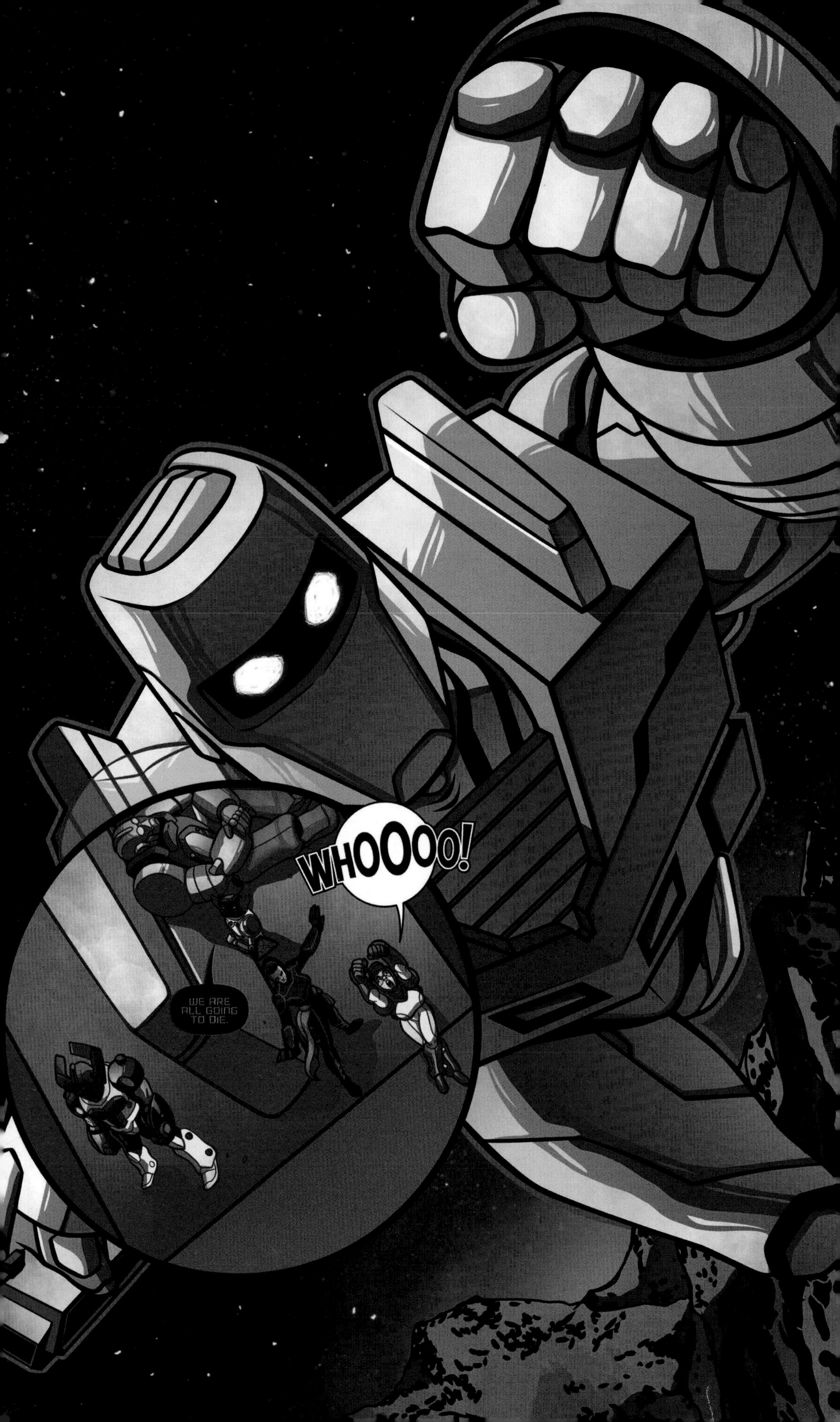
WHOOOO!
WE ARE ALL GOING TO DIE.

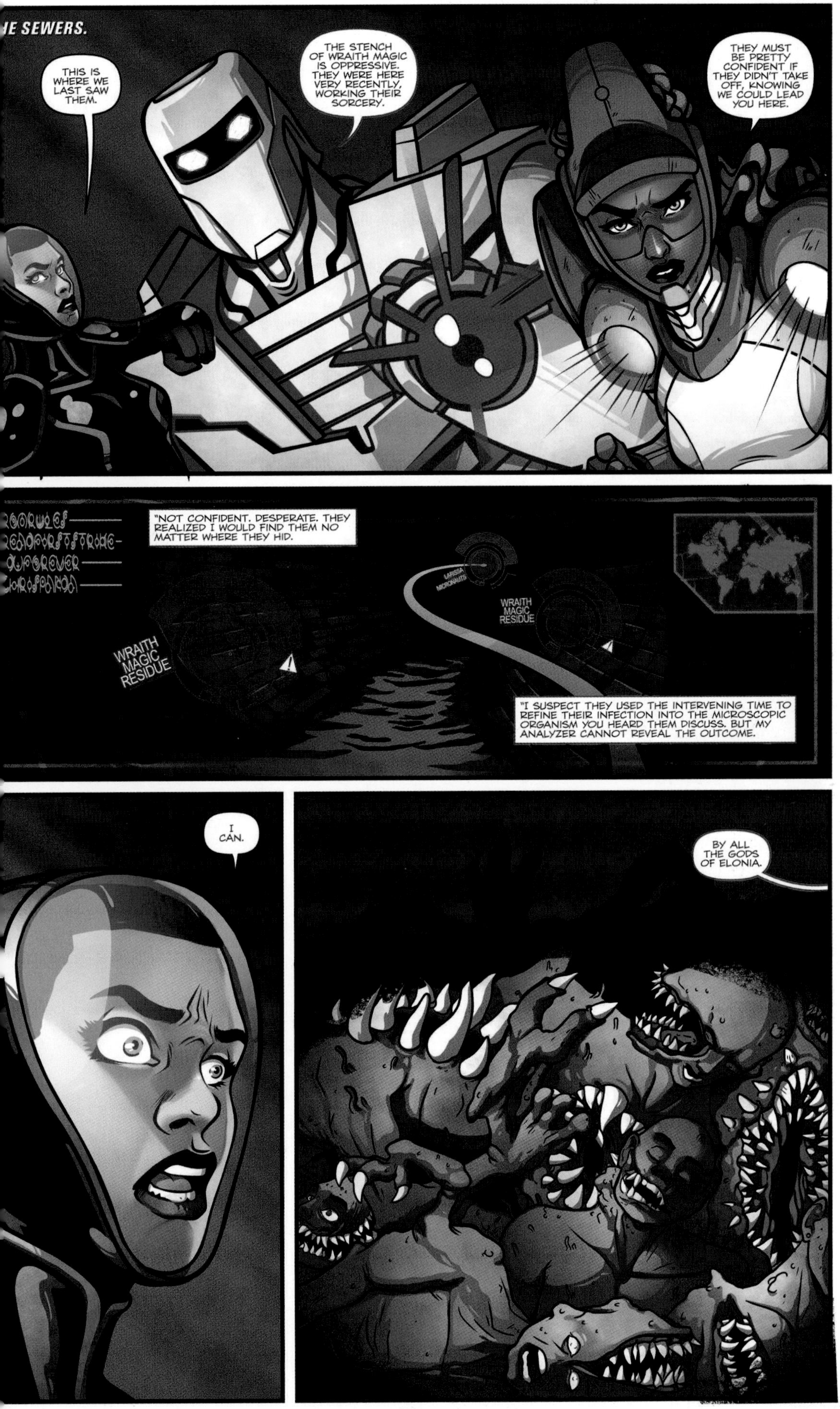

...E SEWERS.
THIS IS WHERE WE LAST SAW THEM.
THE STENCH OF WRAITH MAGIC IS OPPRESSIVE. THEY WERE HERE VERY RECENTLY, WORKING THEIR SORCERY.
THEY MUST BE PRETTY CONFIDENT IF THEY DIDN'T TAKE OFF, KNOWING WE COULD LEAD YOU HERE.
"NOT CONFIDENT. DESPERATE. THEY REALIZED I WOULD FIND THEM NO MATTER WHERE THEY HID.
LARISSA MICRONAUTS
WRAITH MAGIC RESIDUE
WRAITH MAGIC RESIDUE
"I SUSPECT THEY USED THE INTERVENING TIME TO REFINE THEIR INFECTION INTO THE MICROSCOPIC ORGANISM YOU HEARD THEM DISCUSS. BUT MY ANALYZER CANNOT REVEAL THE OUTCOME.
I CAN.
BY ALL THE GODS OF ELONIA.

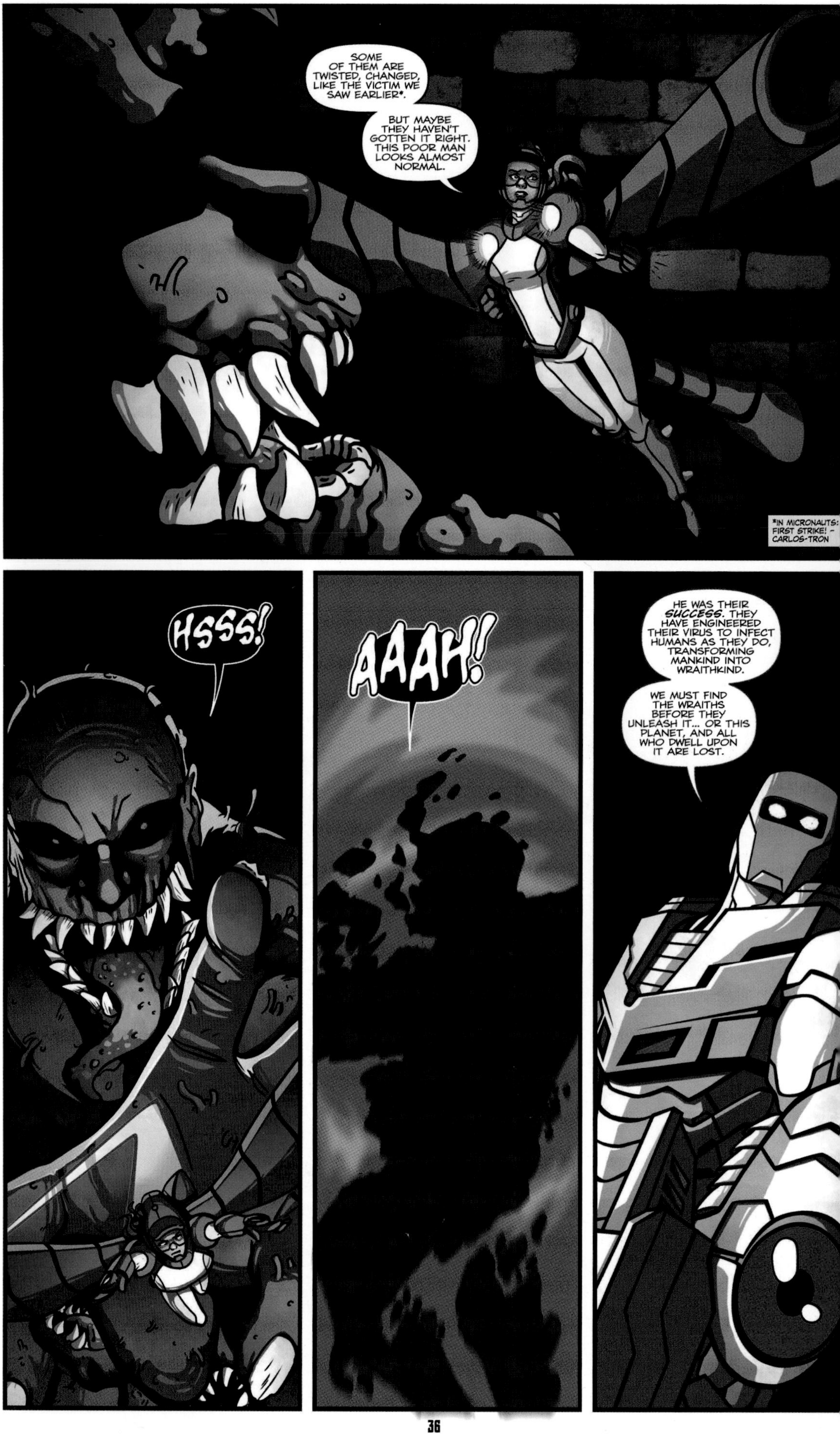
SOME OF THEM ARE TWISTED, CHANGED, LIKE THE VICTIM WE SAW EARLIER*.
BUT MAYBE THEY HAVEN'T GOTTEN IT RIGHT. THIS POOR MAN LOOKS ALMOST NORMAL.
*IN MICRONAUTS: FIRST STRIKE! – CARLOS-TRON
HSSS!
AAAH!
HE WAS THEIR SUCCESS. THEY HAVE ENGINEERED THEIR VIRUS TO INFECT HUMANS AS THEY DO, TRANSFORMING MANKIND INTO WRAITHKIND.
WE MUST FIND THE WRAITHS BEFORE THEY UNLEASH IT... OR THIS PLANET, AND ALL WHO DWELL UPON IT ARE LOST.

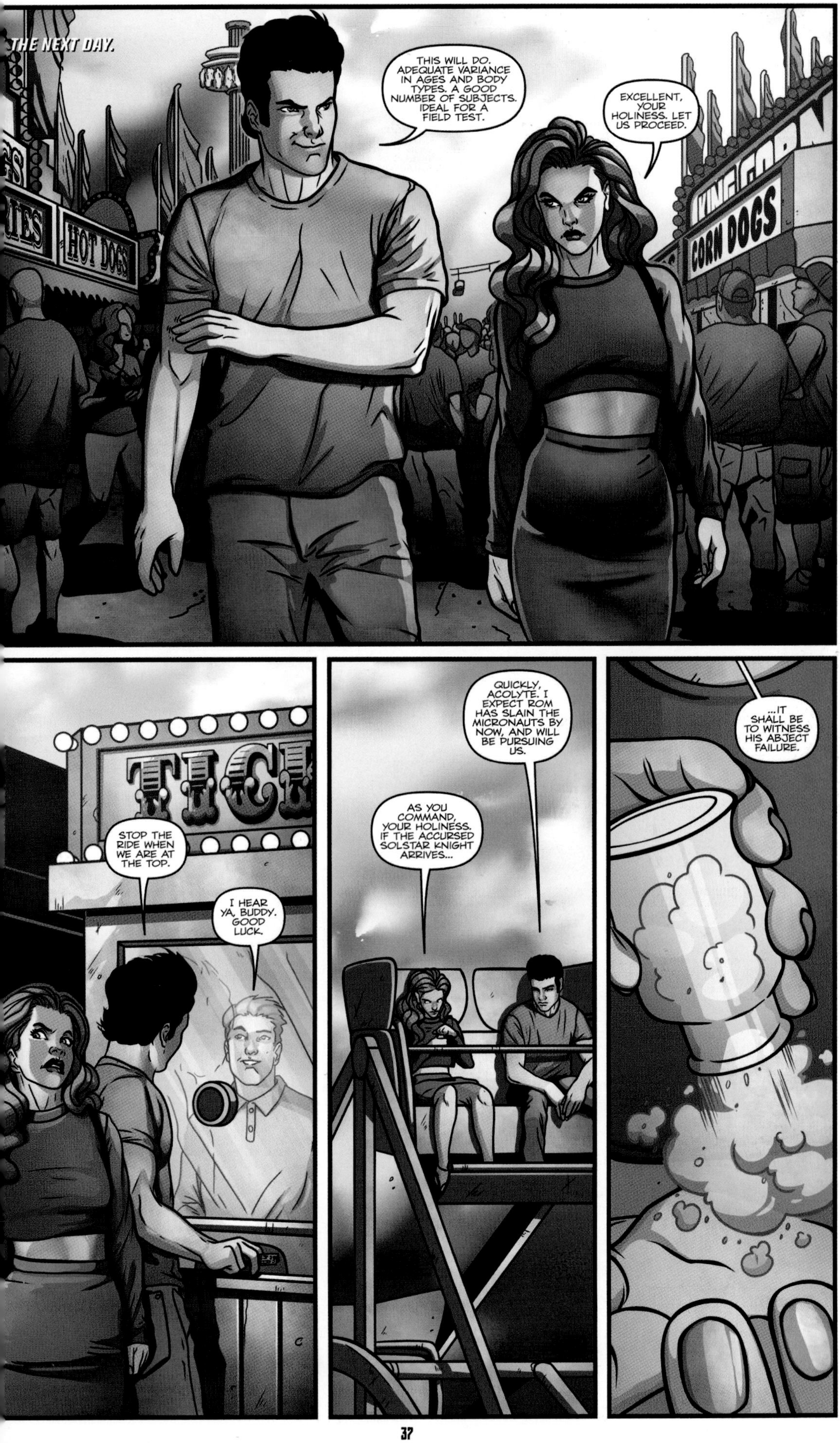
THE NEXT DAY.
THIS WILL DO. ADEQUATE VARIANCE IN AGES AND BODY TYPES. A GOOD NUMBER OF SUBJECTS. IDEAL FOR A FIELD TEST.
EXCELLENT, YOUR HOLINESS. LET US PROCEED.
HOT DOGS
CORN DOGS
KING CORN
STOP THE RIDE WHEN WE ARE AT THE TOP.
I HEAR YA, BUDDY. GOOD LUCK.
QUICKLY, ACOLYTE. I EXPECT ROM HAS SLAIN THE MICRONAUTS BY NOW, AND WILL BE PURSUING US.
AS YOU COMMAND, YOUR HOLINESS. IF THE ACCURSED SOLSTAR KNIGHT ARRIVES...
...IT SHALL BE TO WITNESS HIS ABJECT FAILURE.

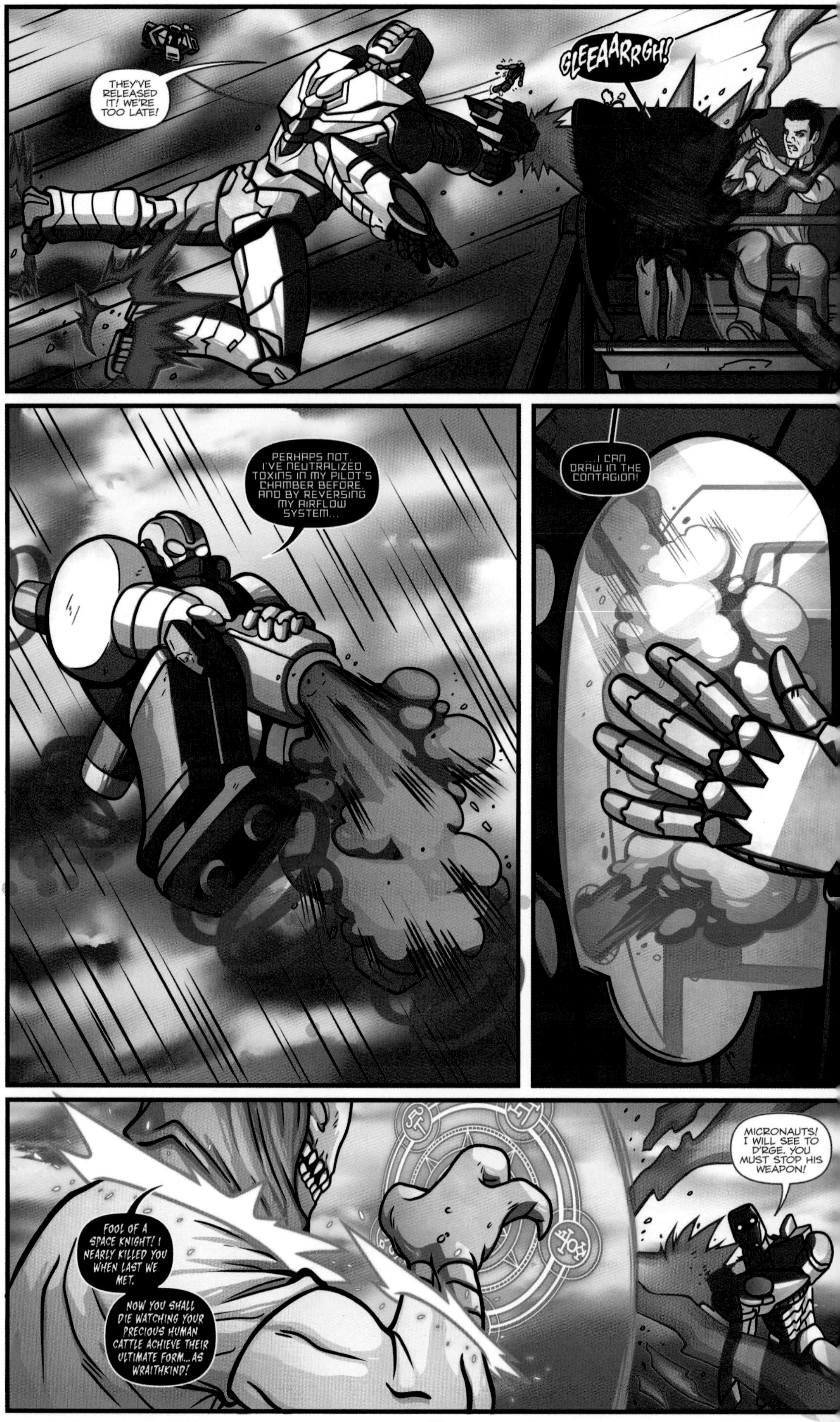
THEY'VE RELEASED IT! WE'RE TOO LATE!
GLEEAARRGH!
PERHAPS NOT. I'VE NEUTRALIZED TOXINS IN MY PILOT'S CHAMBER BEFORE. AND BY REVERSING MY AIRFLOW SYSTEM...
...I CAN DRAW IN THE CONTAGION!
FOOL OF A SPACE KNIGHT! I NEARLY KILLED YOU WHEN LAST WE MET.
NOW YOU SHALL DIE WATCHING YOUR PRECIOUS HUMAN CATTLE ACHIEVE THEIR ULTIMATE FORM...AS WRAITHKIND!
MICRONAUTS! I WILL SEE TO D'RGE. YOU MUST STOP HIS WEAPON!

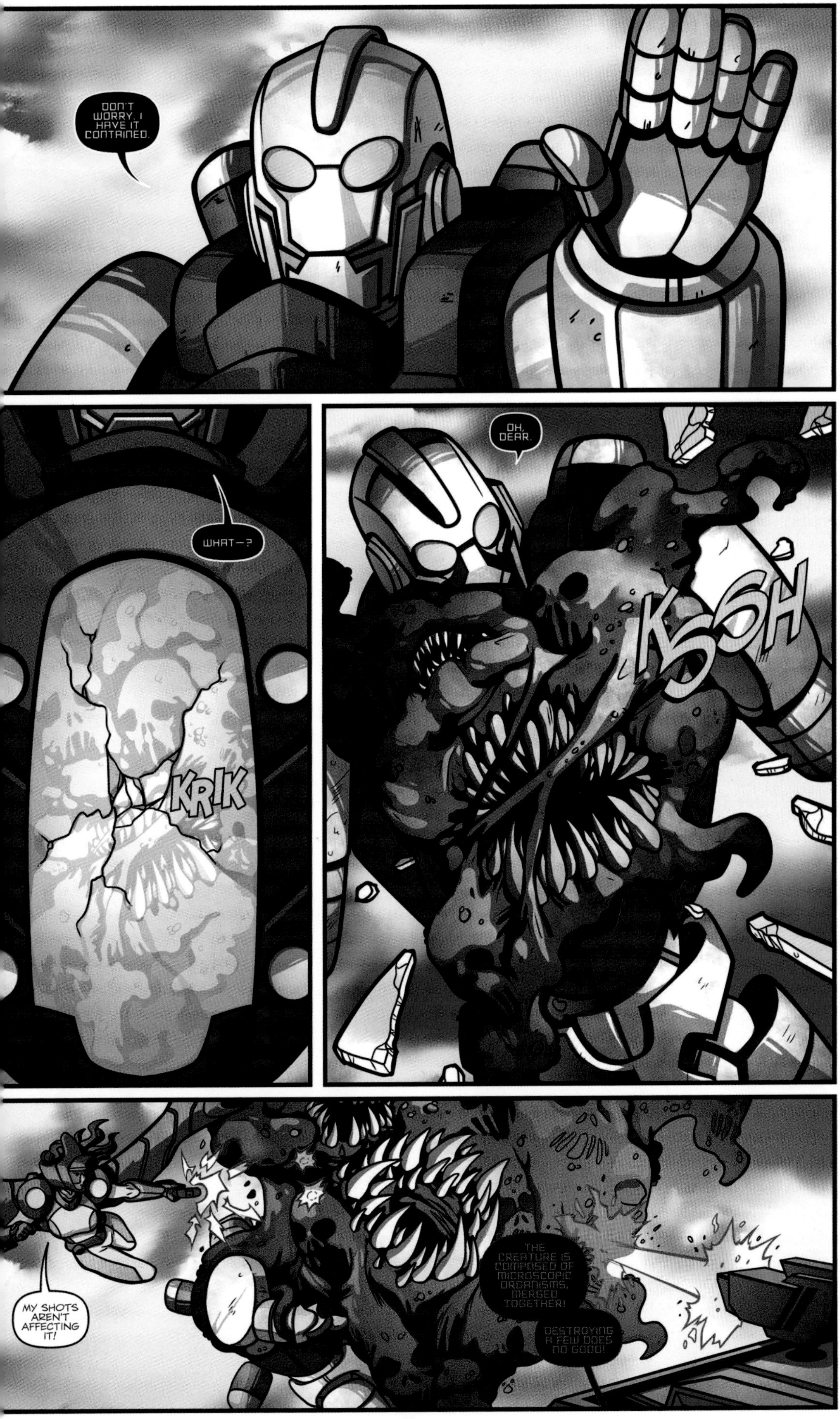
DON'T WORRY. I HAVE IT CONTAINED.
WHAT—?
KRIK
OH, DEAR.
KSSH
MY SHOTS AREN'T AFFECTING IT!
THE CREATURE IS COMPOSED OF MICROSCOPIC ORGANISMS, MERGED TOGETHER!
DESTROYING A FEW DOES NO GOOD!

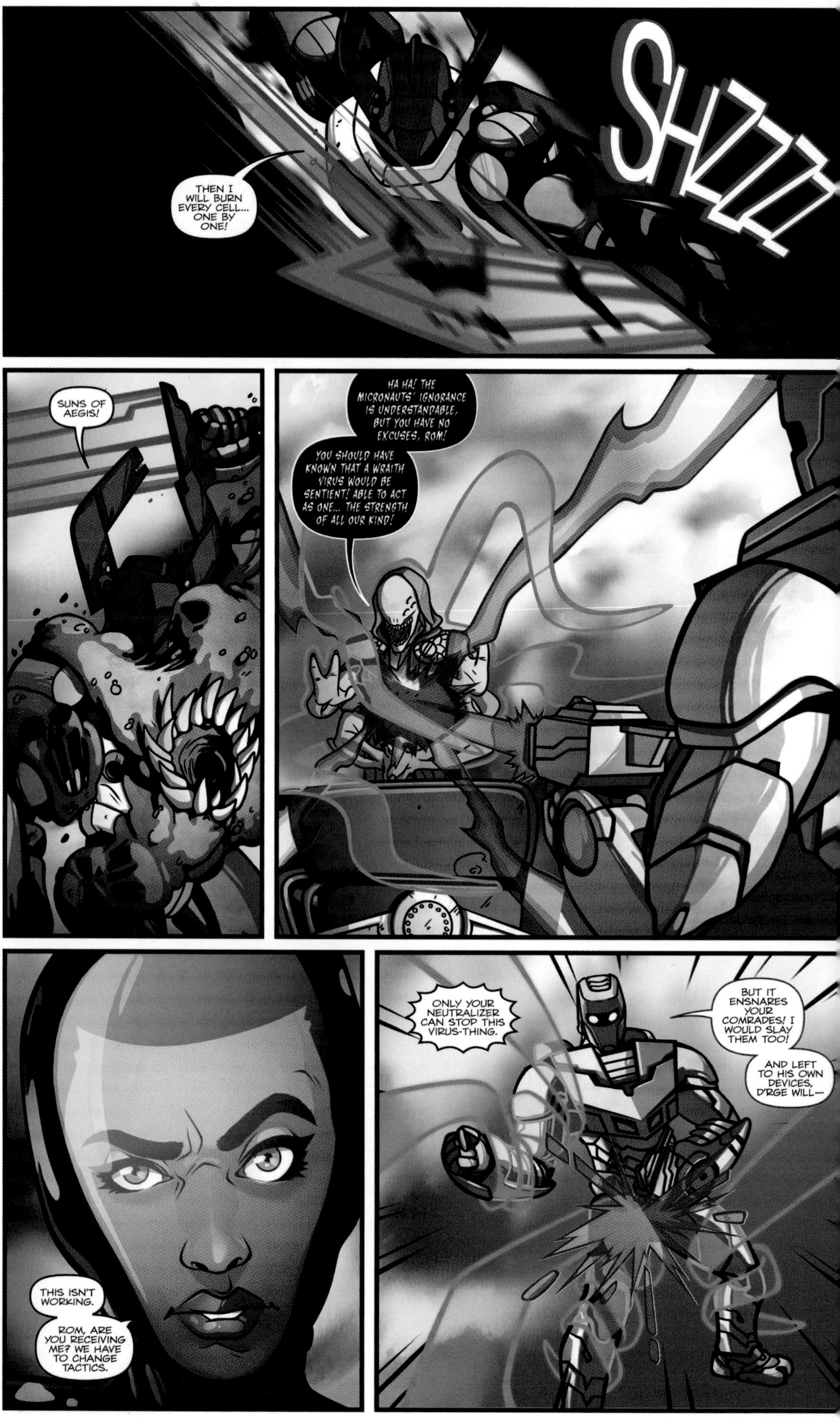
THEN I WILL BURN EVERY CELL... ONE BY ONE!
SHZZZT
SUNS OF AEGIS!
HA HA! THE MICRONAUTS' IGNORANCE IS UNDERSTANDABLE, BUT YOU HAVE NO EXCUSES, ROM!
YOU SHOULD HAVE KNOWN THAT A WRAITH VIRUS WOULD BE SENTIENT! ABLE TO ACT AS ONE... THE STRENGTH OF ALL OUR KIND!
THIS ISN'T WORKING.
ROM, ARE YOU RECEIVING ME? WE HAVE TO CHANGE TACTICS.
ONLY YOUR NEUTRALIZER CAN STOP THIS VIRUS-THING.
BUT IT ENSNARES YOUR COMRADES! I WOULD SLAY THEM TOO!
AND LEFT TO HIS OWN DEVICES, D'RGE WILL—

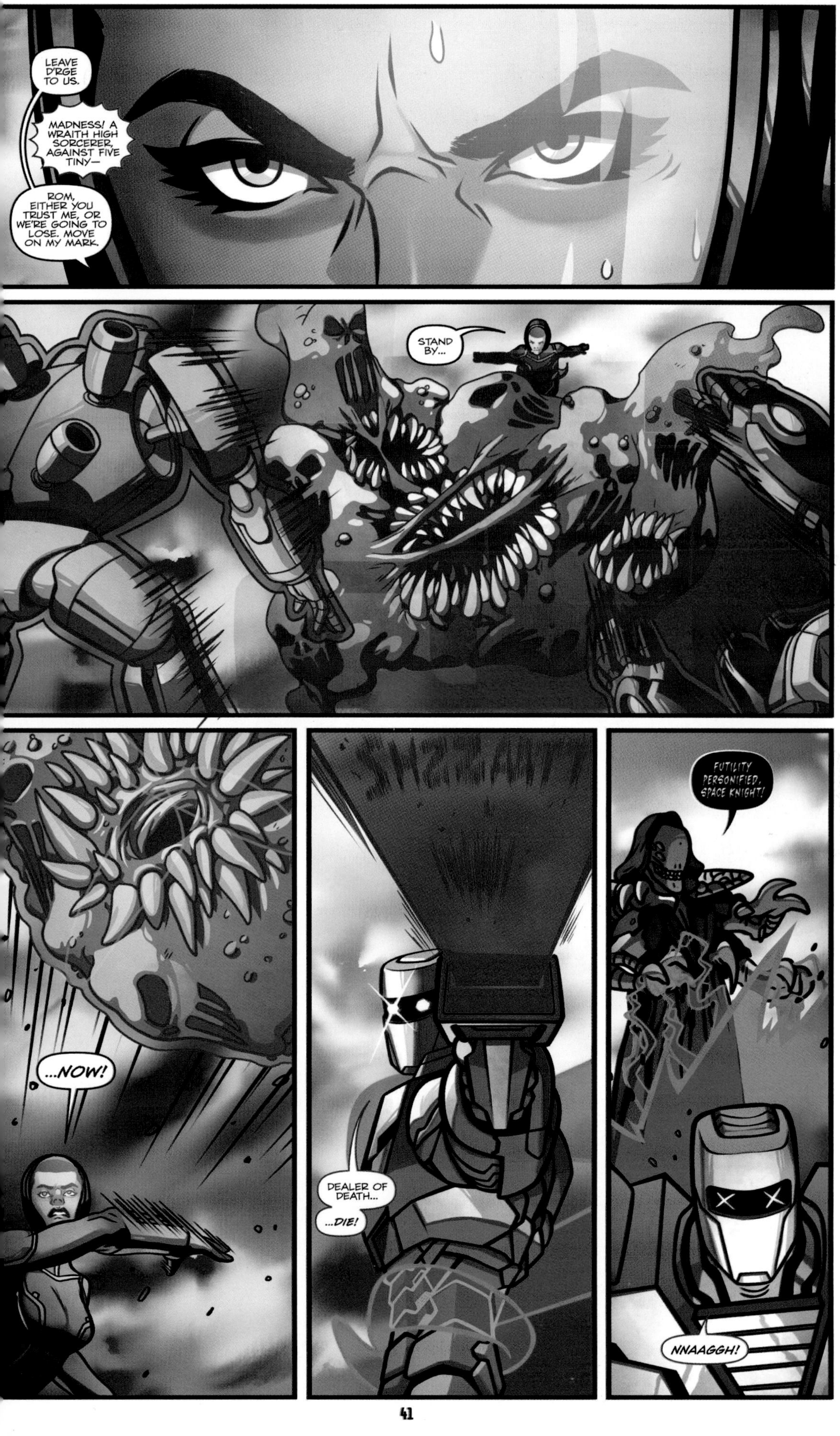
LEAVE D'RGE TO US.
MADNESS! A WRAITH HIGH SORCERER, AGAINST FIVE TINY—
ROM, EITHER YOU TRUST ME, OR WE'RE GOING TO LOSE. MOVE ON MY MARK.
STAND BY...
...NOW!
DEALER OF DEATH...
...DIE!
FUTILITY PERSONIFIED, SPACE KNIGHT!
NNAAGGH!

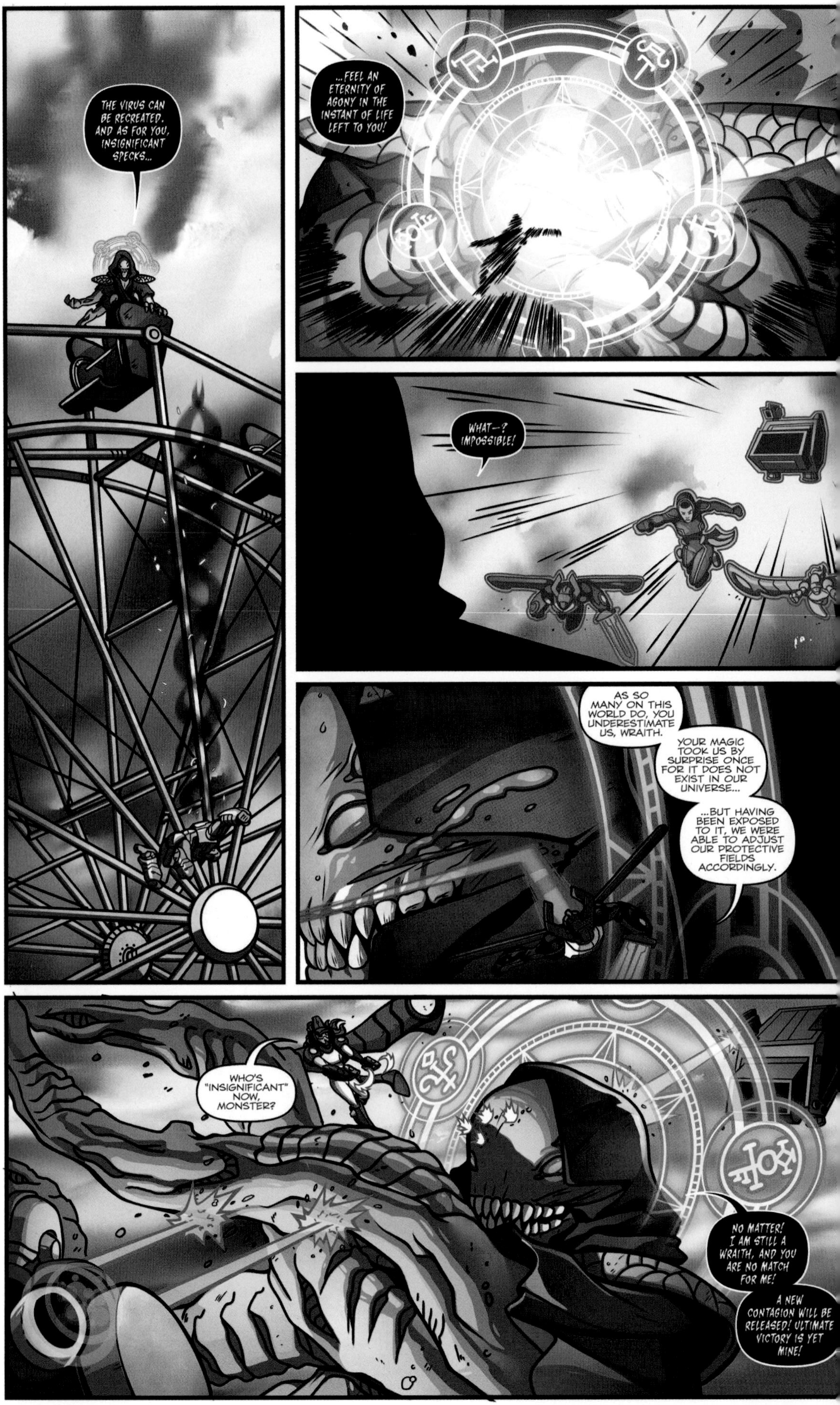
THE VIRUS CAN BE RECREATED. AND AS FOR YOU, INSIGNIFICANT SPECKS...
...FEEL AN ETERNITY OF AGONY IN THE INSTANT OF LIFE LEFT TO YOU!
WHAT--? IMPOSSIBLE!
AS SO MANY ON THIS WORLD DO, YOU UNDERESTIMATE US, WRAITH.
YOUR MAGIC TOOK US BY SURPRISE ONCE FOR IT DOES NOT EXIST IN OUR UNIVERSE...
...BUT HAVING BEEN EXPOSED TO IT, WE WERE ABLE TO ADJUST OUR PROTECTIVE FIELDS ACCORDINGLY.
WHO'S "INSIGNIFICANT" NOW, MONSTER?
NO MATTER! I AM STILL A WRAITH, AND YOU ARE NO MATCH FOR ME!
A NEW CONTAGION WILL BE RELEASED! ULTIMATE VICTORY IS YET MINE!

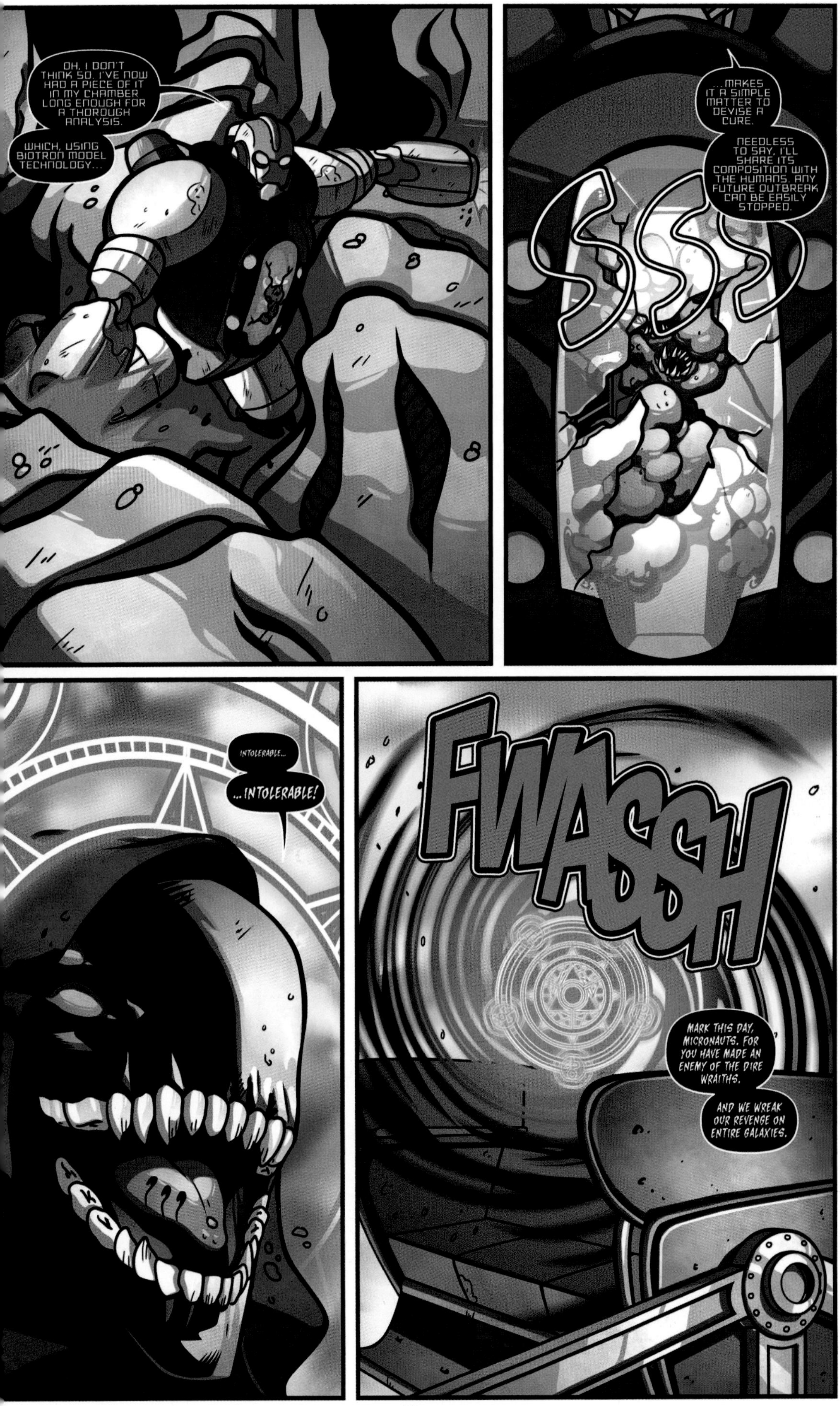
OH, I DON'T THINK SO. I'VE NOW HAD A PIECE OF IT IN MY CHAMBER LONG ENOUGH FOR A THOROUGH ANALYSIS.
WHICH, USING BIOTRON MODEL TECHNOLOGY...
...MAKES IT A SIMPLE MATTER TO DEVISE A CURE.
NEEDLESS TO SAY, I'LL SHARE ITS COMPOSITION WITH THE HUMANS. ANY FUTURE OUTBREAK CAN BE EASILY STOPPED.
SSSS
INTOLERABLE...
...INTOLERABLE!
FWASSH
MARK THIS DAY, MICRONAUTS. FOR YOU HAVE MADE AN ENEMY OF THE DIRE WRAITHS.
AND WE WREAK OUR REVENGE ON ENTIRE GALAXIES.

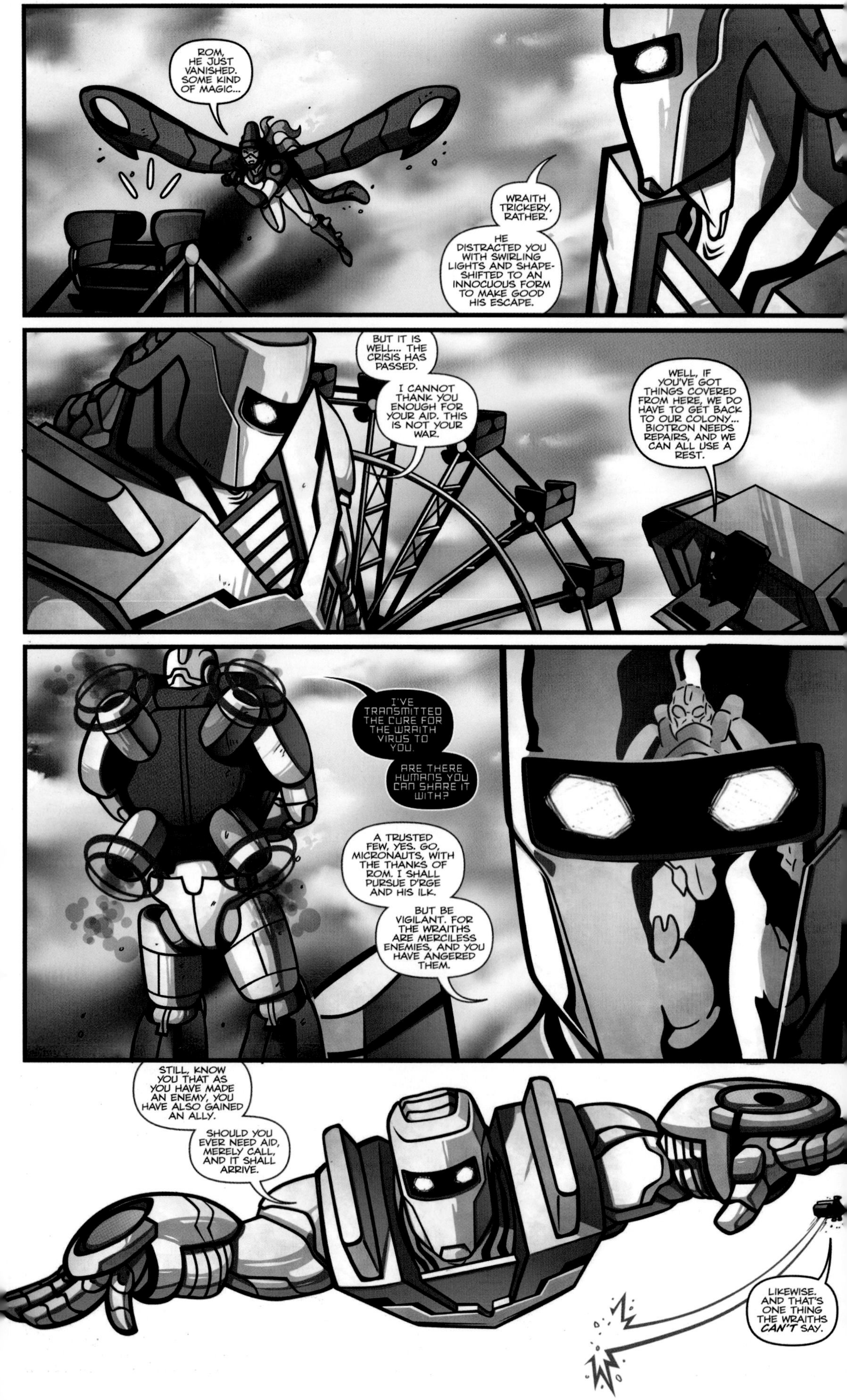
ROM, HE JUST VANISHED. SOME KIND OF MAGIC...
WRAITH TRICKERY, RATHER.
HE DISTRACTED YOU WITH SWIRLING LIGHTS AND SHAPE-SHIFTED TO AN INNOCUOUS FORM TO MAKE GOOD HIS ESCAPE.
BUT IT IS WELL... THE CRISIS HAS PASSED.
I CANNOT THANK YOU ENOUGH FOR YOUR AID. THIS IS NOT YOUR WAR.
WELL, IF YOU'VE GOT THINGS COVERED FROM HERE, WE DO HAVE TO GET BACK TO OUR COLONY... BIOTRON NEEDS REPAIRS, AND WE CAN ALL USE A REST.
I'VE TRANSMITTED THE CURE FOR THE WRAITH VIRUS TO YOU.
ARE THERE HUMANS YOU CAN SHARE IT WITH?
A TRUSTED FEW, YES. GO, MICRONAUTS, WITH THE THANKS OF ROM. I SHALL PURSUE D'RGE AND HIS ILK.
BUT BE VIGILANT. FOR THE WRAITHS ARE MERCILESS ENEMIES, AND YOU HAVE ANGERED THEM.
STILL, KNOW YOU THAT AS YOU HAVE MADE AN ENEMY, YOU HAVE ALSO GAINED AN ALLY.
SHOULD YOU EVER NEED AID, MERELY CALL, AND IT SHALL ARRIVE.
LIKEWISE. AND THAT'S ONE THING THE WRAITHS *CAN'T* SAY.

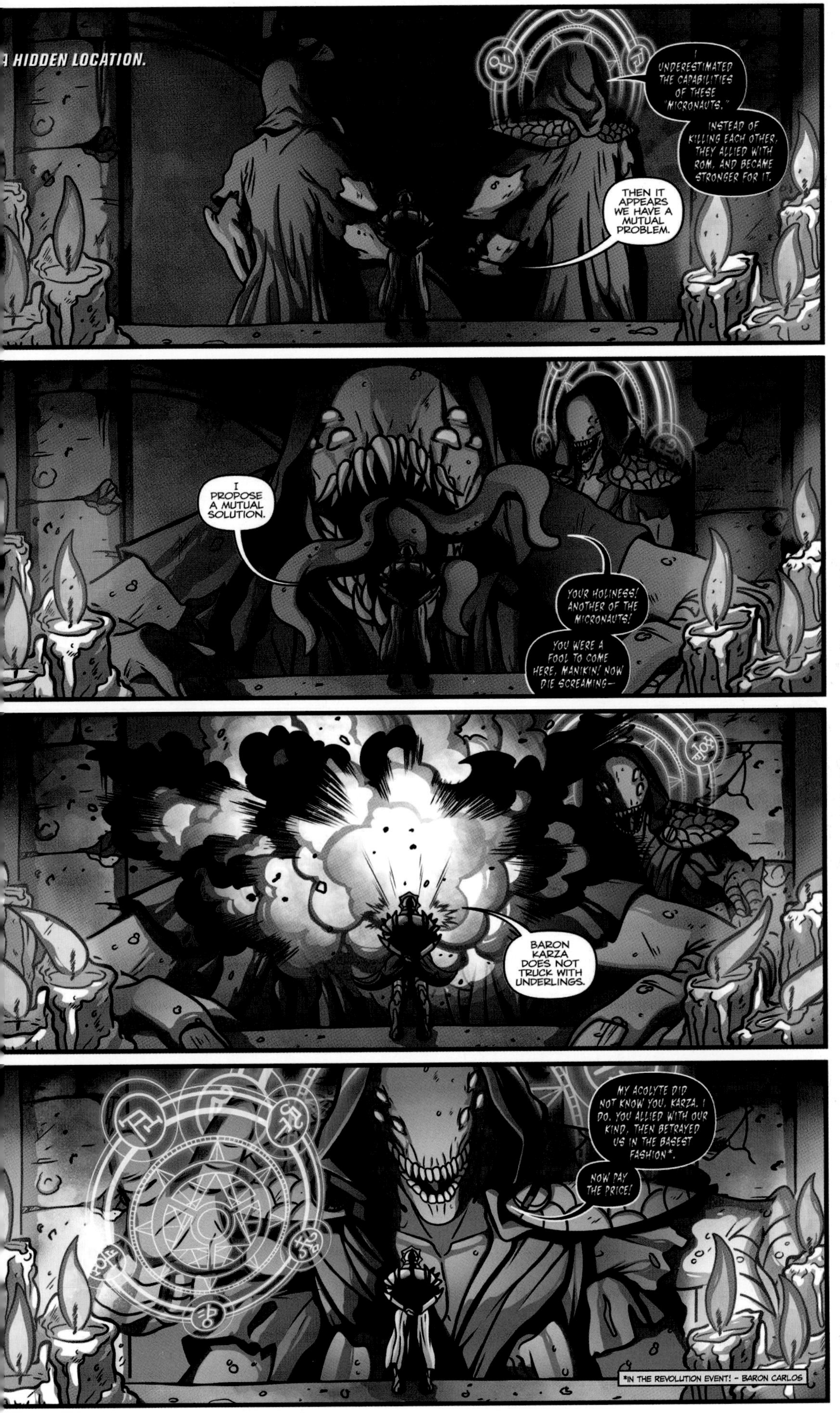
A HIDDEN LOCATION.
I UNDERESTIMATED THE CAPABILITIES OF THESE "MICRONAUTS."
INSTEAD OF KILLING EACH OTHER, THEY ALLIED WITH ROM, AND BECAME STRONGER FOR IT.
THEN IT APPEARS WE HAVE A MUTUAL PROBLEM.
I PROPOSE A MUTUAL SOLUTION.
YOUR HOLINESS! ANOTHER OF THE MICRONAUTS!
YOU WERE A FOOL TO COME HERE, MANIKIN! NOW DIE SCREAMING—
BARON KARZA DOES NOT TRUCK WITH UNDERLINGS.
MY ACOLYTE DID NOT KNOW YOU, KARZA. I DO. YOU ALLIED WITH OUR KIND, THEN BETRAYED US IN THE BASEST FASHION*.
NOW PAY THE PRICE!
*IN THE REVOLUTION EVENT! - BARON CARLOS

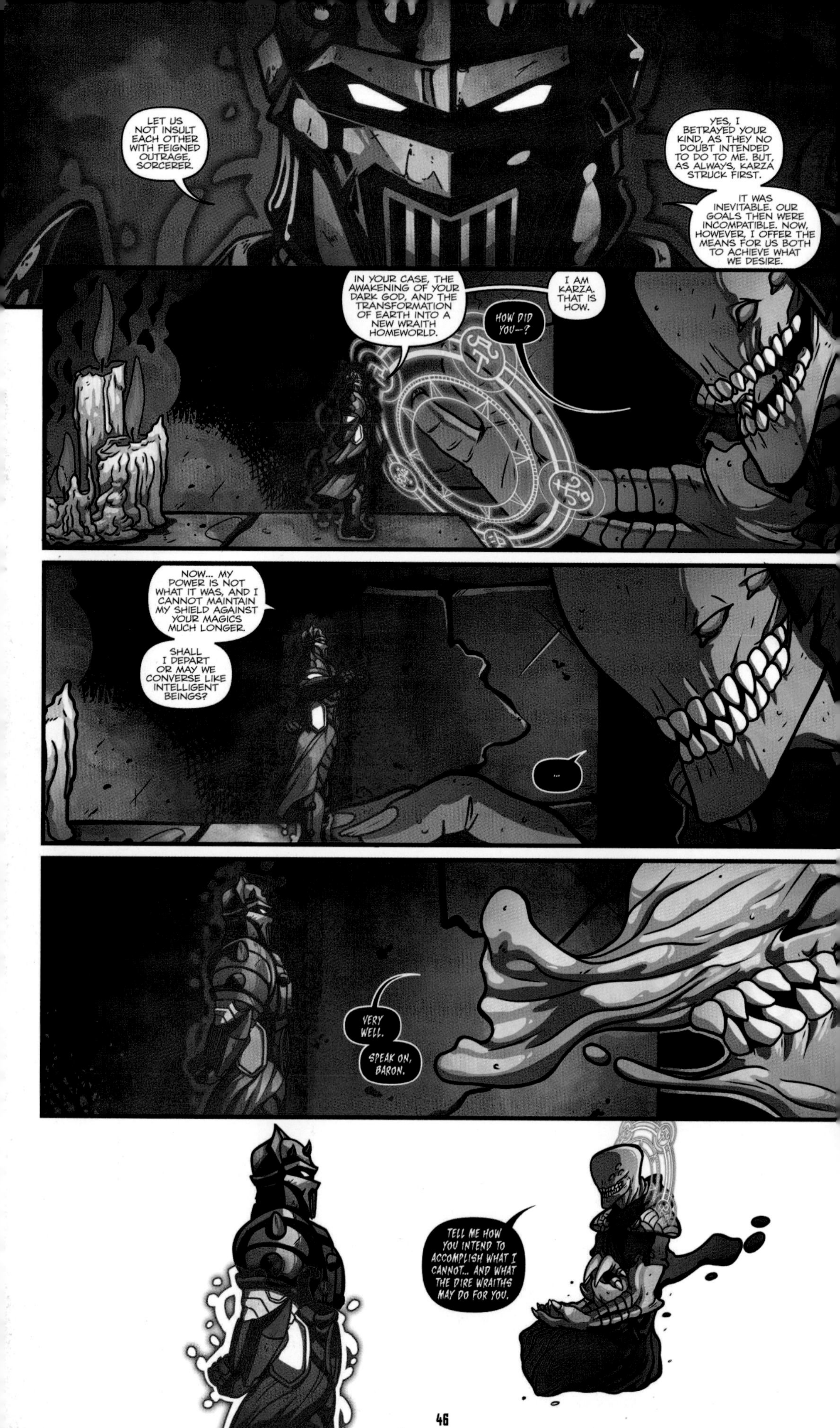
LET US NOT INSULT EACH OTHER WITH FEIGNED OUTRAGE, SORCERER.
YES, I BETRAYED YOUR KIND, AS THEY NO DOUBT INTENDED TO DO TO ME. BUT, AS ALWAYS, KARZA STRUCK FIRST.
IT WAS INEVITABLE. OUR GOALS THEN WERE INCOMPATIBLE. NOW, HOWEVER, I OFFER THE MEANS FOR US BOTH TO ACHIEVE WHAT WE DESIRE.
IN YOUR CASE, THE AWAKENING OF YOUR DARK GOD, AND THE TRANSFORMATION OF EARTH INTO A NEW WRAITH HOMEWORLD.
HOW DID YOU--?
I AM KARZA. THAT IS HOW.
NOW... MY POWER IS NOT WHAT IT WAS, AND I CANNOT MAINTAIN MY SHIELD AGAINST YOUR MAGICS MUCH LONGER.
SHALL I DEPART OR MAY WE CONVERSE LIKE INTELLIGENT BEINGS?
...
VERY WELL.
SPEAK ON, BARON.
TELL ME HOW YOU INTEND TO ACCOMPLISH WHAT I CANNOT... AND WHAT THE DIRE WRAITHS MAY DO FOR YOU.

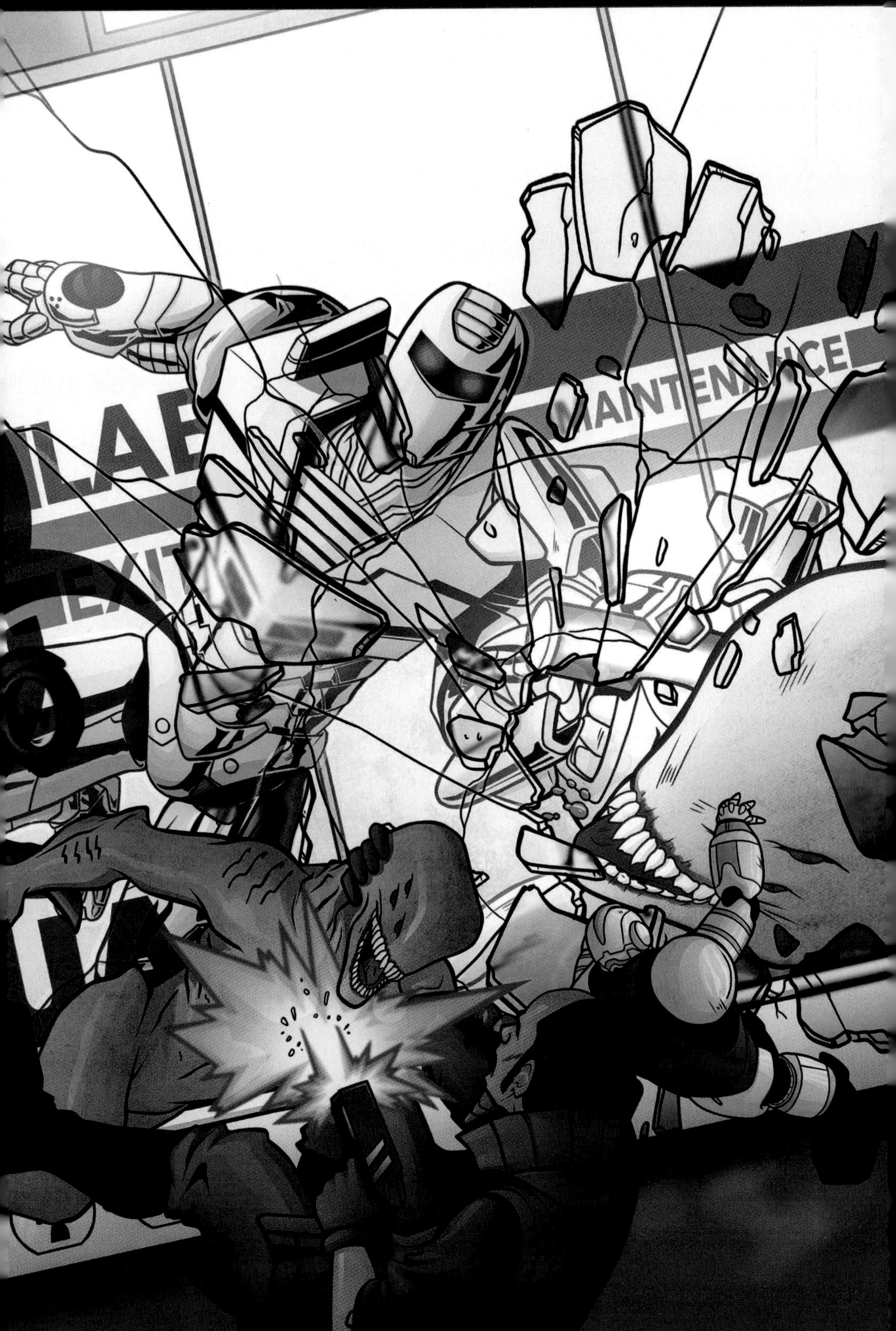
LAB

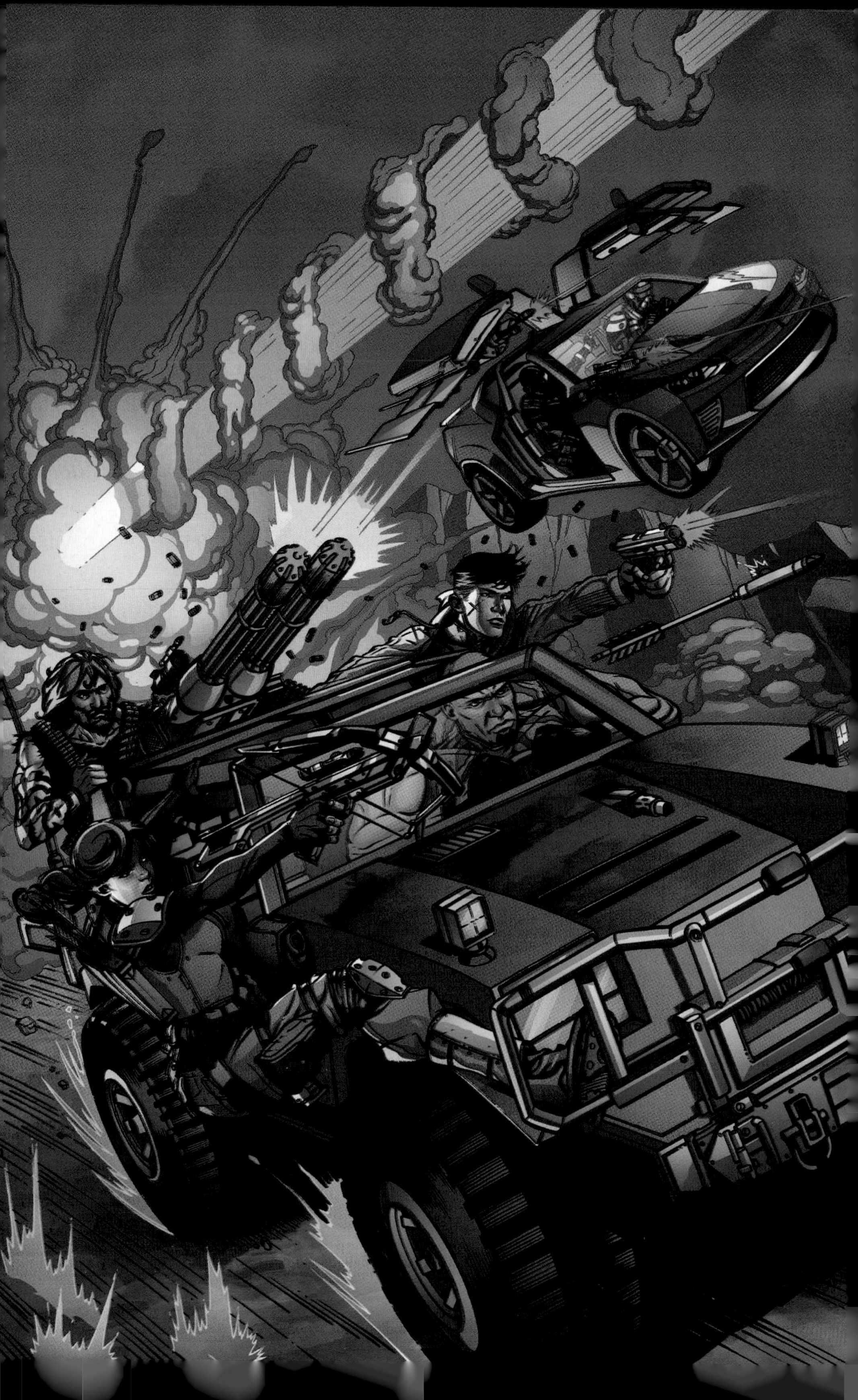

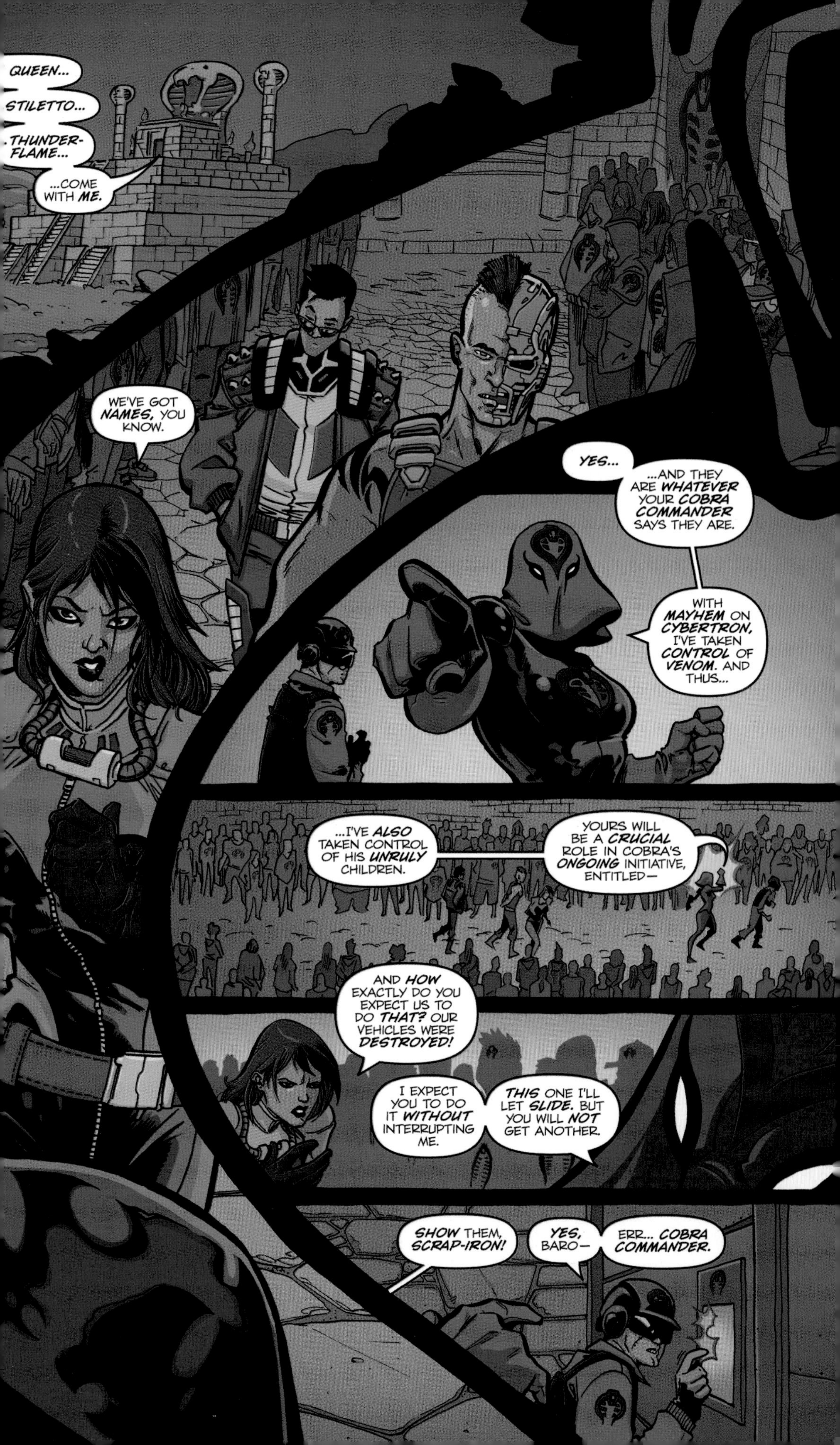
QUEEN...
STILETTO...
...THUNDER-FLAME...
...COME WITH ME.
WE'VE GOT NAMES, YOU KNOW.
YES...
...AND THEY ARE WHATEVER YOUR COBRA COMMANDER SAYS THEY ARE.
WITH MAYHEM ON CYBERTRON, I'VE TAKEN CONTROL OF VENOM. AND THUS...
...I'VE ALSO TAKEN CONTROL OF HIS UNRULY CHILDREN.
YOURS WILL BE A CRUCIAL ROLE IN COBRA'S ONGOING INITIATIVE, ENTITLED—
AND HOW EXACTLY DO YOU EXPECT US TO DO THAT? OUR VEHICLES WERE DESTROYED!
I EXPECT YOU TO DO IT WITHOUT INTERRUPTING ME.
THIS ONE I'LL LET SLIDE. BUT YOU WILL NOT GET ANOTHER.
SHOW THEM, SCRAP-IRON!
YES, BARO—
ERR... COBRA COMMANDER.

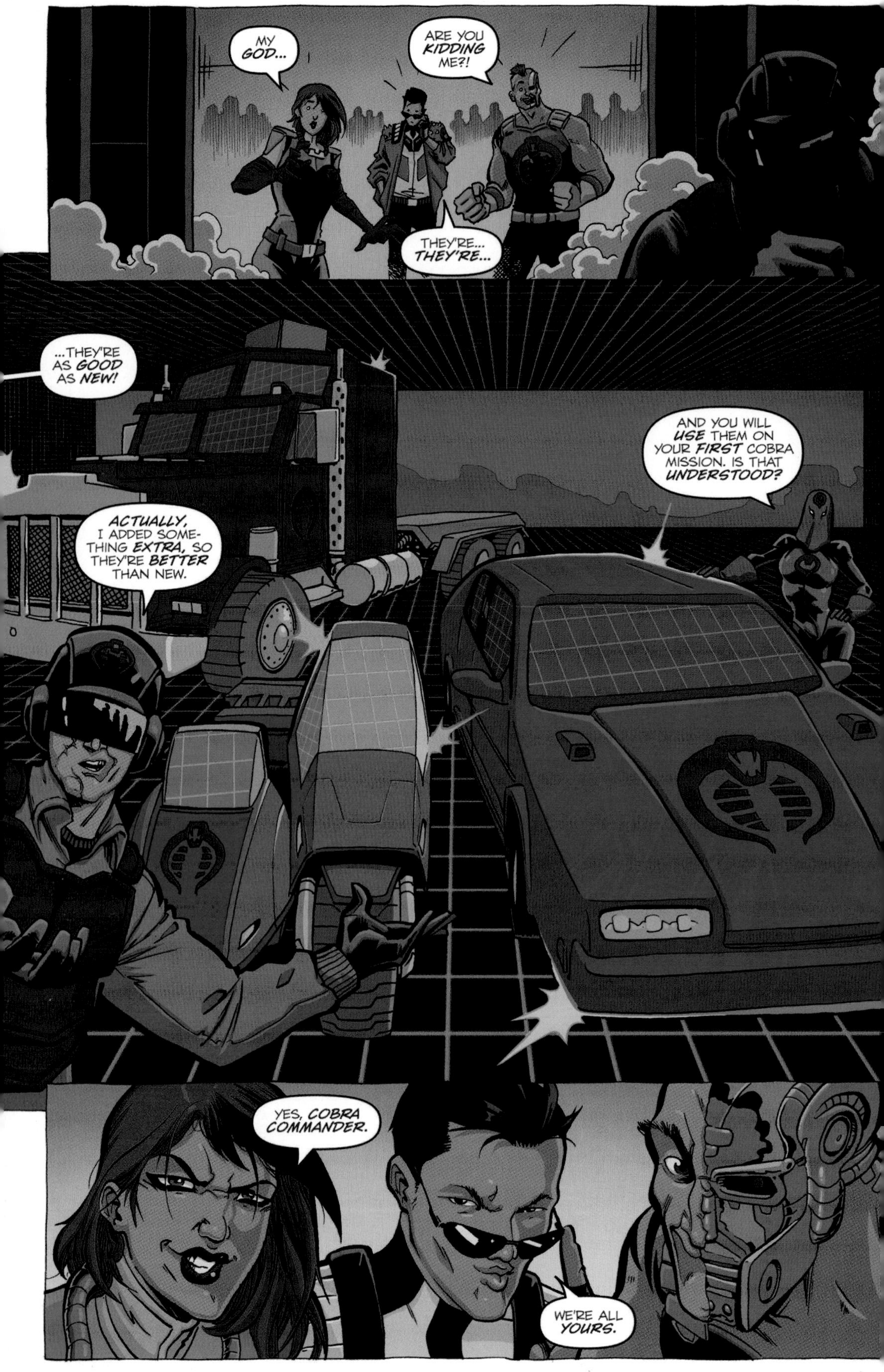
MY GOD...
ARE YOU KIDDING ME?!
THEY'RE... THEY'RE...
...THEY'RE AS GOOD AS NEW!
ACTUALLY, I ADDED SOMETHING EXTRA, SO THEY'RE BETTER THAN NEW.
AND YOU WILL USE THEM ON YOUR FIRST COBRA MISSION. IS THAT UNDERSTOOD?
YES, COBRA COMMANDER.
WE'RE ALL YOURS.

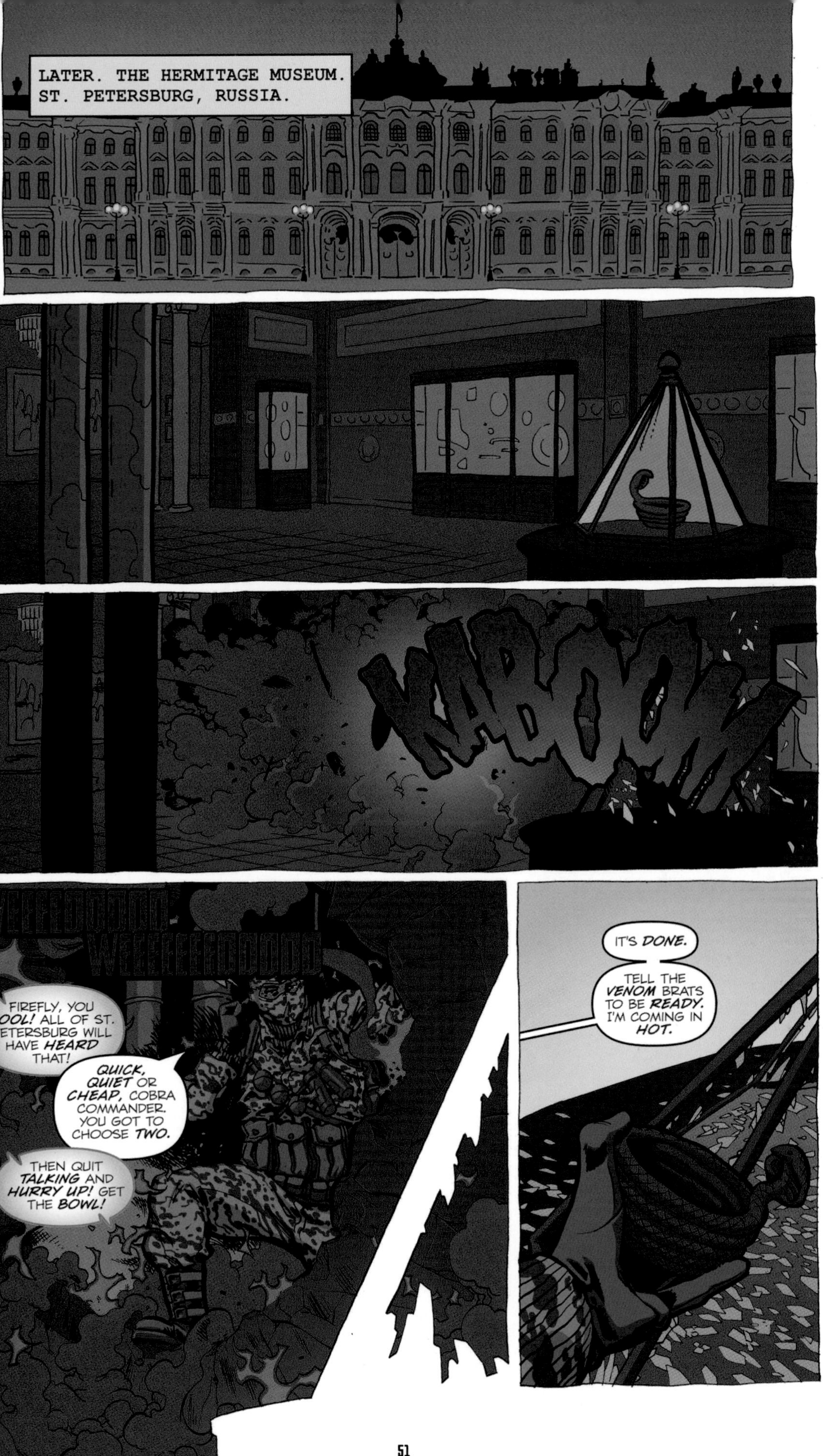

LATER. THE HERMITAGE MUSEUM. ST. PETERSBURG, RUSSIA.
KABOOM
FIREFLY, YOU FOOL! ALL OF ST. PETERSBURG WILL HAVE HEARD THAT!
QUICK, QUIET OR CHEAP, COBRA COMMANDER. YOU GOT TO CHOOSE TWO.
THEN QUIT TALKING AND HURRY UP! GET THE BOWL!
IT'S DONE.
TELL THE VENOM BRATS TO BE READY. I'M COMING IN HOT.

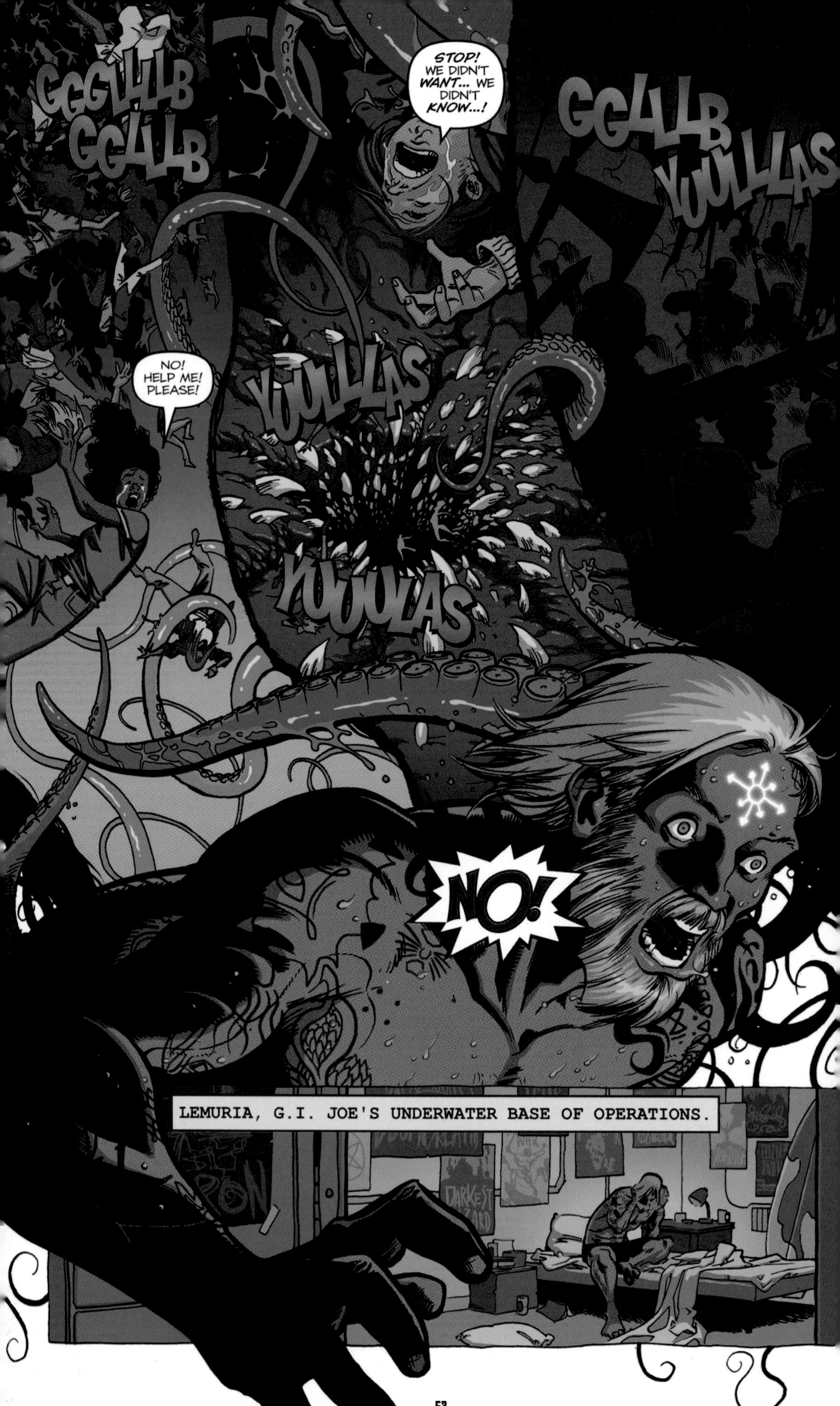
GGGLLLLB GGLLLB
STOP! WE DIDN'T WANT... WE DIDN'T KNOW...!
GGLLLB YUULLLAS
NO! HELP ME! PLEASE!
YUULLLAS
YUUULAS
NO!
LEMURIA, G.I. JOE'S UNDERWATER BASE OF OPERATIONS.

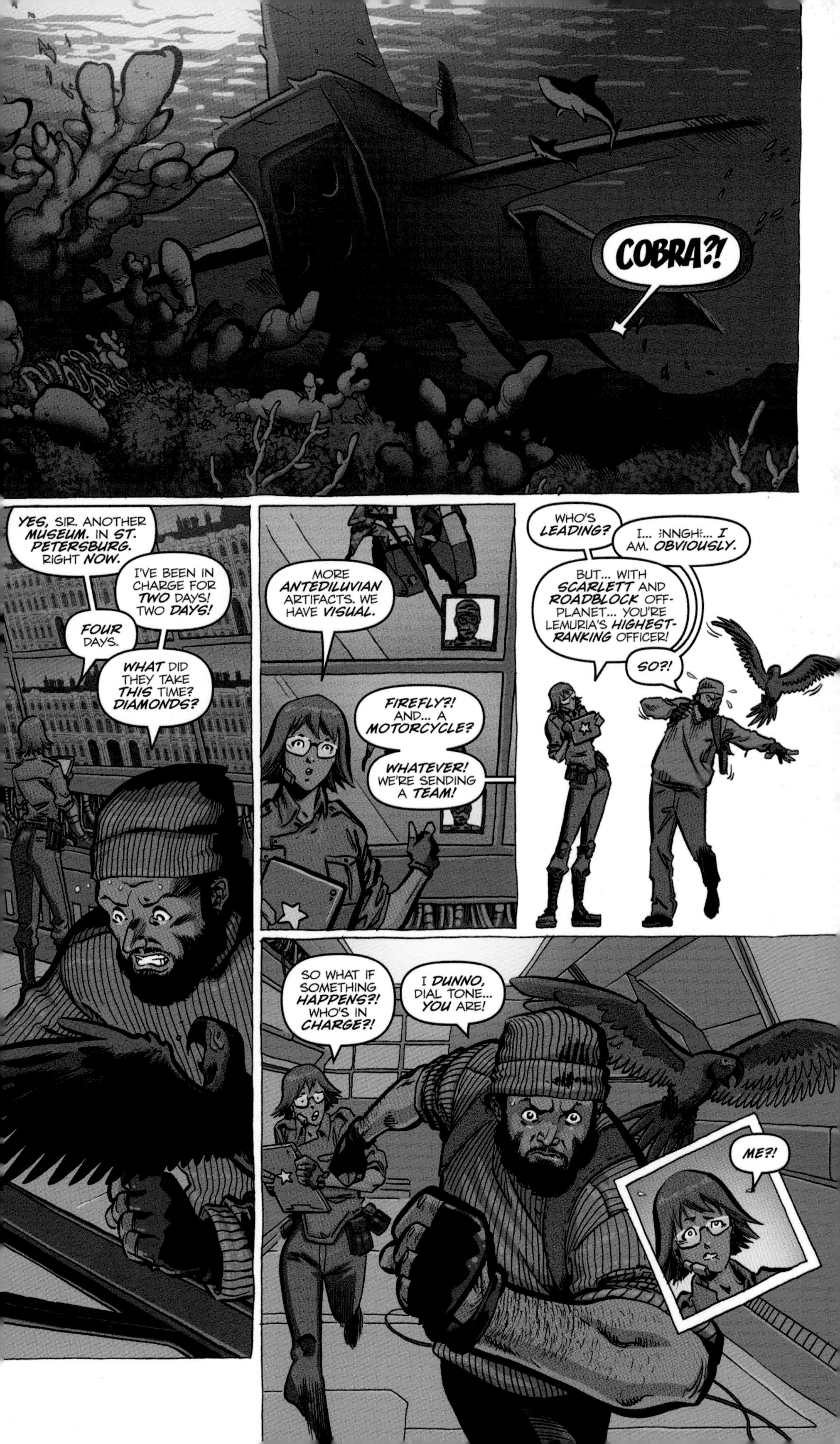
COBRA?!
YES, SIR. ANOTHER MUSEUM. IN ST. PETERSBURG. RIGHT NOW.
I'VE BEEN IN CHARGE FOR TWO DAYS! TWO DAYS!
FOUR DAYS.
WHAT DID THEY TAKE THIS TIME? DIAMONDS?
MORE ANTEDILUVIAN ARTIFACTS. WE HAVE VISUAL.
FIREFLY?! AND... A MOTORCYCLE?
WHATEVER! WE'RE SENDING A TEAM!
WHO'S LEADING?
I... NNGH... I AM. OBVIOUSLY.
BUT... WITH SCARLETT AND ROADBLOCK OFF-PLANET... YOU'RE LEMURIA'S HIGHEST-RANKING OFFICER!
SO?!
SO WHAT IF SOMETHING HAPPENS?! WHO'S IN CHARGE?!
I DUNNO, DIAL TONE... YOU ARE!
ME?!

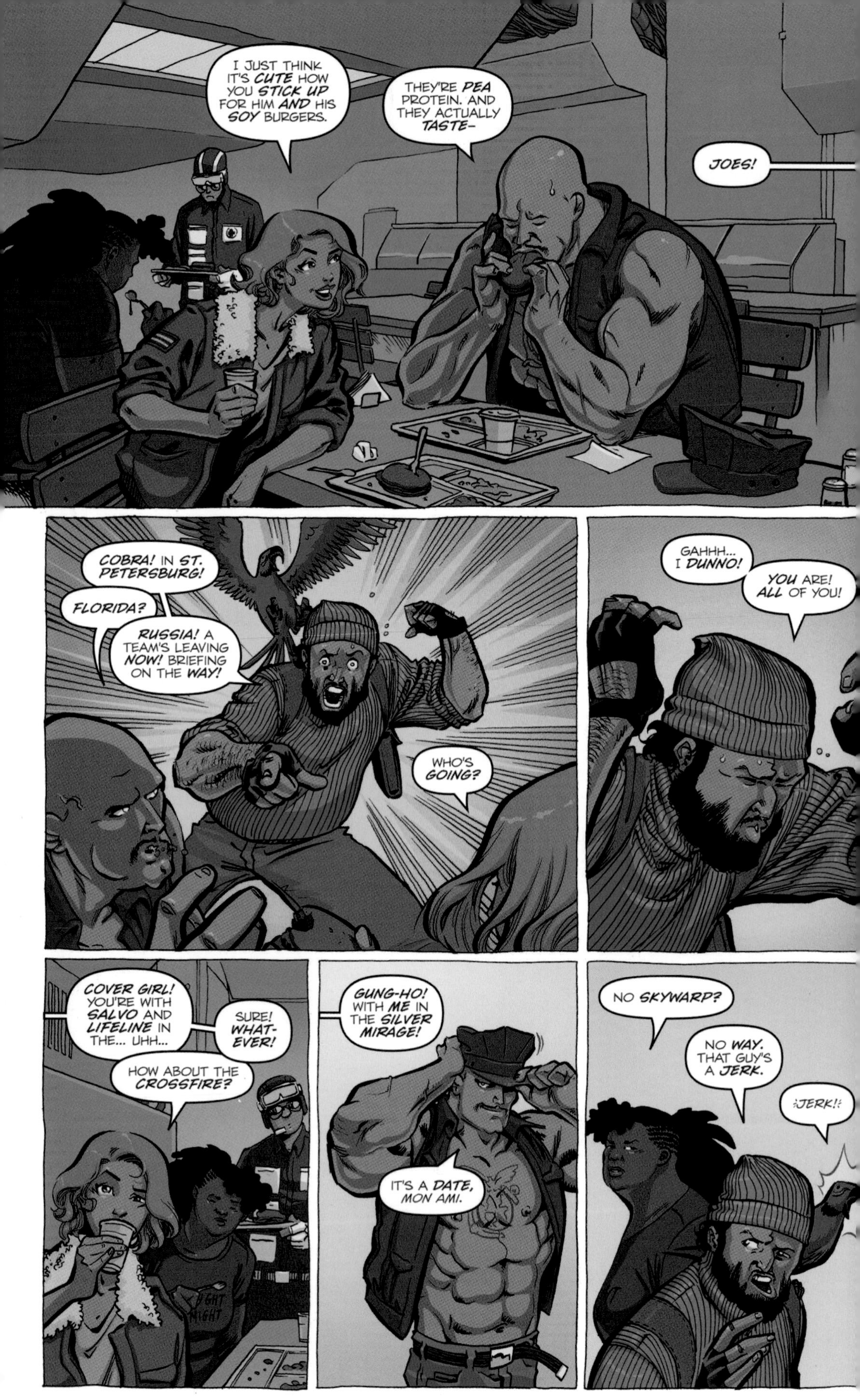

I JUST THINK IT'S CUTE HOW YOU STICK UP FOR HIM AND HIS SOY BURGERS.
THEY'RE PEA PROTEIN. AND THEY ACTUALLY TASTE–
JOES!
COBRA! IN ST. PETERSBURG!
FLORIDA?
RUSSIA! A TEAM'S LEAVING NOW! BRIEFING ON THE WAY!
WHO'S GOING?
GAHHH... I DUNNO!
YOU ARE! ALL OF YOU!
COVER GIRL! YOU'RE WITH SALVO AND LIFELINE IN THE... UHH...
SURE! WHAT-EVER!
HOW ABOUT THE CROSSFIRE?
GUNG-HO! WITH ME IN THE SILVER MIRAGE!
IT'S A DATE, MON AMI.
NO SKYWARP?
NO WAY. THAT GUY'S A JERK.
JERK!

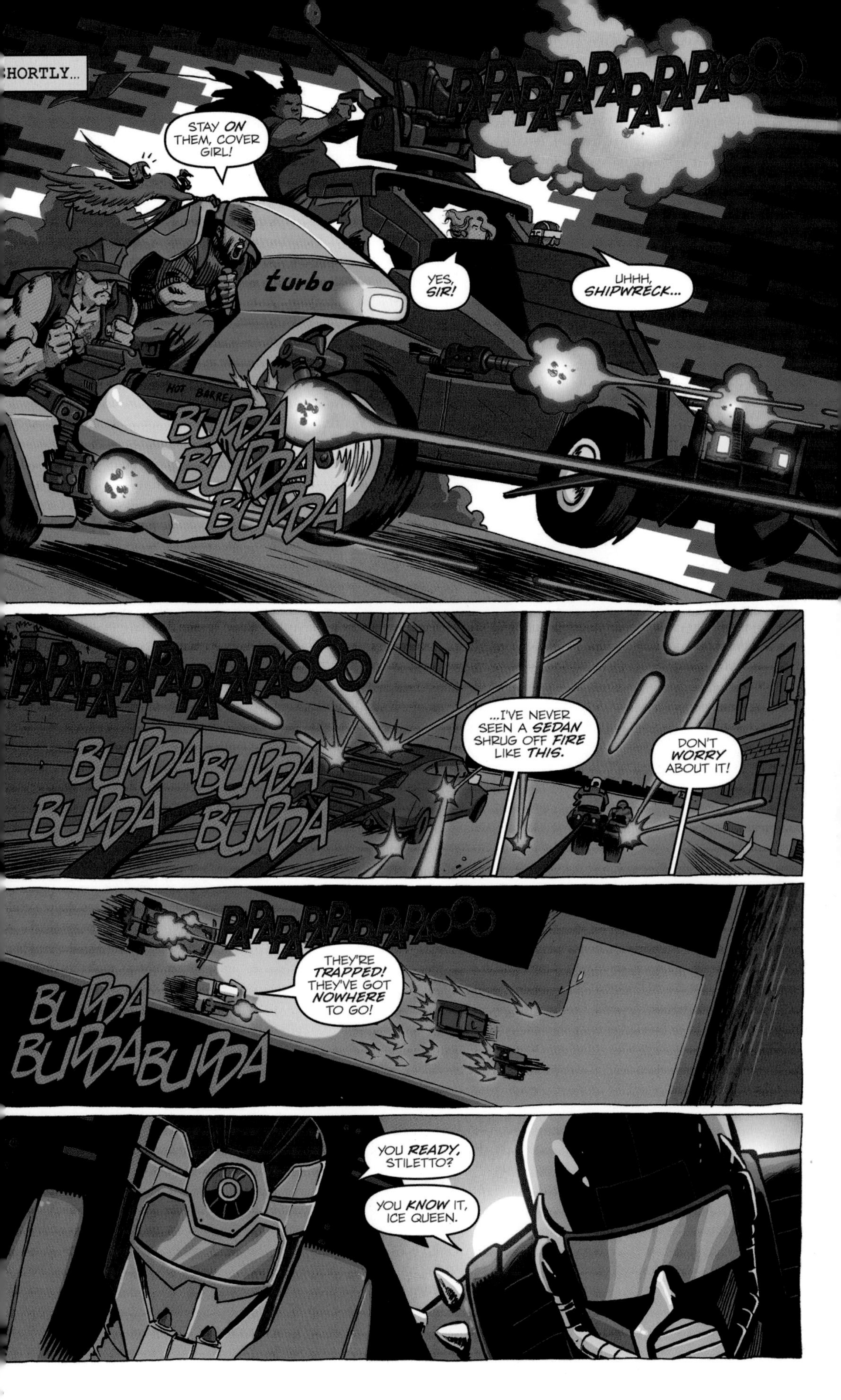
SHORTLY...
STAY ON THEM, COVER GIRL!
YES, SIR!
UHHH, SHIPWRECK...
BUDDA BUDDA BUDDA
...I'VE NEVER SEEN A SEDAN SHRUG OFF FIRE LIKE THIS.
DON'T WORRY ABOUT IT!
BUDDABUDDA BUDDA BUDDA
THEY'RE TRAPPED! THEY'VE GOT NOWHERE TO GO!
BUDDA BUDDABUDDA
YOU READY, STILETTO?
YOU KNOW IT, ICE QUEEN.

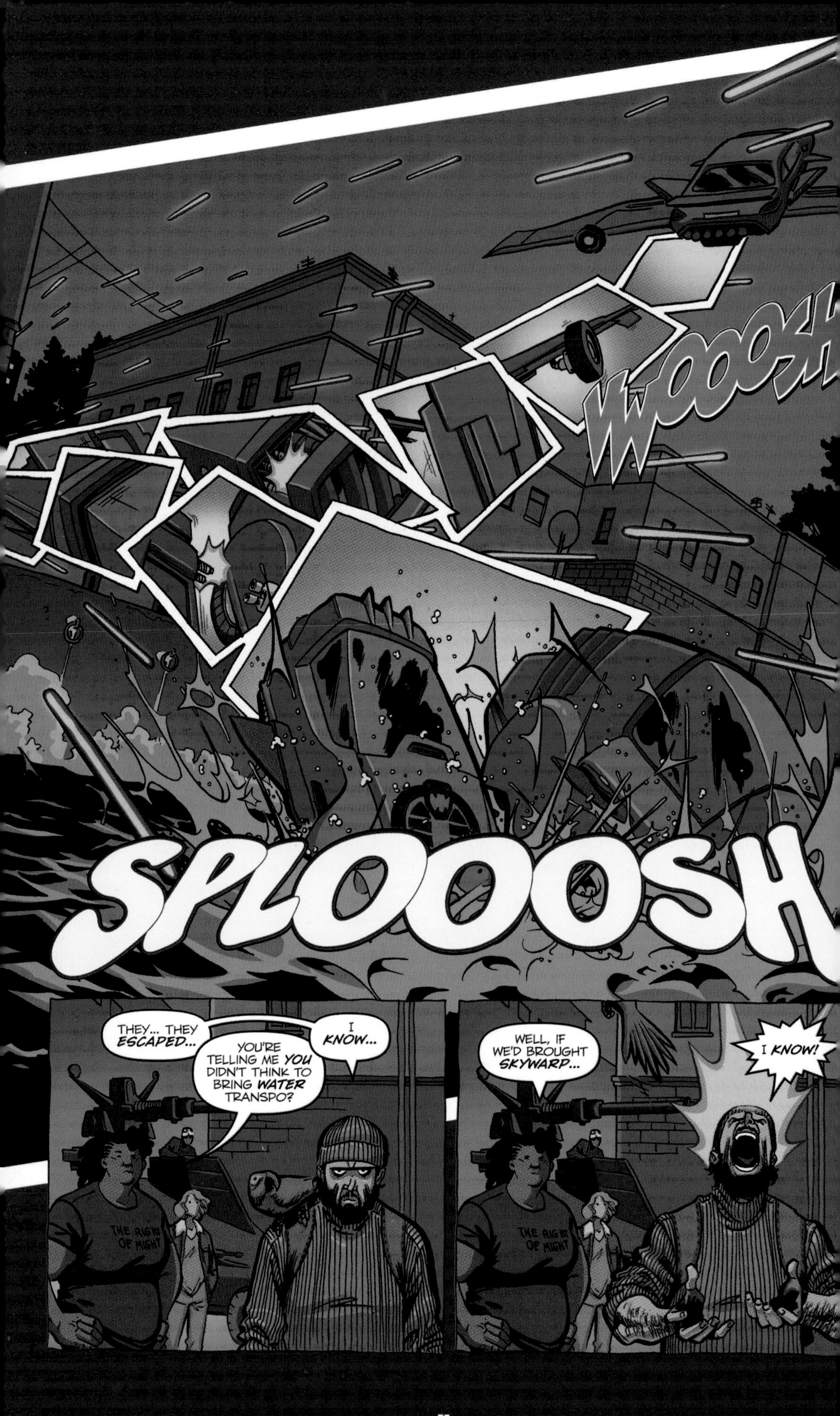
WOOOSH
SPLOOOSH
THEY... THEY ESCAPED...
I KNOW...
YOU'RE TELLING ME YOU DIDN'T THINK TO BRING WATER TRANSPO?
THE RIGHT OF MIGHT
WELL, IF WE'D BROUGHT SKYWARP...
I KNOW!
THE RIGHT OF MIGHT

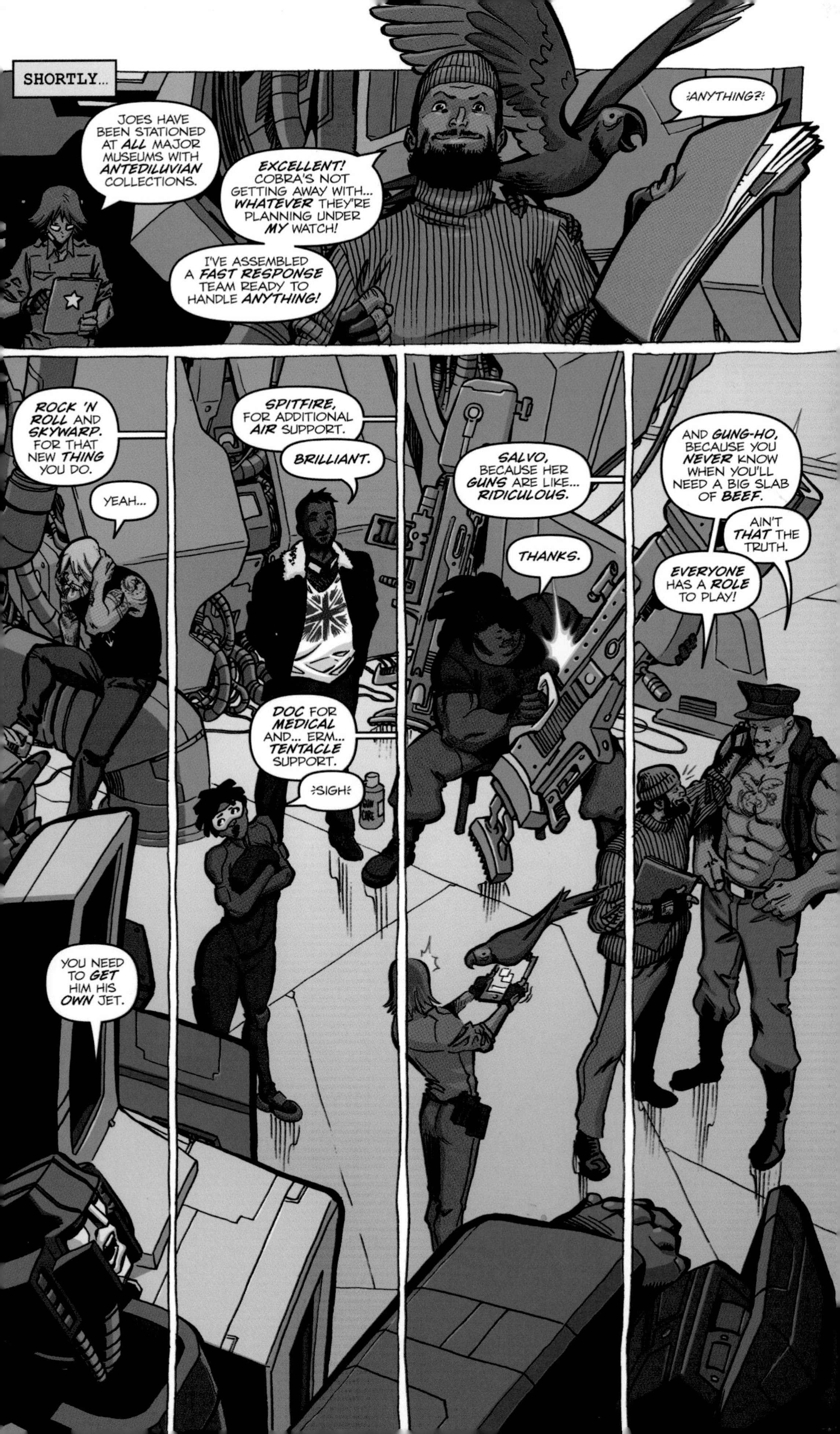
SHORTLY...
JOES HAVE BEEN STATIONED AT ALL MAJOR MUSEUMS WITH ANTEDILUVIAN COLLECTIONS.
EXCELLENT! COBRA'S NOT GETTING AWAY WITH... WHATEVER THEY'RE PLANNING UNDER MY WATCH!
I'VE ASSEMBLED A FAST RESPONSE TEAM READY TO HANDLE ANYTHING!
:ANYTHING?:
ROCK 'N ROLL AND SKYWARP. FOR THAT NEW THING YOU DO.
YEAH...
YOU NEED TO GET HIM HIS OWN JET.
SPITFIRE, FOR ADDITIONAL AIR SUPPORT.
BRILLIANT.
DOC FOR MEDICAL AND... ERM... TENTACLE SUPPORT.
:SIGH:
SALVO, BECAUSE HER GUNS ARE LIKE... RIDICULOUS.
THANKS.
AND GUNG-HO, BECAUSE YOU NEVER KNOW WHEN YOU'LL NEED A BIG SLAB OF BEEF.
AIN'T THAT THE TRUTH.
EVERYONE HAS A ROLE TO PLAY!

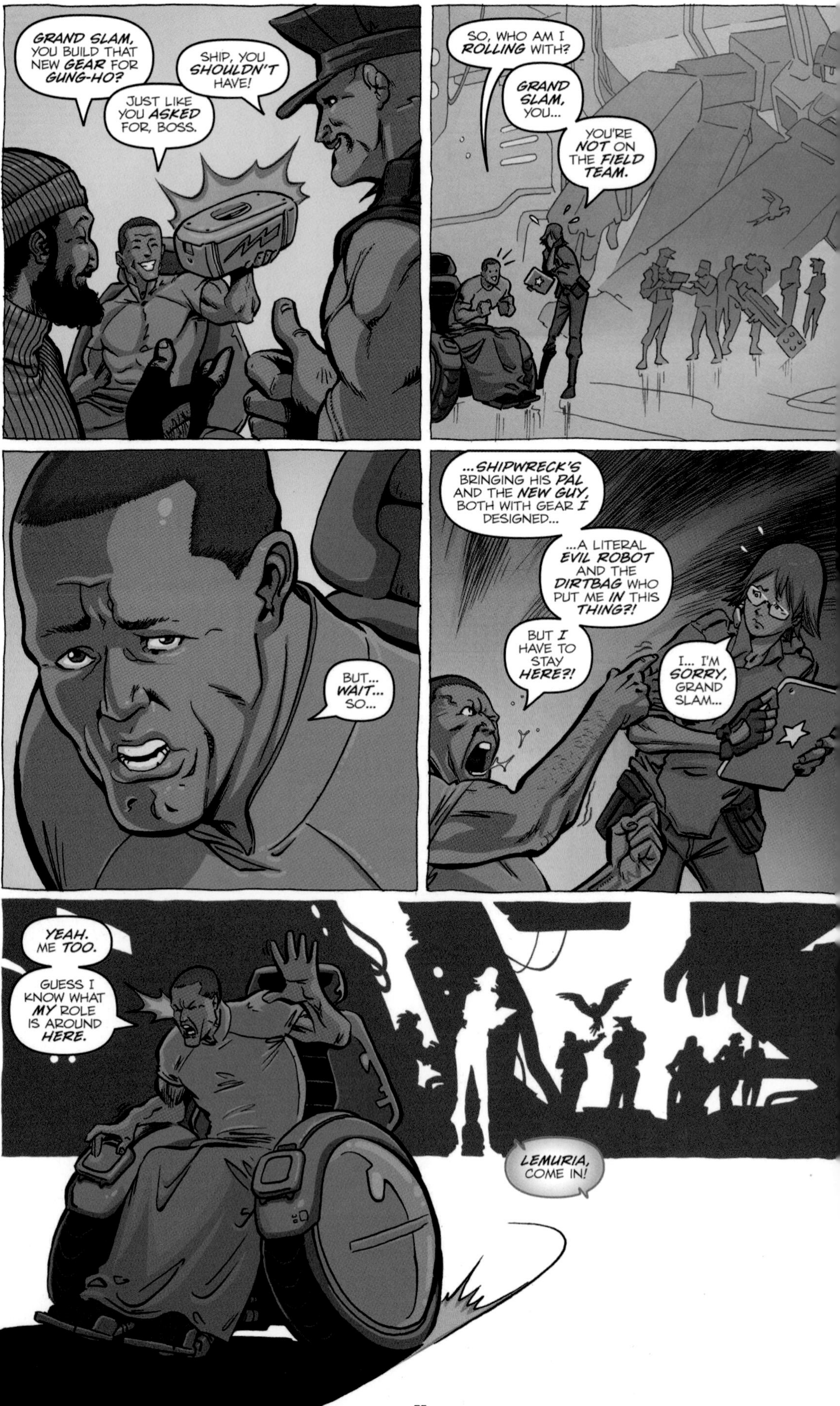
GRAND SLAM, YOU BUILD THAT NEW GEAR FOR GUNG-HO?
JUST LIKE YOU ASKED FOR, BOSS.
SHIP, YOU SHOULDN'T HAVE!
SO, WHO AM I ROLLING WITH?
GRAND SLAM, YOU...
YOU'RE NOT ON THE FIELD TEAM.
BUT... WAIT... SO...
...SHIPWRECK'S BRINGING HIS PAL AND THE NEW GUY, BOTH WITH GEAR I DESIGNED...
...A LITERAL EVIL ROBOT AND THE DIRTBAG WHO PUT ME IN THIS THING?!
BUT I HAVE TO STAY HERE?!
I... I'M SORRY, GRAND SLAM...
YEAH. ME TOO.
GUESS I KNOW WHAT MY ROLE IS AROUND HERE.
LEMURIA, COME IN!

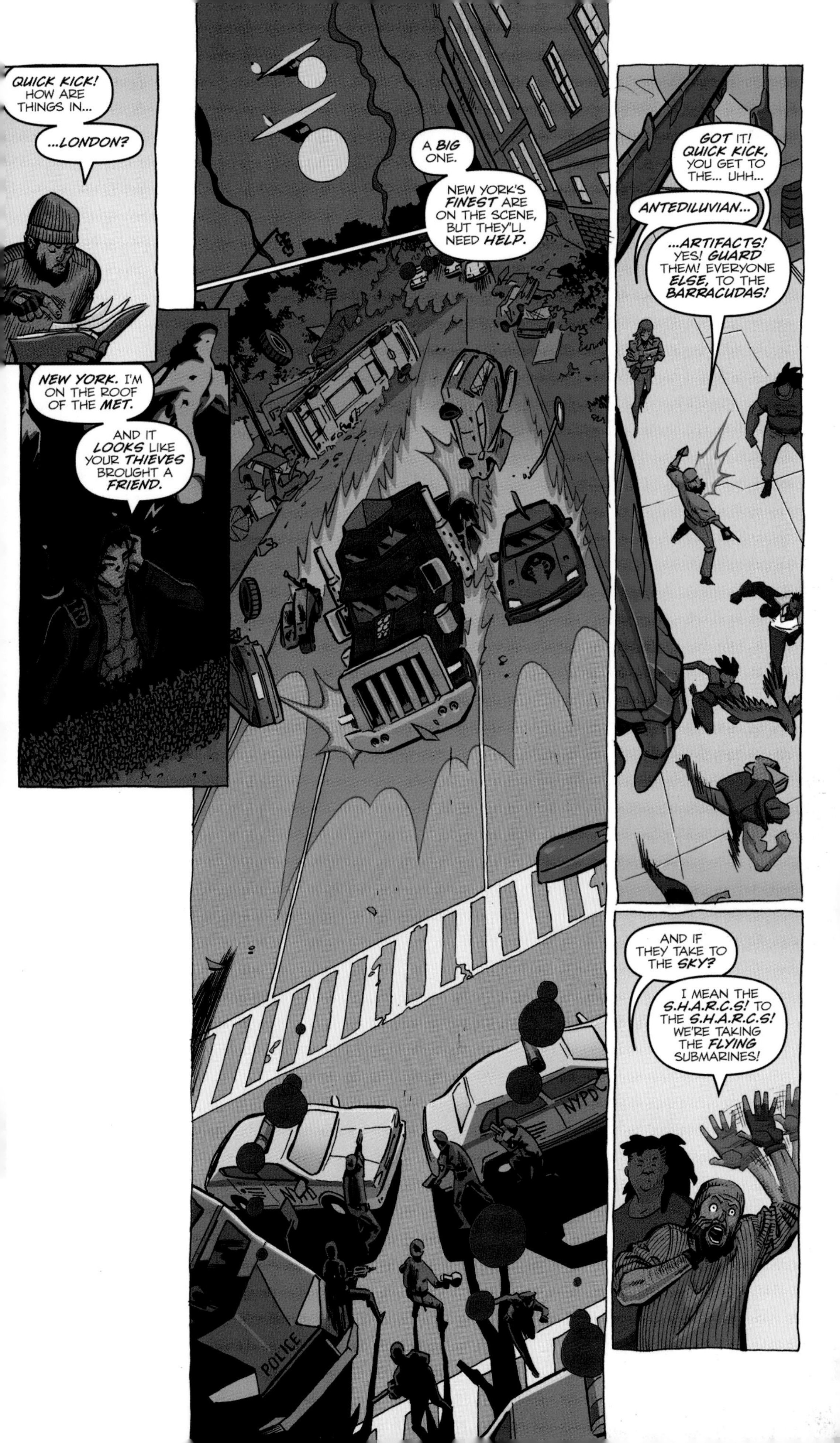
QUICK KICK! HOW ARE THINGS IN...
...LONDON?
NEW YORK. I'M ON THE ROOF OF THE MET.
AND IT LOOKS LIKE YOUR THIEVES BROUGHT A FRIEND.
A BIG ONE.
NEW YORK'S FINEST ARE ON THE SCENE, BUT THEY'LL NEED HELP.
NYPD
POLICE
GOT IT! QUICK KICK, YOU GET TO THE... UHH...
ANTEDILUVIAN...
...ARTIFACTS! YES! GUARD THEM! EVERYONE ELSE, TO THE BARRACUDAS!
AND IF THEY TAKE TO THE SKY?
I MEAN THE S.H.A.R.C.S! TO THE S.H.A.R.C.S! WE'RE TAKING THE FLYING SUBMARINES!

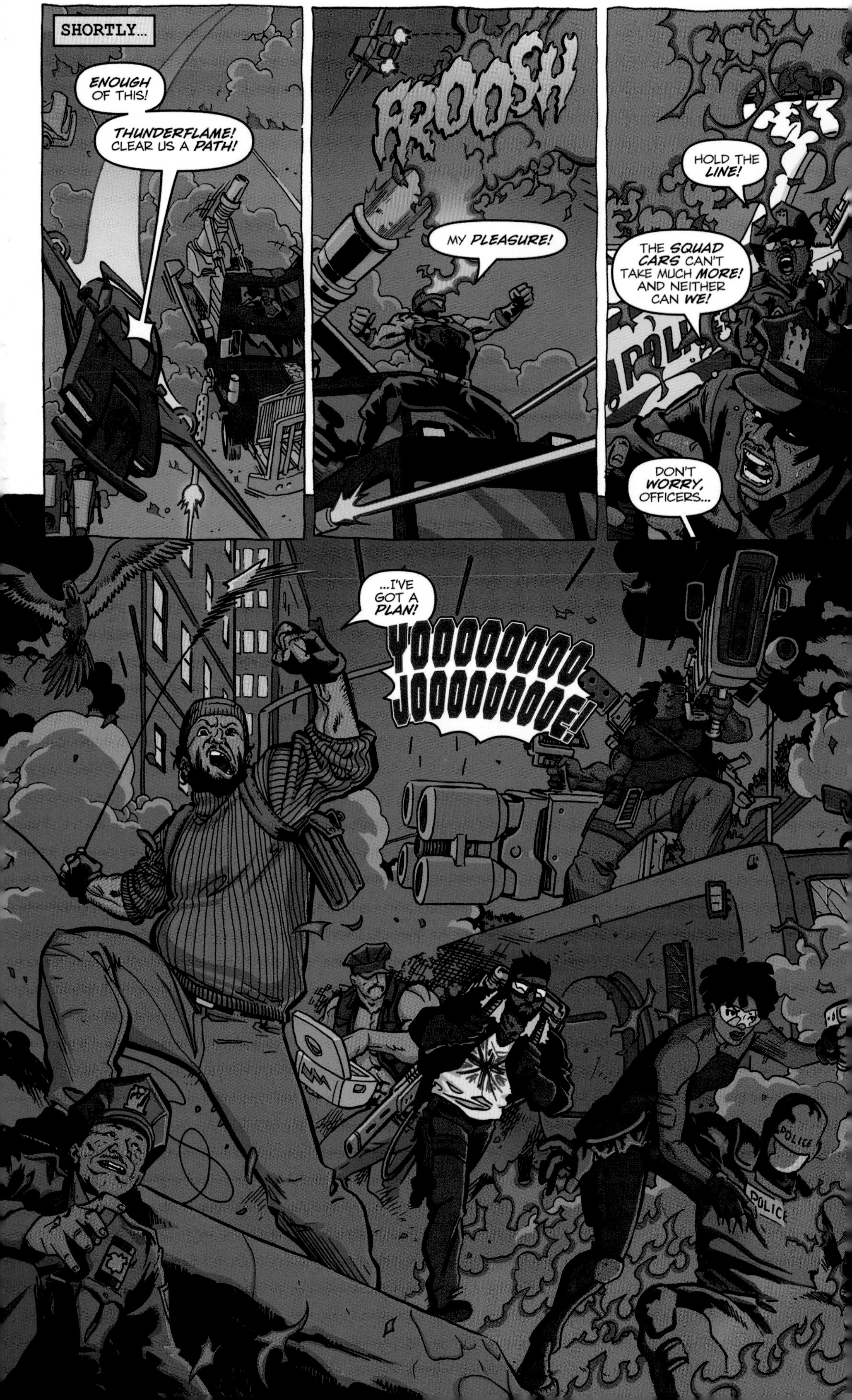
SHORTLY...
ENOUGH OF THIS!
THUNDERFLAME! CLEAR US A PATH!
FROOSH
MY PLEASURE!
HOLD THE LINE!
THE SQUAD CARS CAN'T TAKE MUCH MORE! AND NEITHER CAN WE!
DON'T WORRY, OFFICERS...
...I'VE GOT A PLAN!
YOOOOOOOO JOOOOOOOOE!
POLICE
POLICE

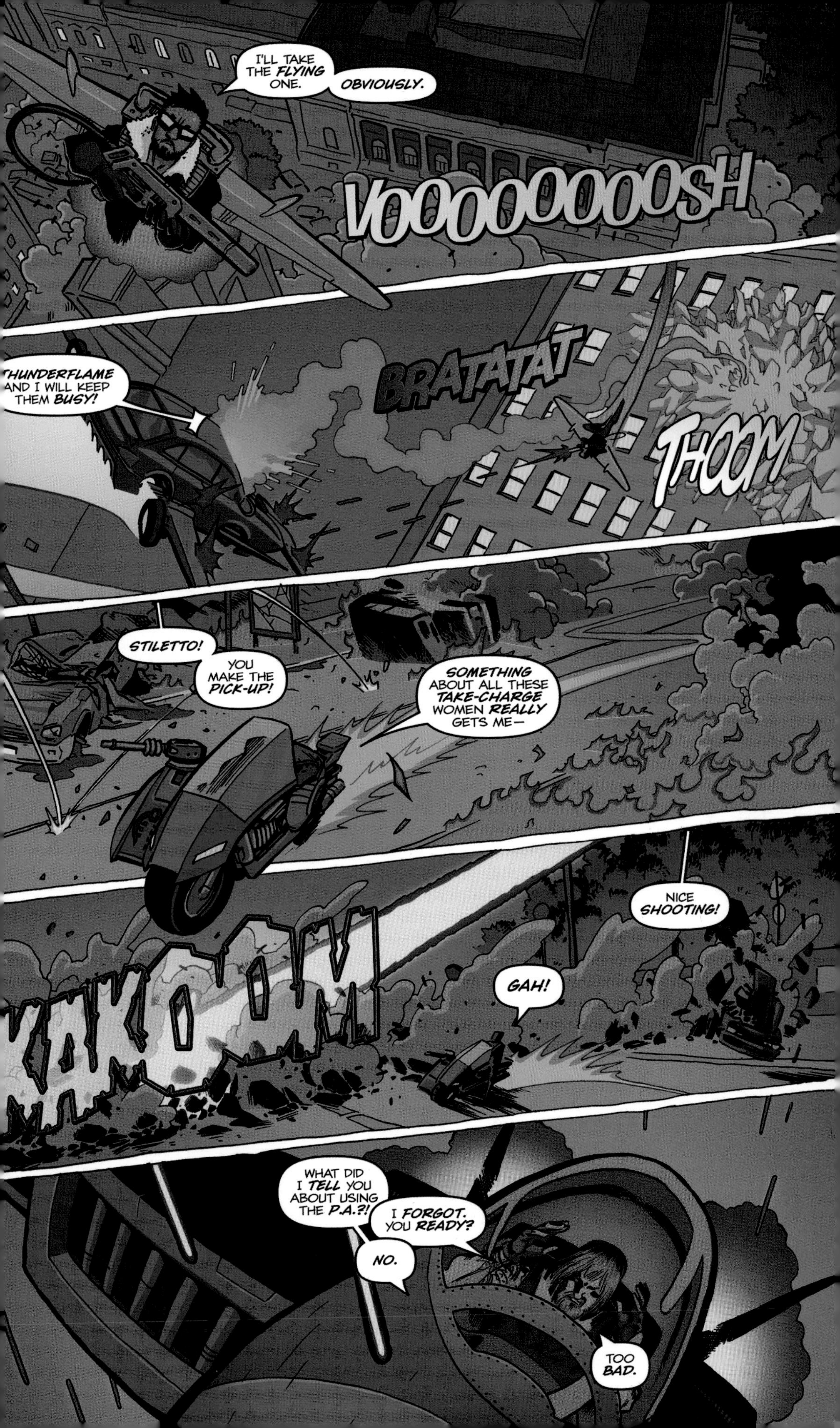
I'LL TAKE THE FLYING ONE.
OBVIOUSLY.
VOOOOOOOOOSH
THUNDERFLAME AND I WILL KEEP THEM BUSY!
BRATATAT
THOOM
STILETTO!
YOU MAKE THE PICK-UP!
SOMETHING ABOUT ALL THESE TAKE-CHARGE WOMEN REALLY GETS ME—
NICE SHOOTING!
GAH!
WHAT DID I TELL YOU ABOUT USING THE P.A.?!
I FORGOT. YOU READY?
NO.
TOO BAD.

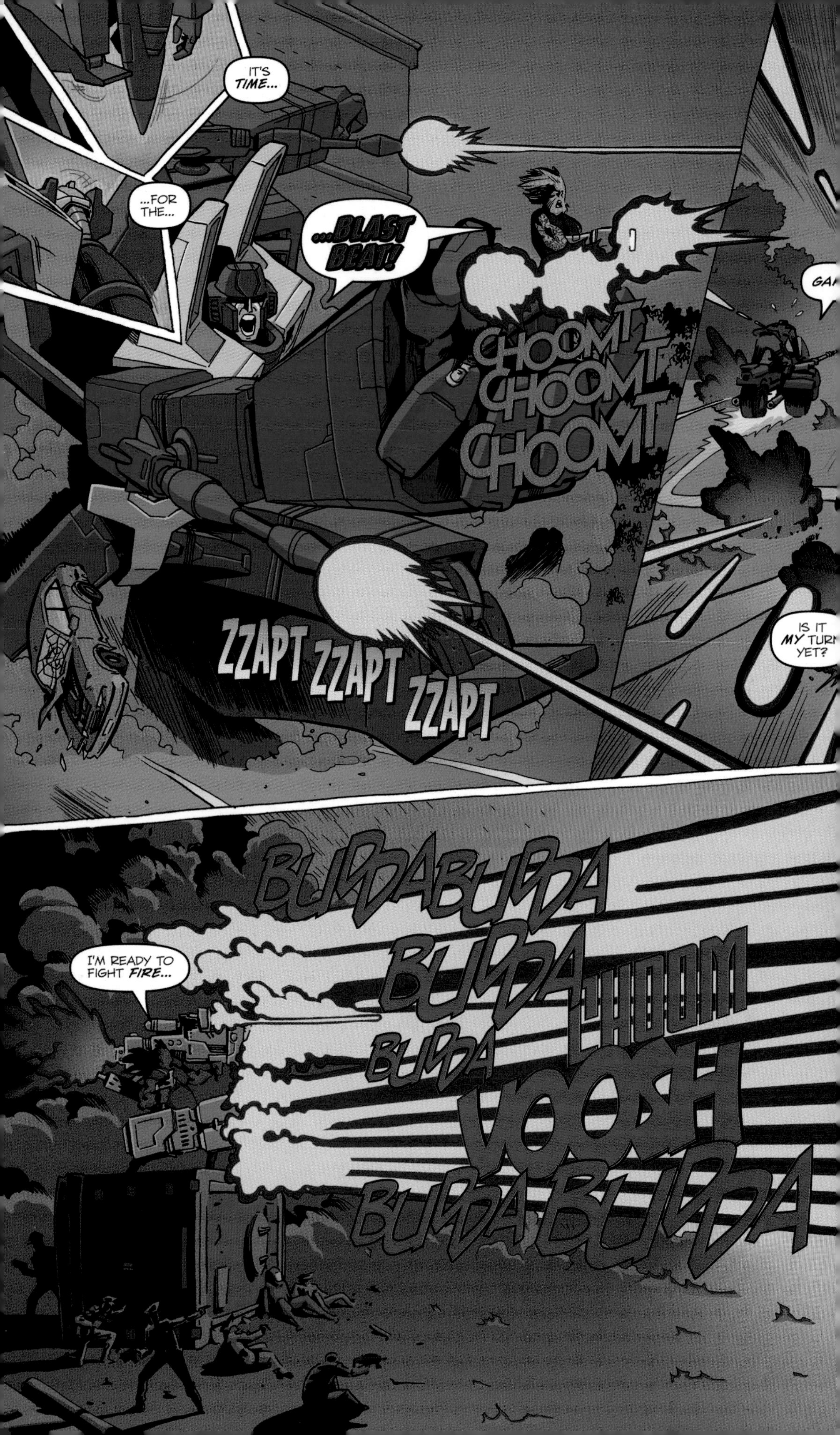
IT'S TIME...
...FOR THE...
...BLAST BEAT!
CHOOMT CHOOMT CHOOMT
ZZAPT ZZAPT ZZAPT
IS IT MY TURN YET?
I'M READY TO FIGHT FIRE...
BUDDABUDDA BUDDA BUDDA
CHOOM
VOOSH
BUDDA BUDDA

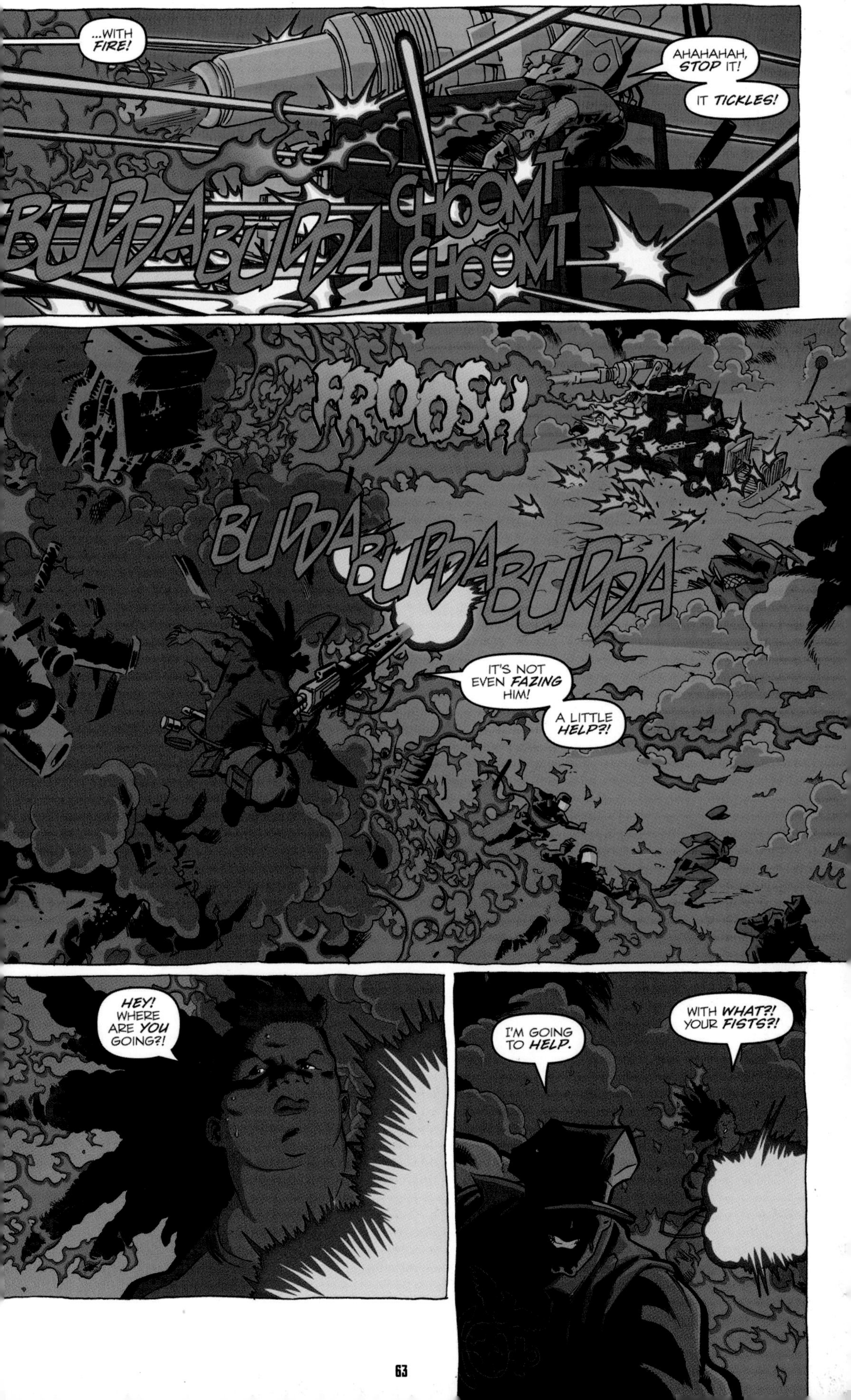
...WITH FIRE!
AHAHAHAH, STOP IT!
IT TICKLES!
BUDDABUDDA
CHOOMT CHOOMT
FROOSH
BUDDA BUDDA BUDDA
IT'S NOT EVEN FAZING HIM!
A LITTLE HELP?!
HEY! WHERE ARE YOU GOING?!
I'M GOING TO HELP.
WITH WHAT?! YOUR FISTS?!

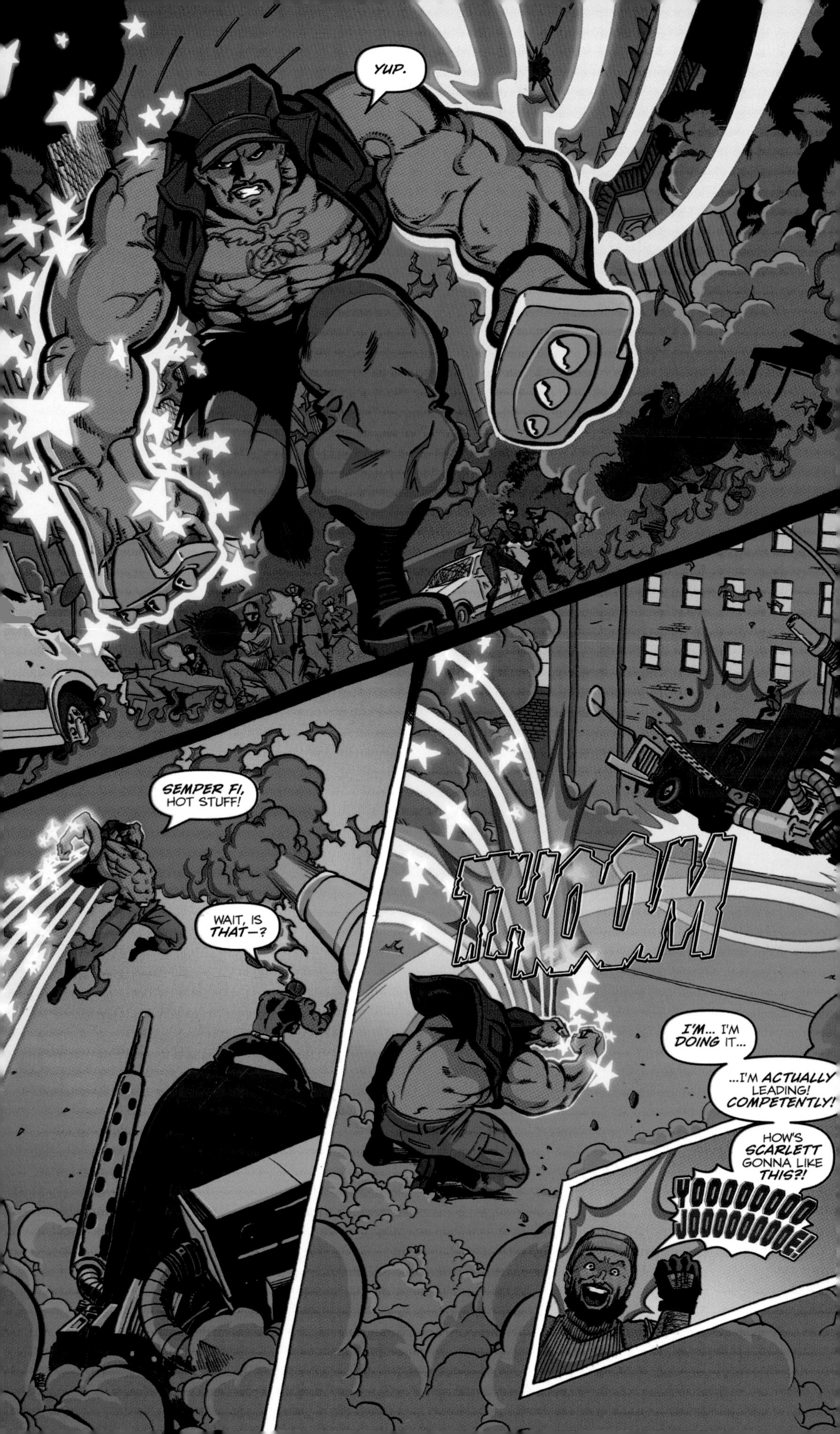
YUP.
SEMPER FI, HOT STUFF!
WAIT, IS THAT—?
THOOM
I'M... I'M DOING IT...
...I'M ACTUALLY LEADING! COMPETENTLY!
HOW'S SCARLETT GONNA LIKE THIS?!
YOOOOOOOO JOOOOOOOOE!

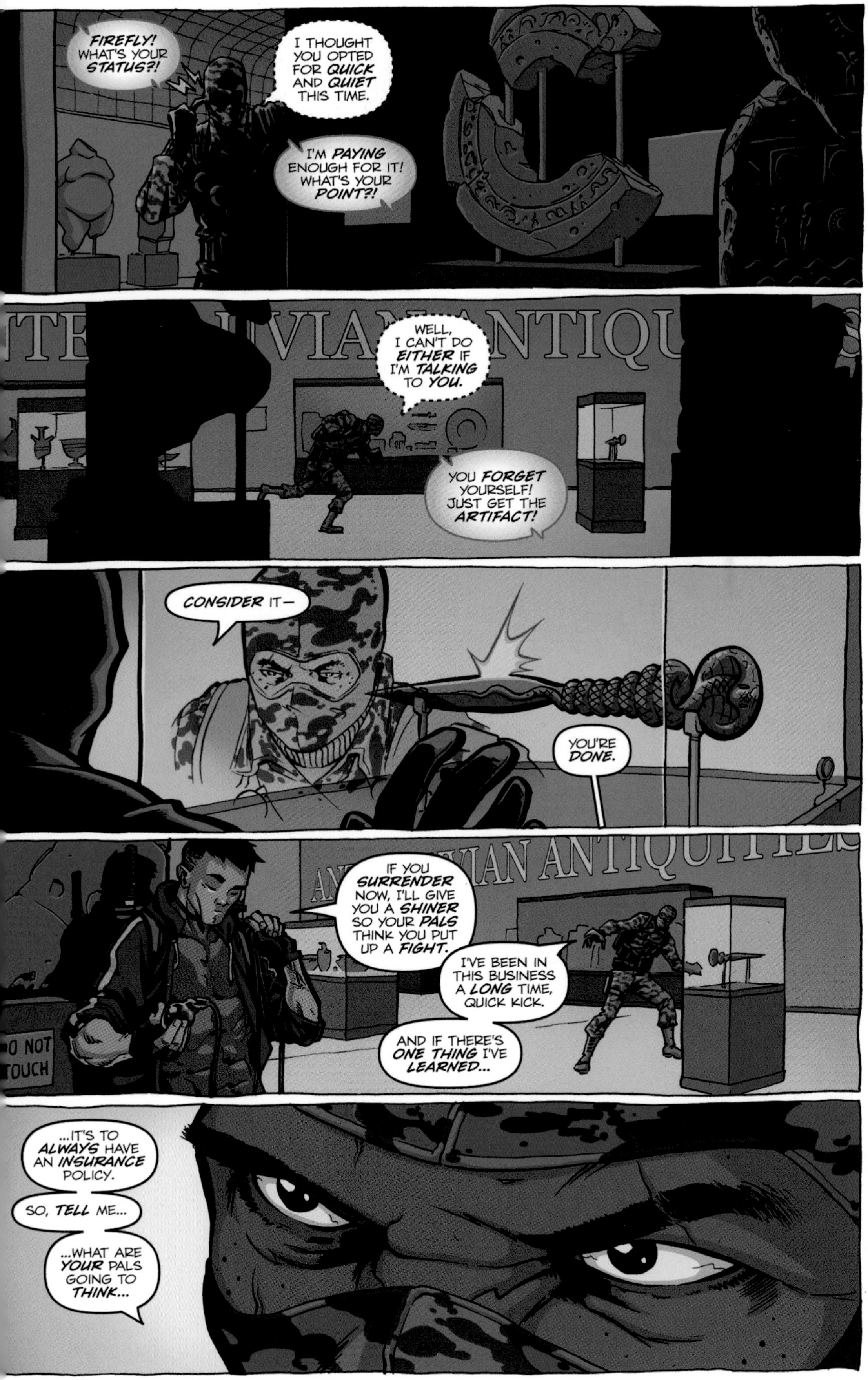
FIREFLY! WHAT'S YOUR STATUS?!
I THOUGHT YOU OPTED FOR QUICK AND QUIET THIS TIME.
I'M PAYING ENOUGH FOR IT! WHAT'S YOUR POINT?!
WELL, I CAN'T DO EITHER IF I'M TALKING TO YOU.
YOU FORGET YOURSELF! JUST GET THE ARTIFACT!
CONSIDER IT—
YOU'RE DONE.
IF YOU SURRENDER NOW, I'LL GIVE YOU A SHINER SO YOUR PALS THINK YOU PUT UP A FIGHT.
I'VE BEEN IN THIS BUSINESS A LONG TIME, QUICK KICK.
AND IF THERE'S ONE THING I'VE LEARNED...
...IT'S TO ALWAYS HAVE AN INSURANCE POLICY.
SO, TELL ME...
...WHAT ARE YOUR PALS GOING TO THINK...

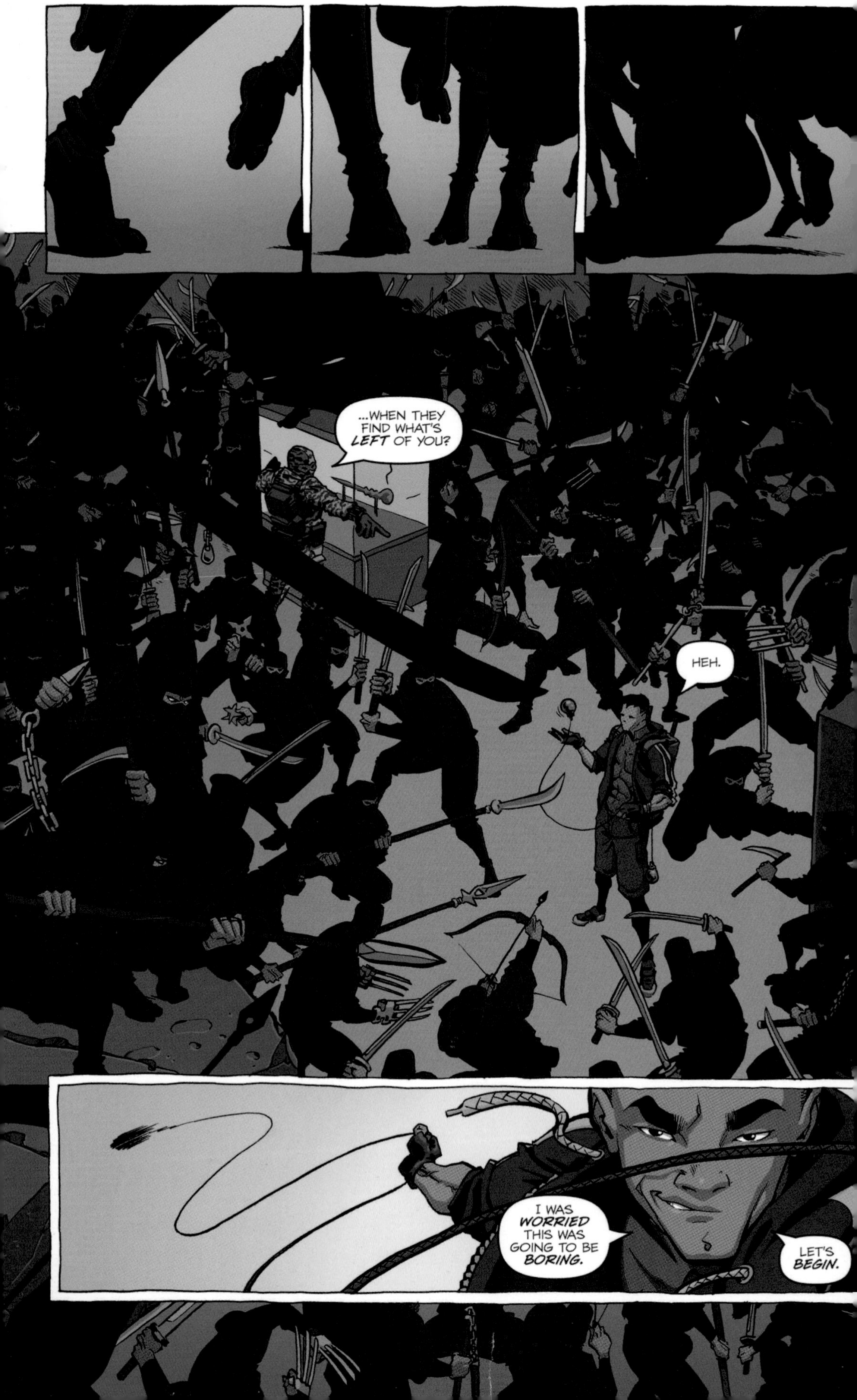
...WHEN THEY FIND WHAT'S LEFT OF YOU?
HEH.
I WAS WORRIED THIS WAS GOING TO BE BORING.
LET'S BEGIN.

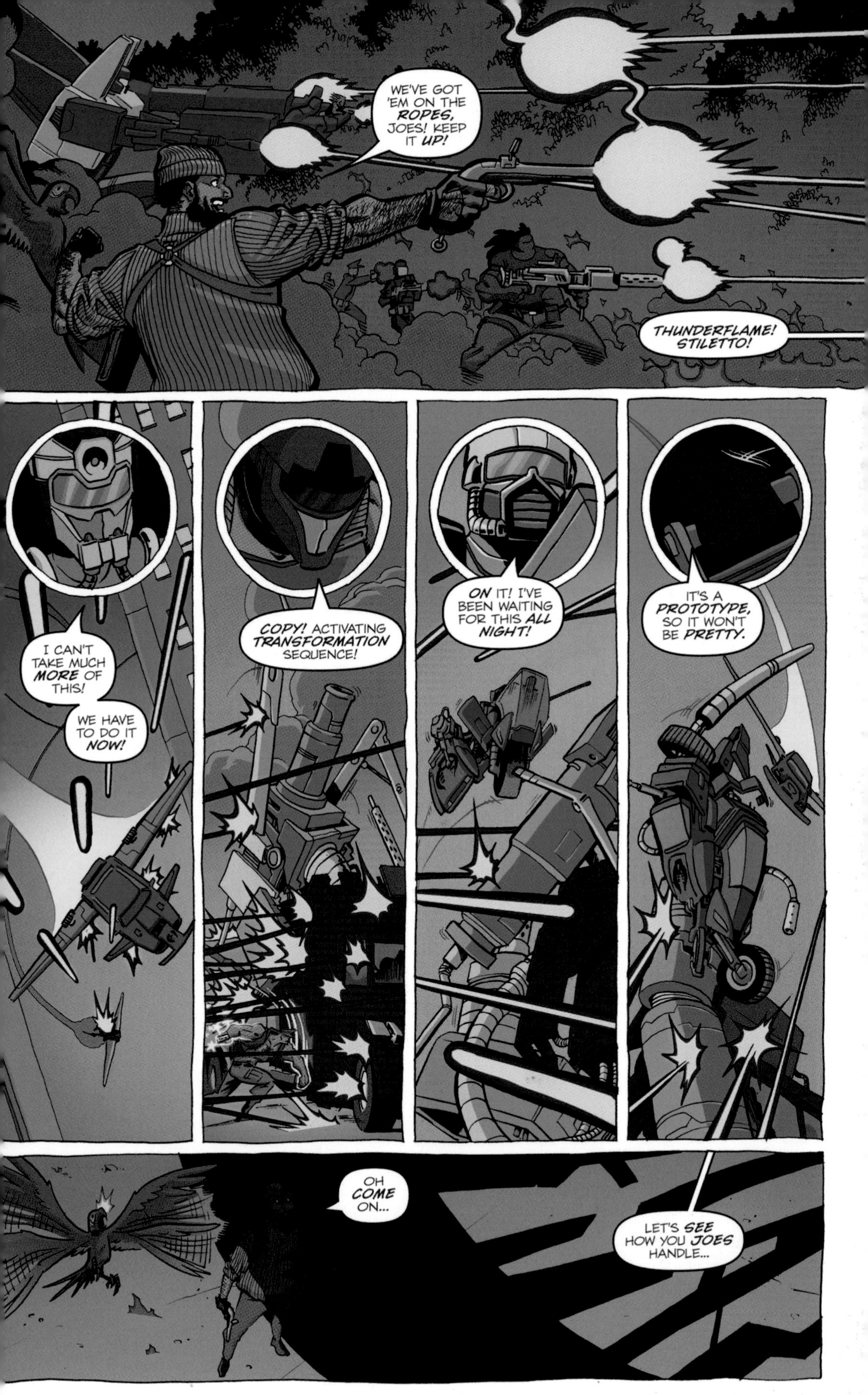
WE'VE GOT 'EM ON THE ROPES, JOES! KEEP IT UP!
THUNDERFLAME! STILETTO!
I CAN'T TAKE MUCH MORE OF THIS!
WE HAVE TO DO IT NOW!
COPY! ACTIVATING TRANSFORMATION SEQUENCE!
ON IT! I'VE BEEN WAITING FOR THIS ALL NIGHT!
IT'S A PROTOTYPE, SO IT WON'T BE PRETTY.
OH COME ON...
LET'S SEE HOW YOU JOES HANDLE...

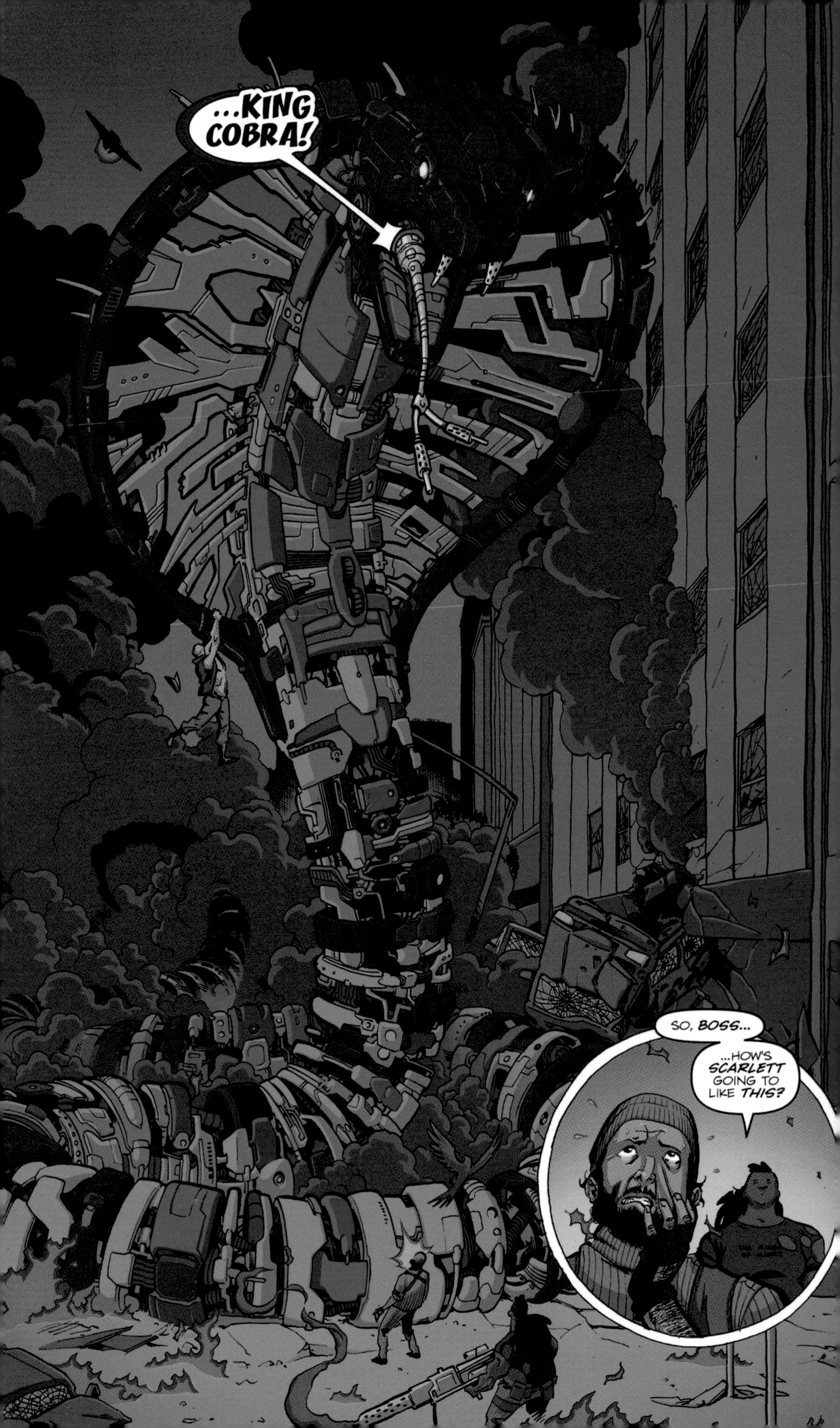
...KING COBRA!
SO, BOSS...
...HOW'S SCARLETT GOING TO LIKE THIS?

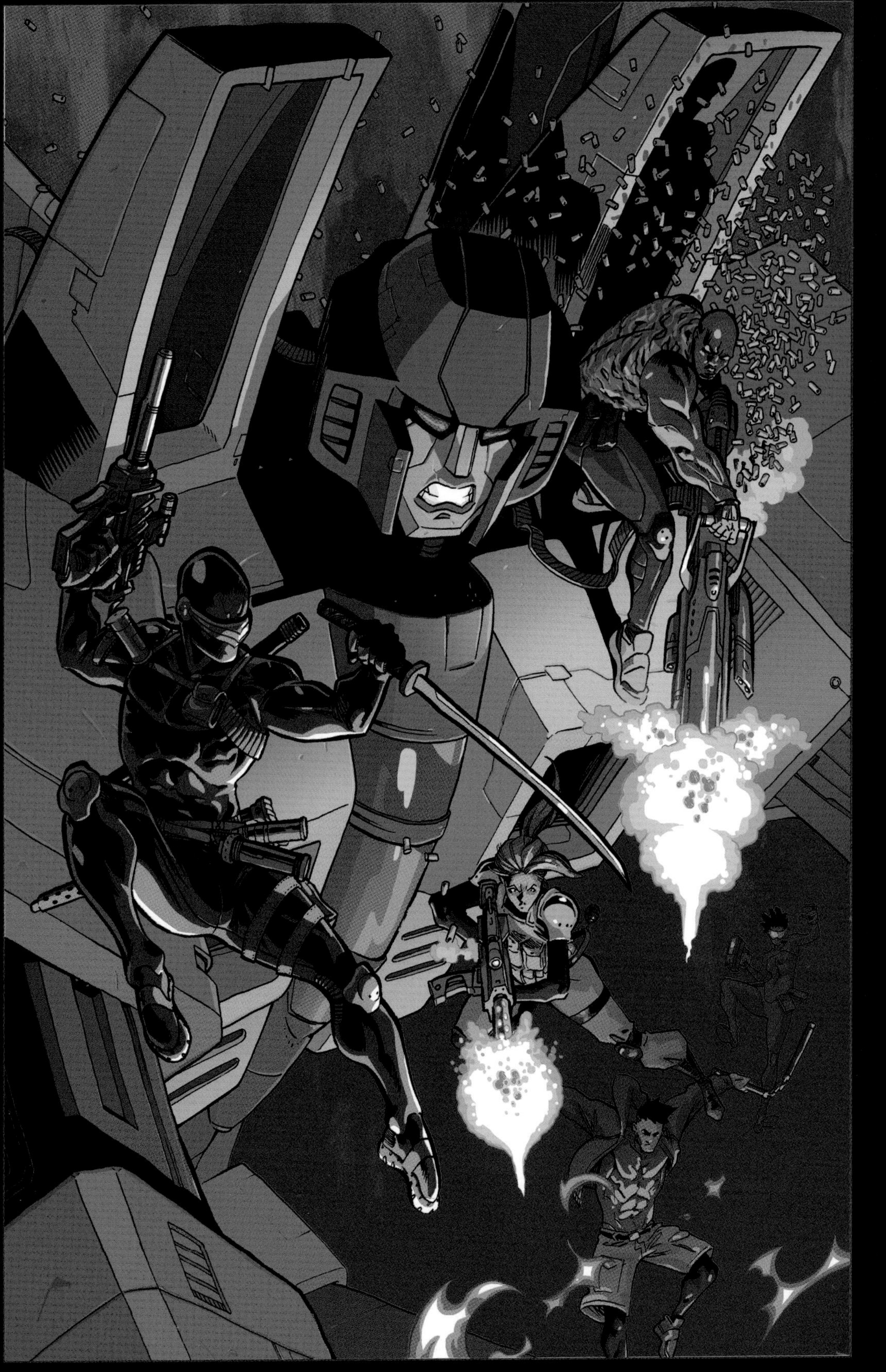

// art by Ilias Kyriazis

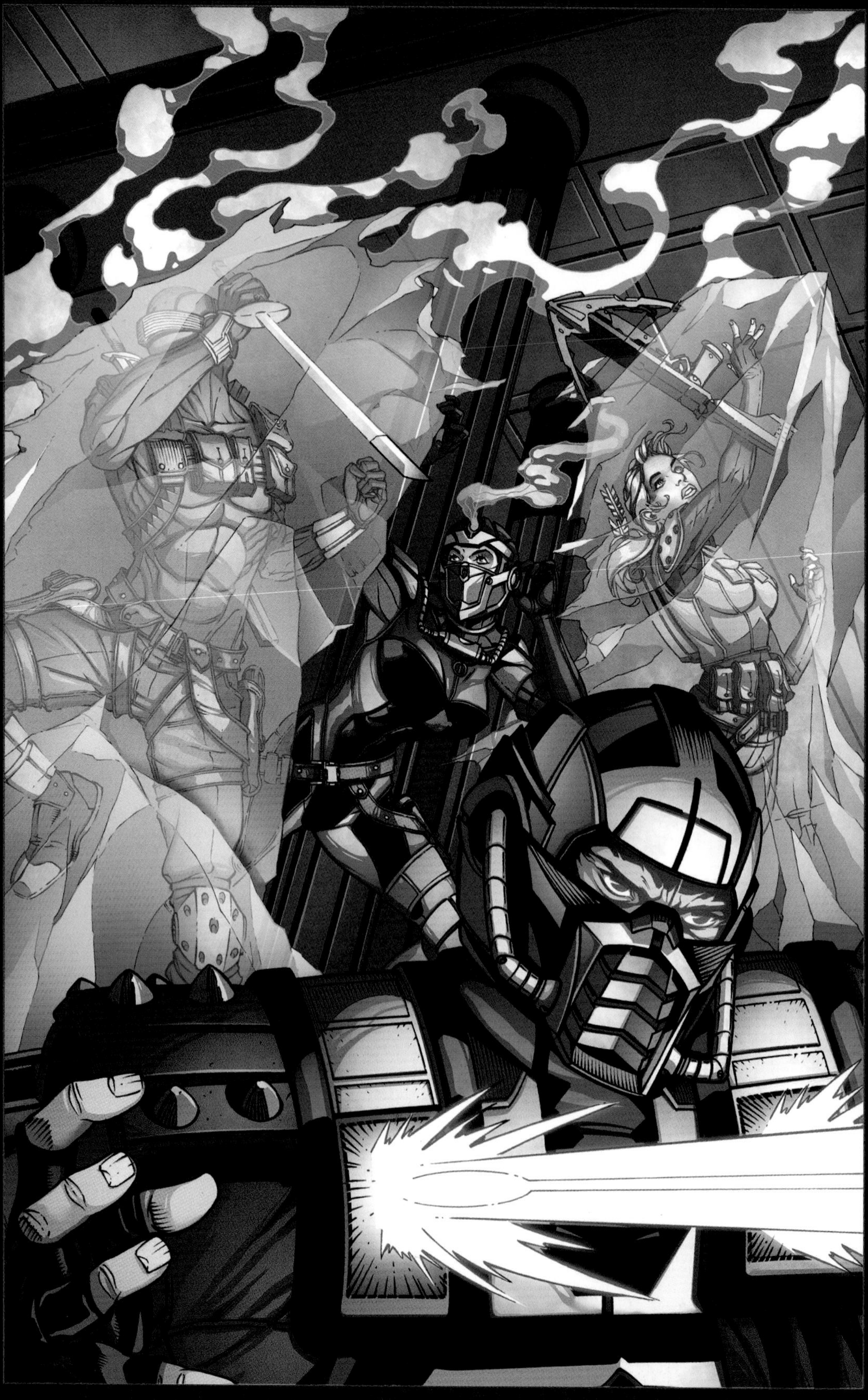

// art by Drew Johnson
// colors by David Garcia Cruz

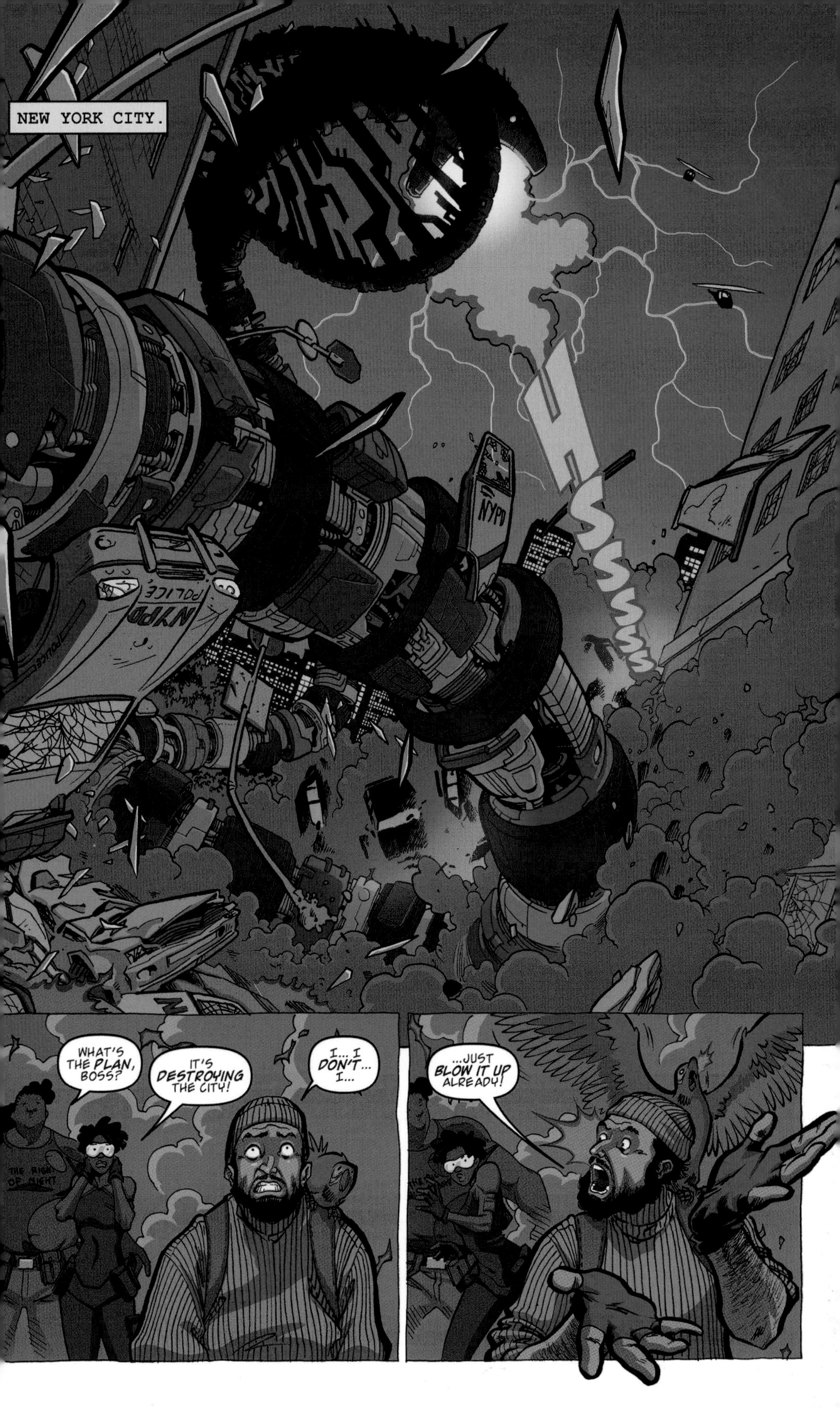
NEW YORK CITY.
NYPD
POLICE
NYPD
FSSSWWW
WHAT'S THE PLAN, BOSS?
IT'S DESTROYING THE CITY!
I... I DON'T... I...
...JUST BLOW IT UP ALREADY!

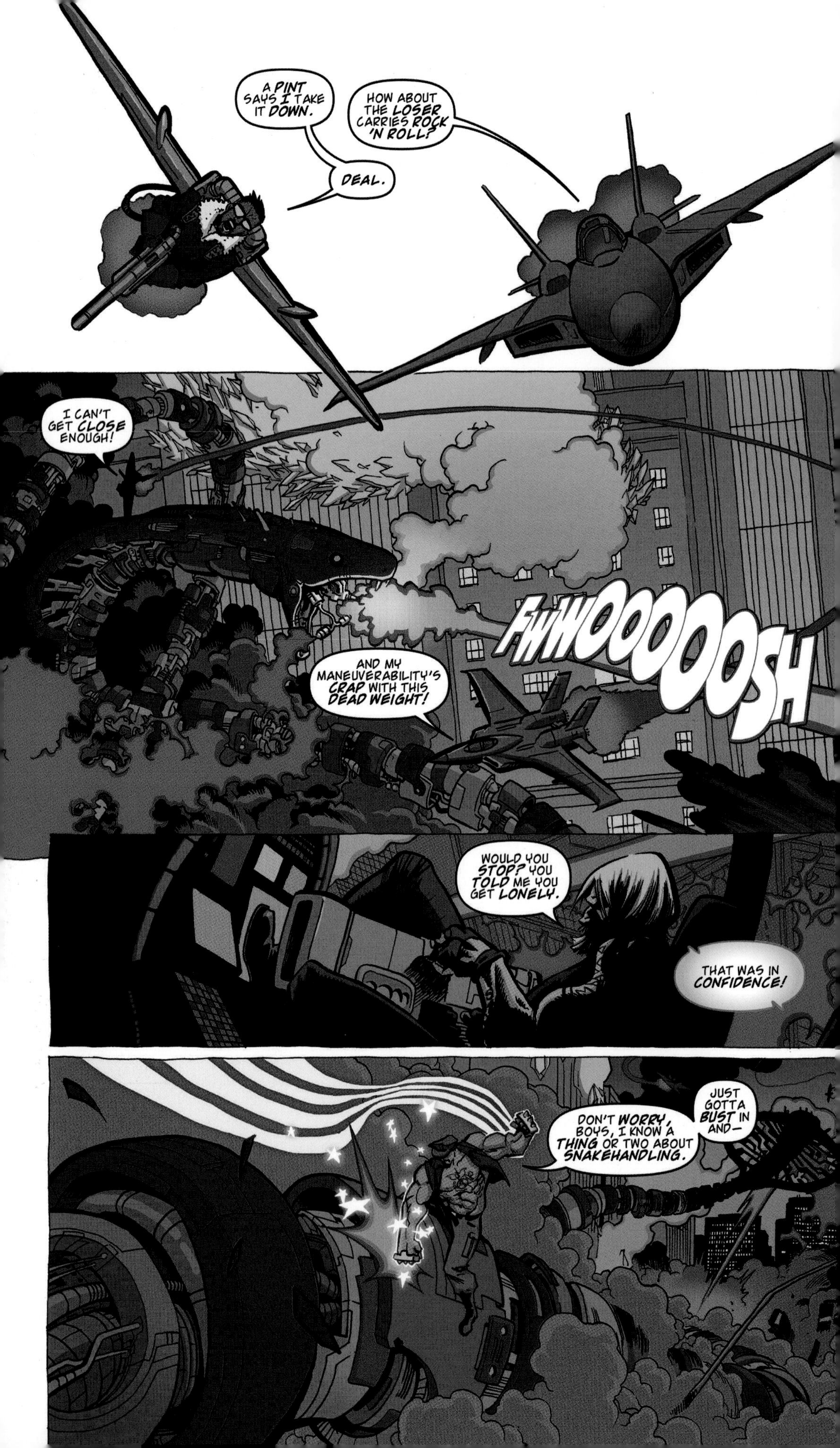
A PINT SAYS I TAKE IT DOWN.
HOW ABOUT THE LOSER CARRIES ROCK 'N ROLL?
DEAL.
I CAN'T GET CLOSE ENOUGH!
AND MY MANEUVERABILITY'S CRAP WITH THIS DEAD WEIGHT!
FWWOOOOOOSH
WOULD YOU STOP? YOU TOLD ME YOU GET LONELY.
THAT WAS IN CONFIDENCE!
DON'T WORRY, BOYS, I KNOW A THING OR TWO ABOUT SNAKEHANDLING.
JUST GOTTA BUST IN AND—

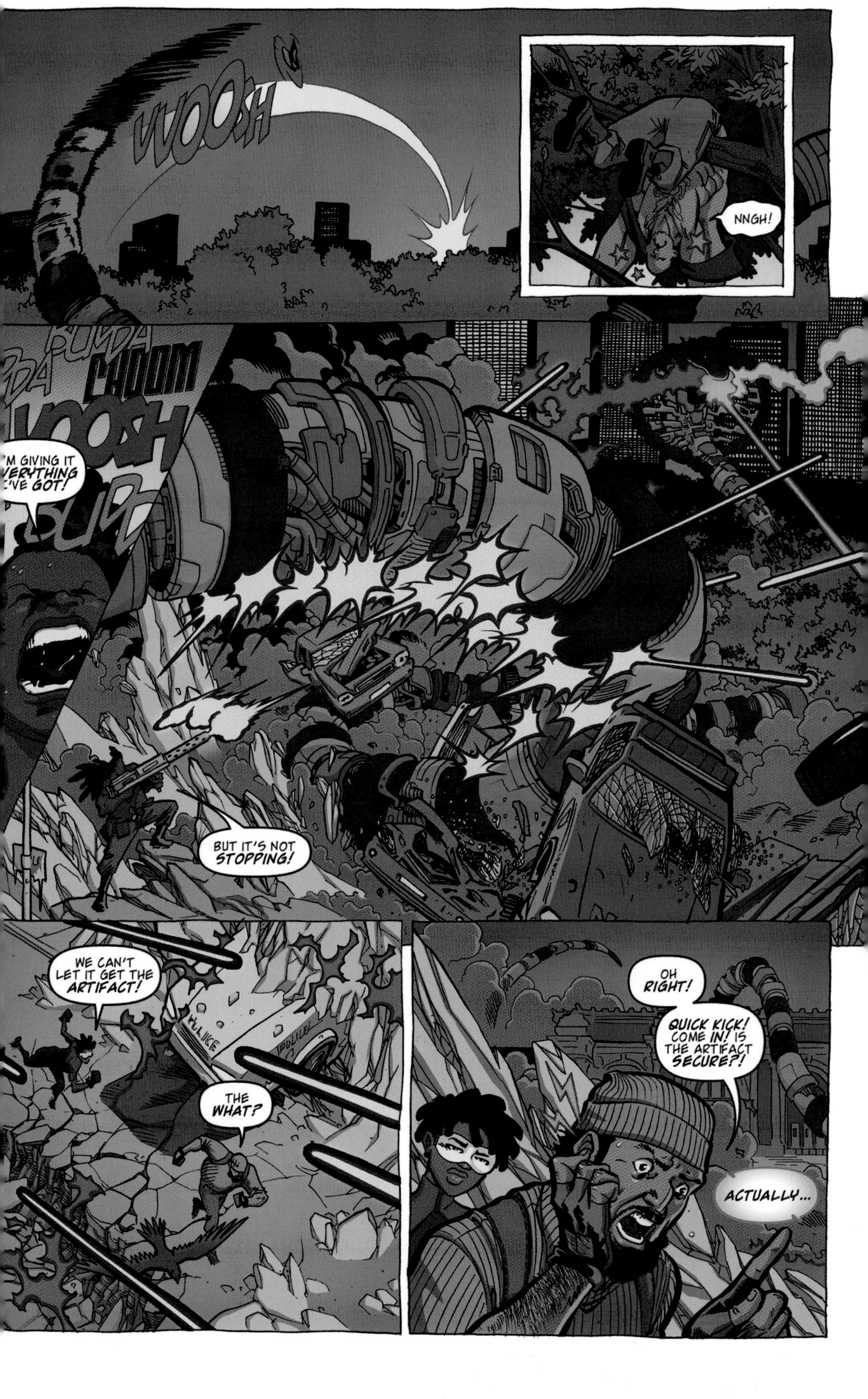
VWOOSH
NNGH!
BUDA
DA
CHOOM
VOOSH
BUZZ
I'M GIVING IT EVERYTHING I'VE GOT!
BUT IT'S NOT STOPPING!
WE CAN'T LET IT GET THE ARTIFACT!
POLICE
POLICE
THE WHAT?
OH RIGHT!
QUICK KICK! COME IN! IS THE ARTIFACT SECURE?!
ACTUALLY...

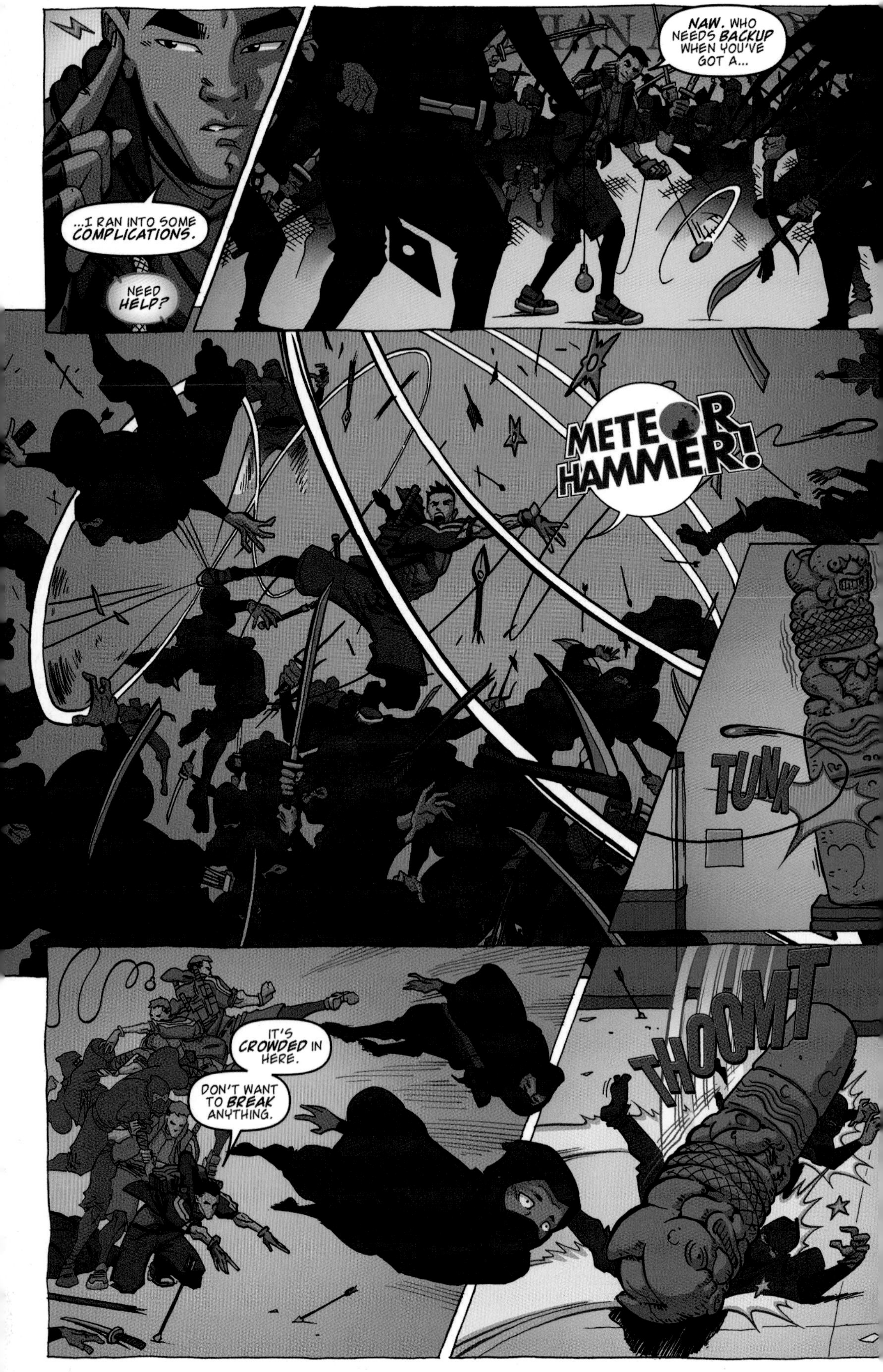
...I RAN INTO SOME COMPLICATIONS.
NEED HELP?
NAW. WHO NEEDS BACKUP WHEN YOU'VE GOT A...
METEOR HAMMER!
TUNK
IT'S CROWDED IN HERE.
DON'T WANT TO BREAK ANYTHING.
THOOMT

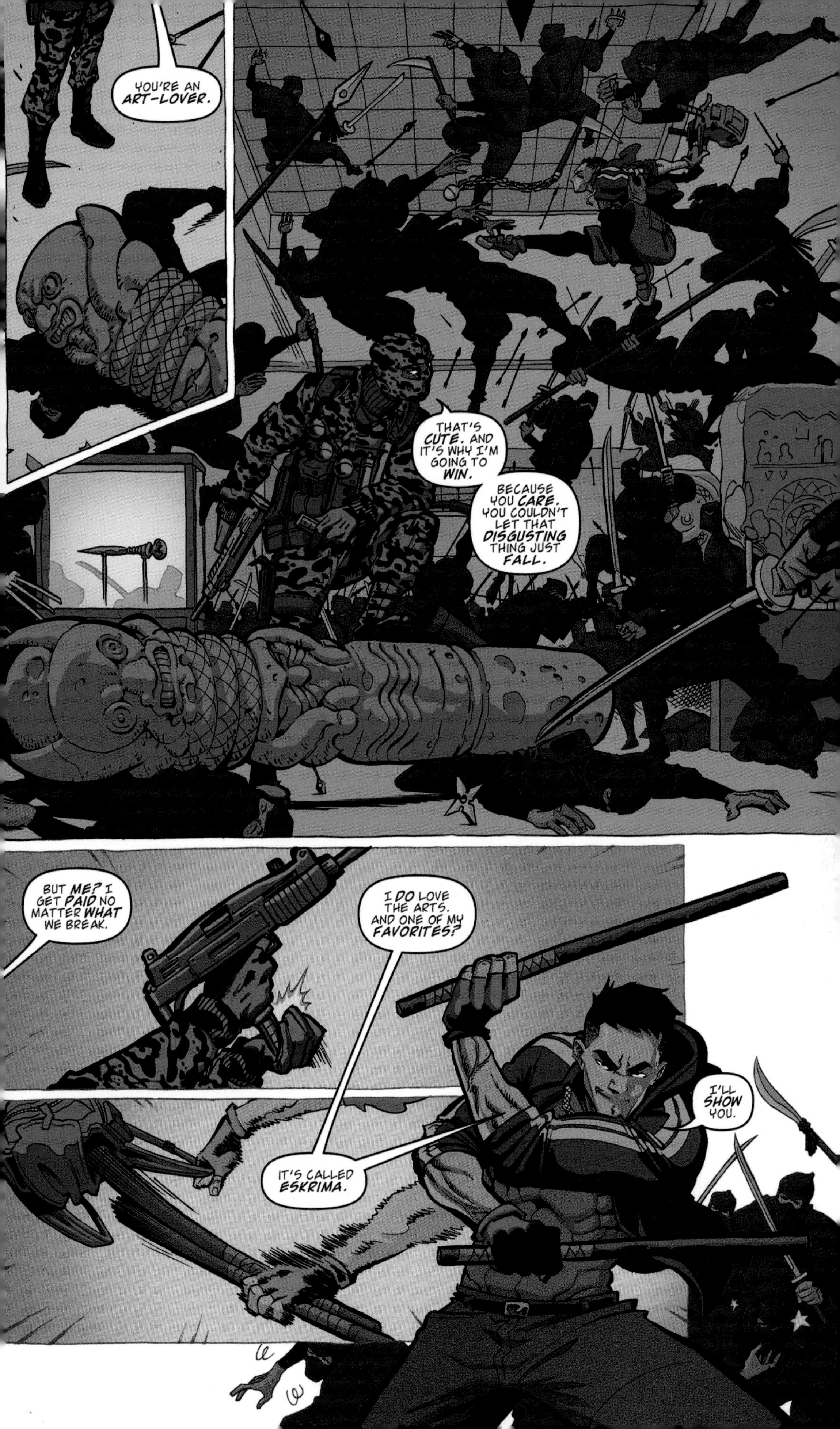
YOU'RE AN ART-LOVER.
THAT'S CUTE. AND IT'S WHY I'M GOING TO WIN.
BECAUSE YOU CARE. YOU COULDN'T LET THAT DISGUSTING THING JUST FALL.
BUT ME? I GET PAID NO MATTER WHAT WE BREAK.
I DO LOVE THE ARTS. AND ONE OF MY FAVORITES?
IT'S CALLED ESKRIMA.
I'LL SHOW YOU.

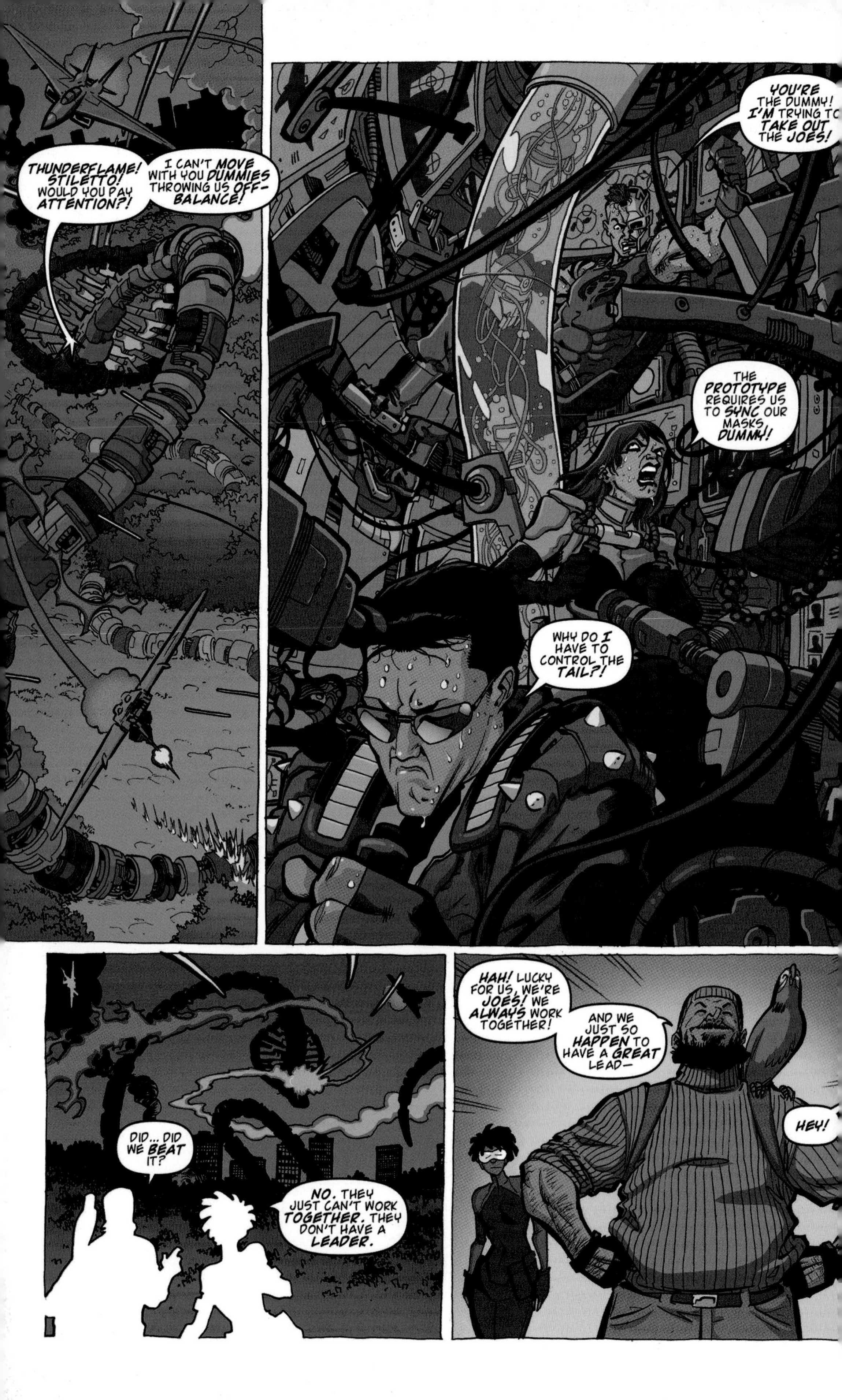
THUNDERFLAME! STILETTO! WOULD YOU PAY ATTENTION?!
I CAN'T MOVE WITH YOU DUMMIES THROWING US OFF-BALANCE!
YOU'RE THE DUMMY! I'M TRYING TO TAKE OUT THE JOES!
THE PROTOTYPE REQUIRES US TO SYNC OUR MASKS, DUMMY!
WHY DO I HAVE TO CONTROL THE TAIL?!
DID... DID WE BEAT IT?
NO. THEY JUST CAN'T WORK TOGETHER. THEY DON'T HAVE A LEADER.
HAH! LUCKY FOR US, WE'RE JOES! WE ALWAYS WORK TOGETHER!
AND WE JUST SO HAPPEN TO HAVE A GREAT LEAD—
HEY!

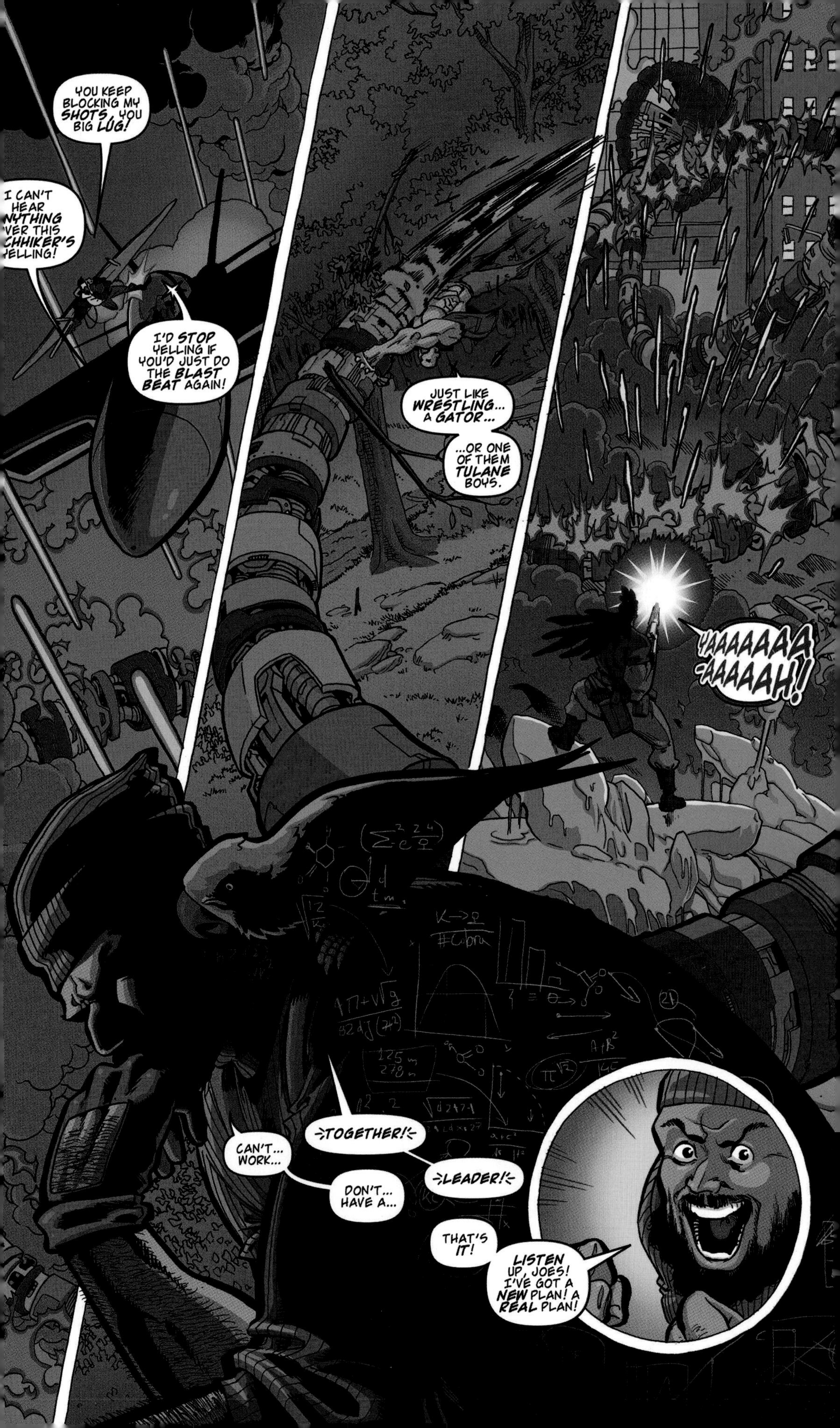

YOU KEEP BLOCKING MY SHOTS, YOU BIG LUG!
I CAN'T HEAR NYTHING VER THIS CHHIKER'S ELLING!
I'D STOP YELLING IF YOU'D JUST DO THE BLAST BEAT AGAIN!
JUST LIKE WRESTLING... A GATOR...
...OR ONE OF THEM TULANE BOYS.
YAAAAAAA-AAAAAH!
CAN'T... WORK...
TOGETHER!
DON'T... HAVE A...
LEADER!
THAT'S IT!
LISTEN UP, JOES! I'VE GOT A NEW PLAN! A REAL PLAN!

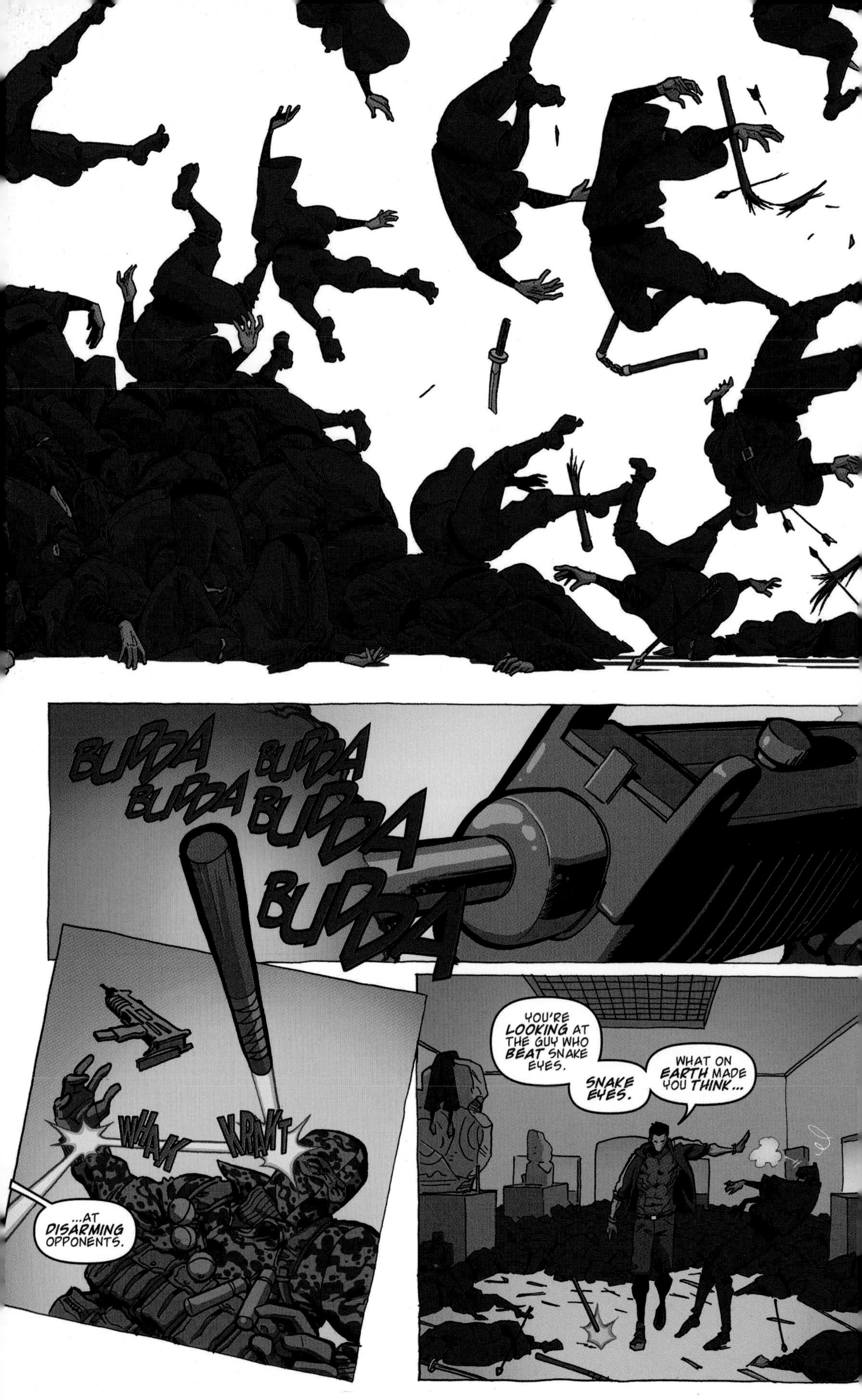
BUDDA BUDDA BUDDA BUDDA BUDDA
WHAK
KRAKT
...AT DISARMING OPPONENTS.
YOU'RE LOOKING AT THE GUY WHO BEAT SNAKE EYES.
SNAKE EYES.
WHAT ON EARTH MADE YOU THINK...

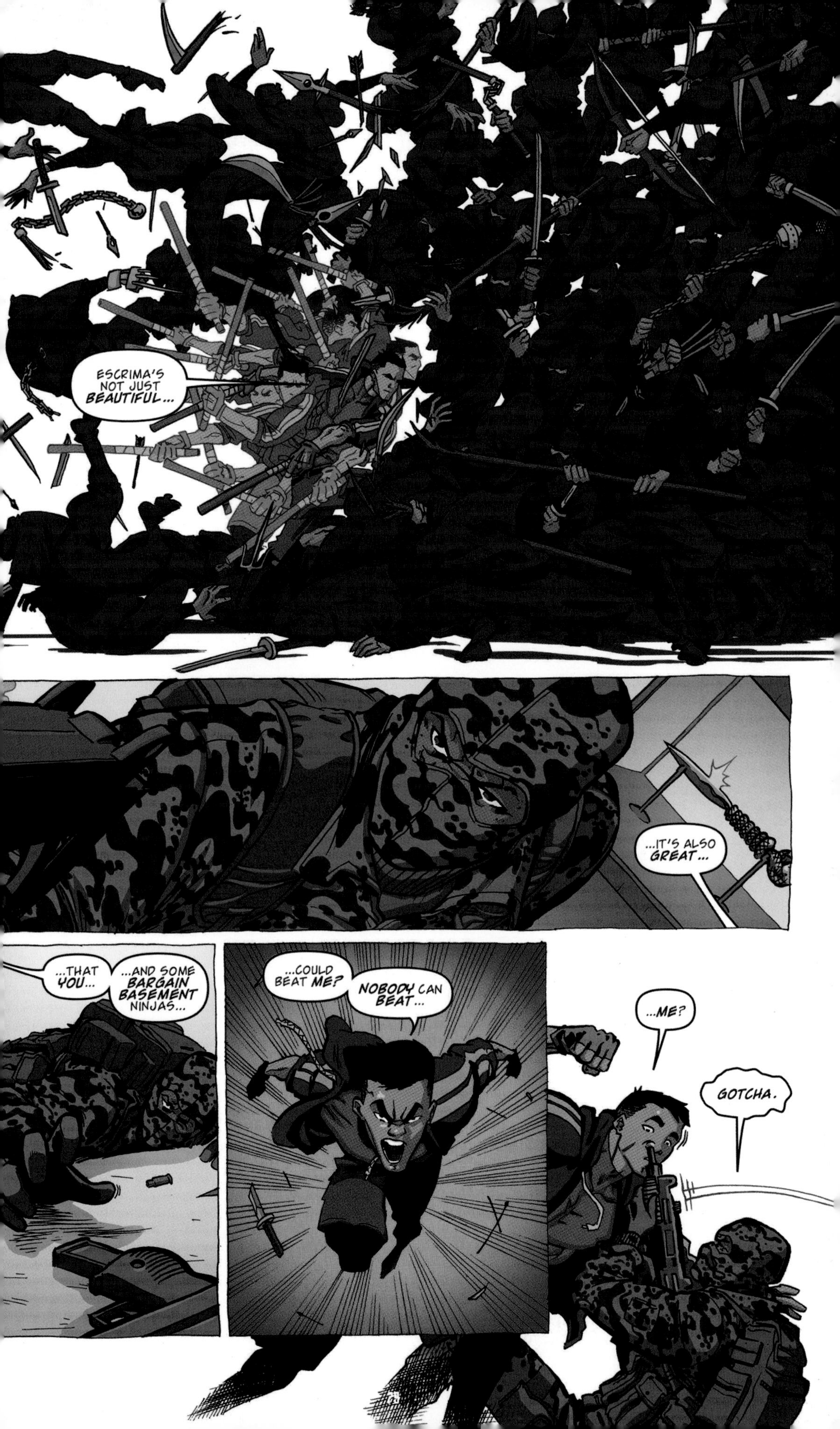
ESCRIMA'S NOT JUST BEAUTIFUL...
...IT'S ALSO GREAT...
...THAT YOU...
...AND SOME BARGAIN BASEMENT NINJAS...
...COULD BEAT ME?
NOBODY CAN BEAT...
...ME?
GOTCHA.

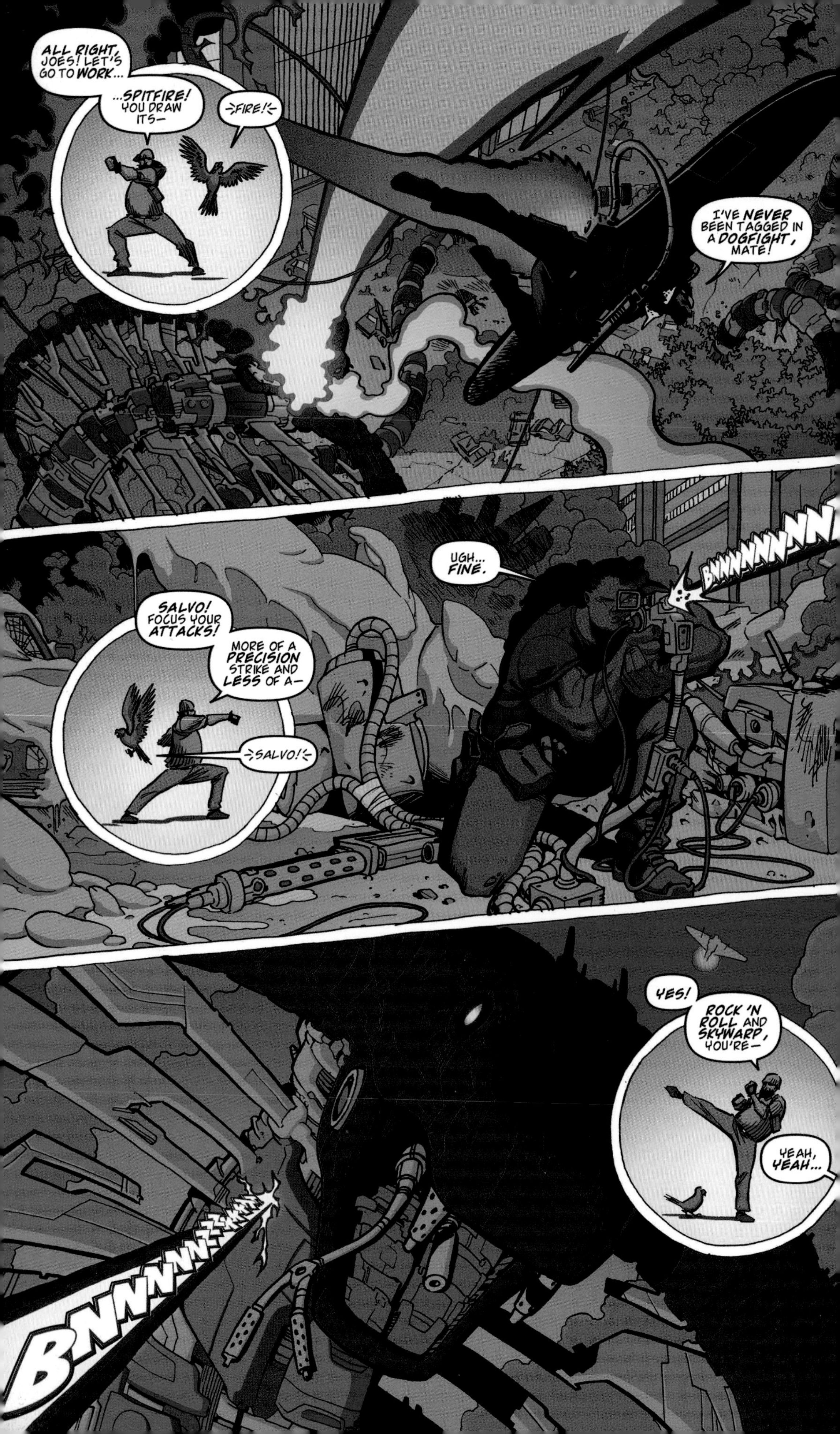
ALL RIGHT, JOES! LET'S GO TO WORK...
...SPITFIRE! YOU DRAW ITS—
FIRE!
I'VE NEVER BEEN TAGGED IN A DOGFIGHT, MATE!
UGH... FINE.
BNNNNNN-NN
SALVO! FOCUS YOUR ATTACKS!
MORE OF A PRECISION STRIKE AND LESS OF A—
SALVO!
YES!
ROCK 'N ROLL AND SKYWARP, YOU'RE—
YEAH, YEAH...
BNNNNN

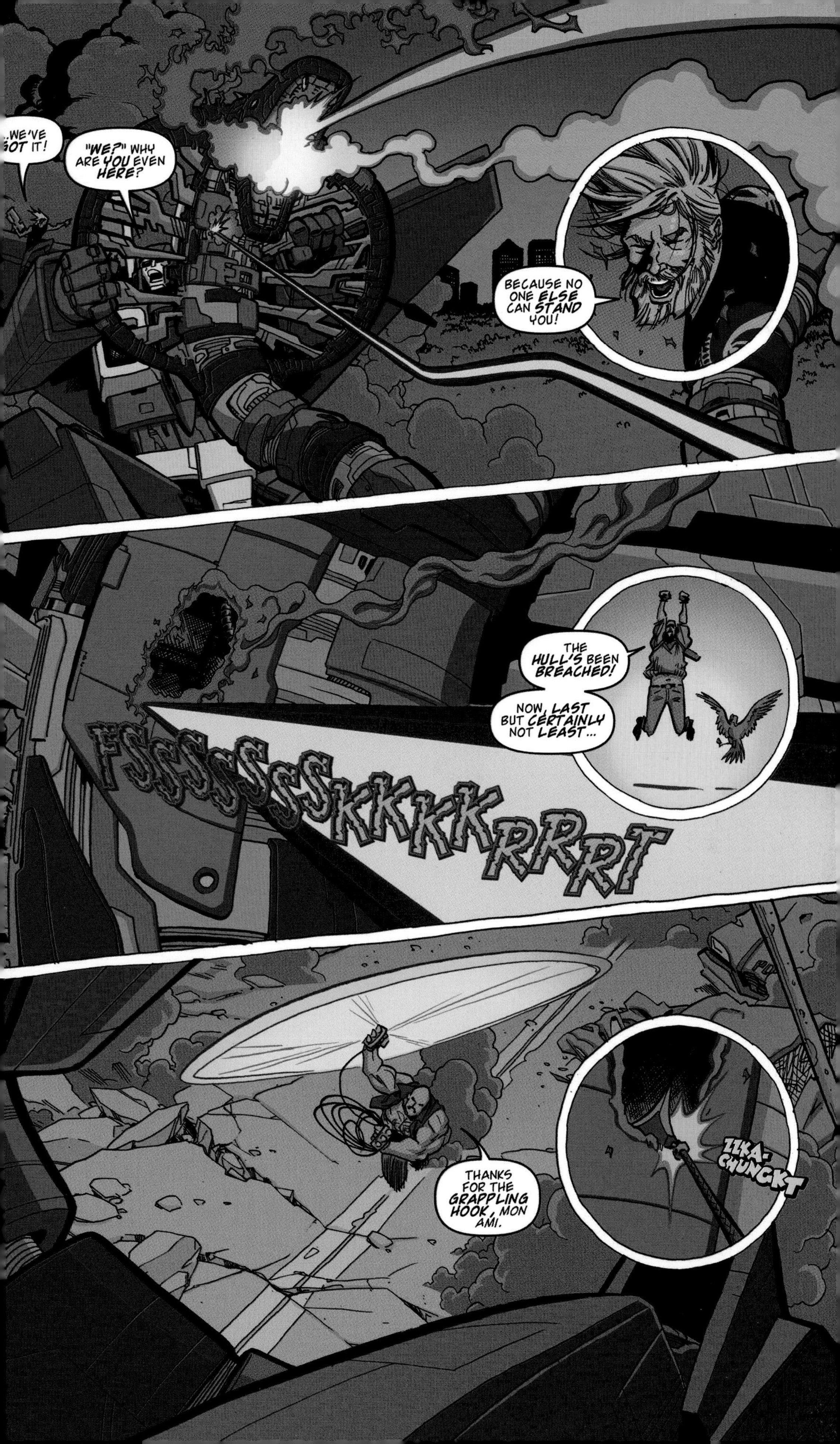
...WE'VE GOT IT!
"WE?" WHY ARE YOU EVEN HERE?
BECAUSE NO ONE ELSE CAN STAND YOU!
THE HULL'S BEEN BREACHED!
NOW, LAST BUT CERTAINLY NOT LEAST...
FSSSSSSKKKKRRRT
THANKS FOR THE GRAPPLING HOOK, MON AMI.
ZZKA-CHUNCKT

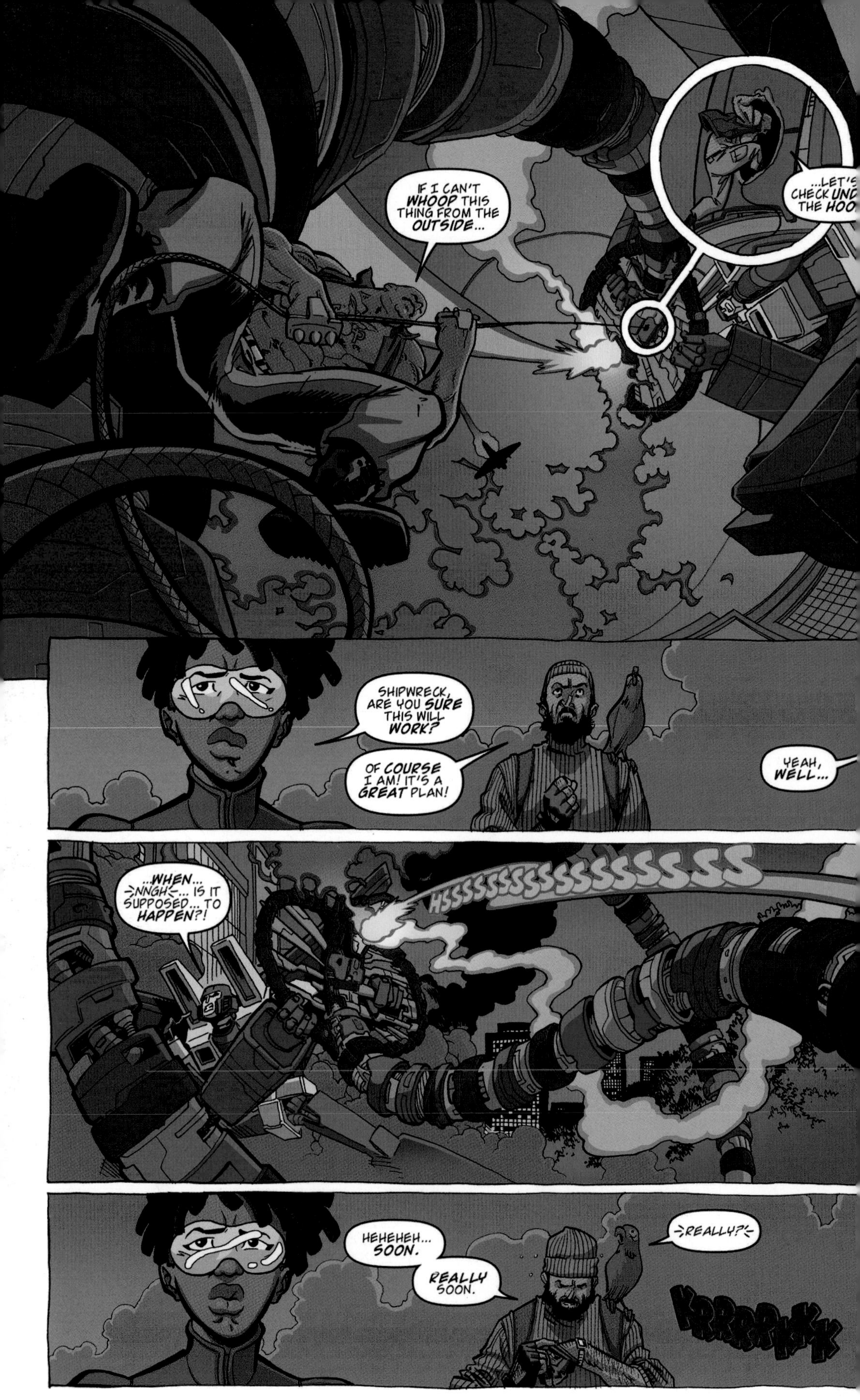
IF I CAN'T WHOOP THIS THING FROM THE OUTSIDE...
...LET'S CHECK UND THE HOO
SHIPWRECK, ARE YOU SURE THIS WILL WORK?
OF COURSE I AM! IT'S A GREAT PLAN!
YEAH, WELL...
...WHEN... NNGH... IS IT SUPPOSED... TO HAPPEN?!
HSSSSSSSSSSSSSSSSS
HEHEHEH... SOON.
REALLY SOON.
REALLY?

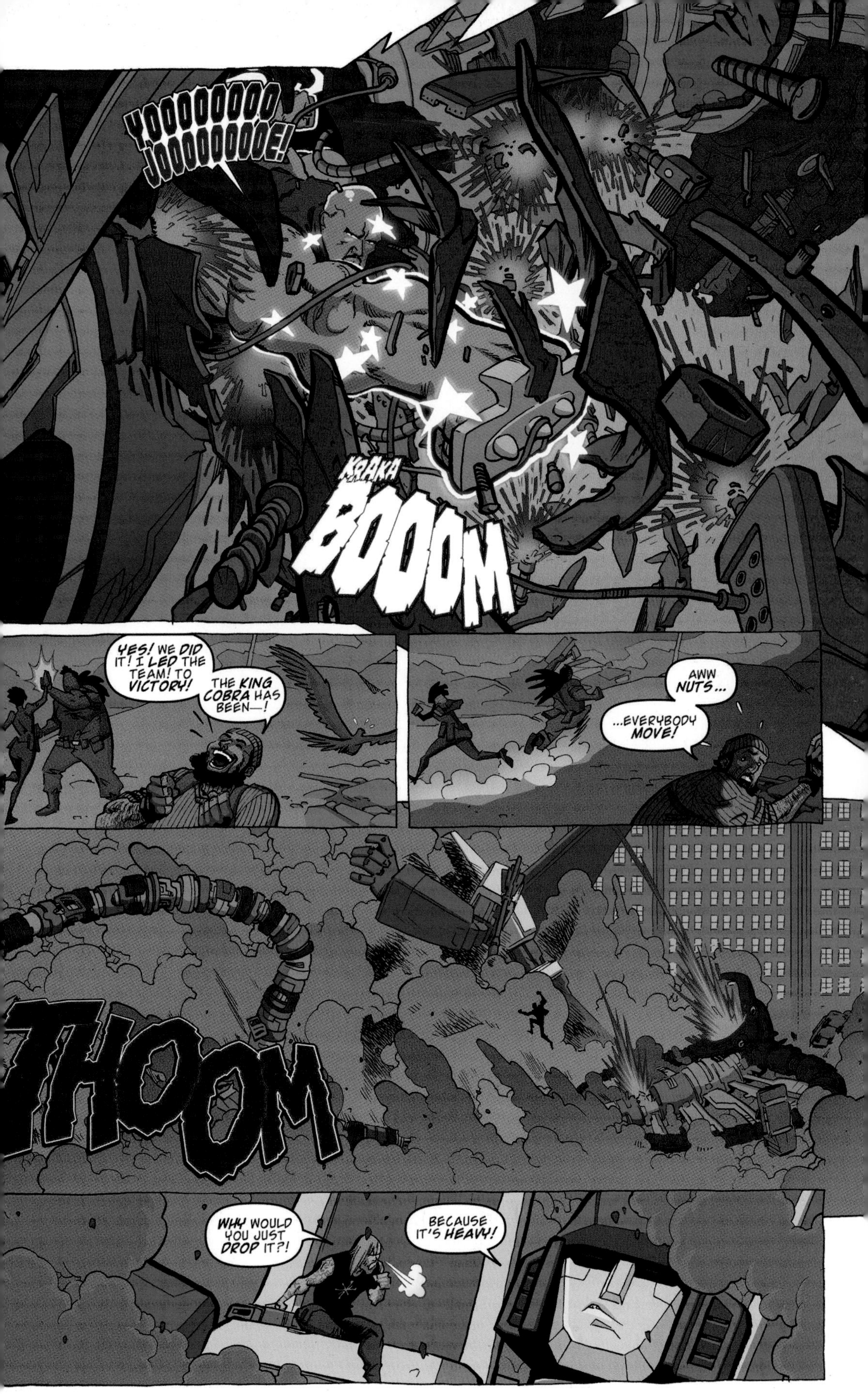

YOOOOOOOO JOOOOOOOOE!
KRAKA BOOOM
YES! WE DID IT! I LED THE TEAM! TO VICTORY!
THE KING COBRA HAS BEEN—!
AWW NUTS...
...EVERYBODY MOVE!
THOOM
WHY WOULD YOU JUST DROP IT?!
BECAUSE IT'S HEAVY!

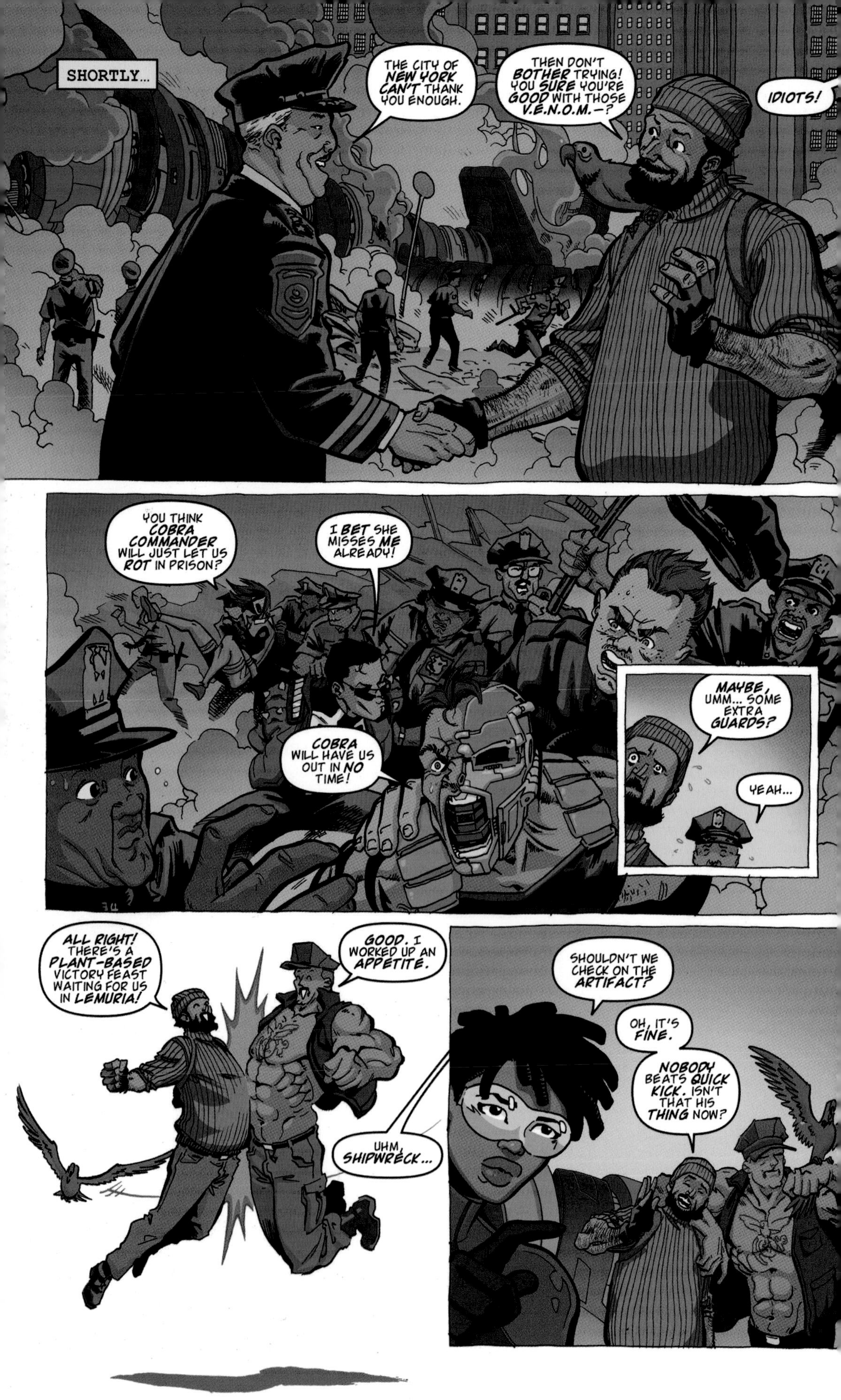
SHORTLY...
THE CITY OF NEW YORK CAN'T THANK YOU ENOUGH.
THEN DON'T BOTHER TRYING! YOU SURE YOU'RE GOOD WITH THOSE V.E.N.O.M.—?
IDIOTS!
YOU THINK COBRA COMMANDER WILL JUST LET US ROT IN PRISON?
I BET SHE MISSES ME ALREADY!
COBRA WILL HAVE US OUT IN NO TIME!
MAYBE, UMM... SOME EXTRA GUARDS?
YEAH...
ALL RIGHT! THERE'S A PLANT-BASED VICTORY FEAST WAITING FOR US IN LEMURIA!
GOOD. I WORKED UP AN APPETITE.
SHOULDN'T WE CHECK ON THE ARTIFACT?
OH, IT'S FINE.
NOBODY BEATS QUICK KICK. ISN'T THAT HIS THING NOW?
UHM, SHIPWRECK...

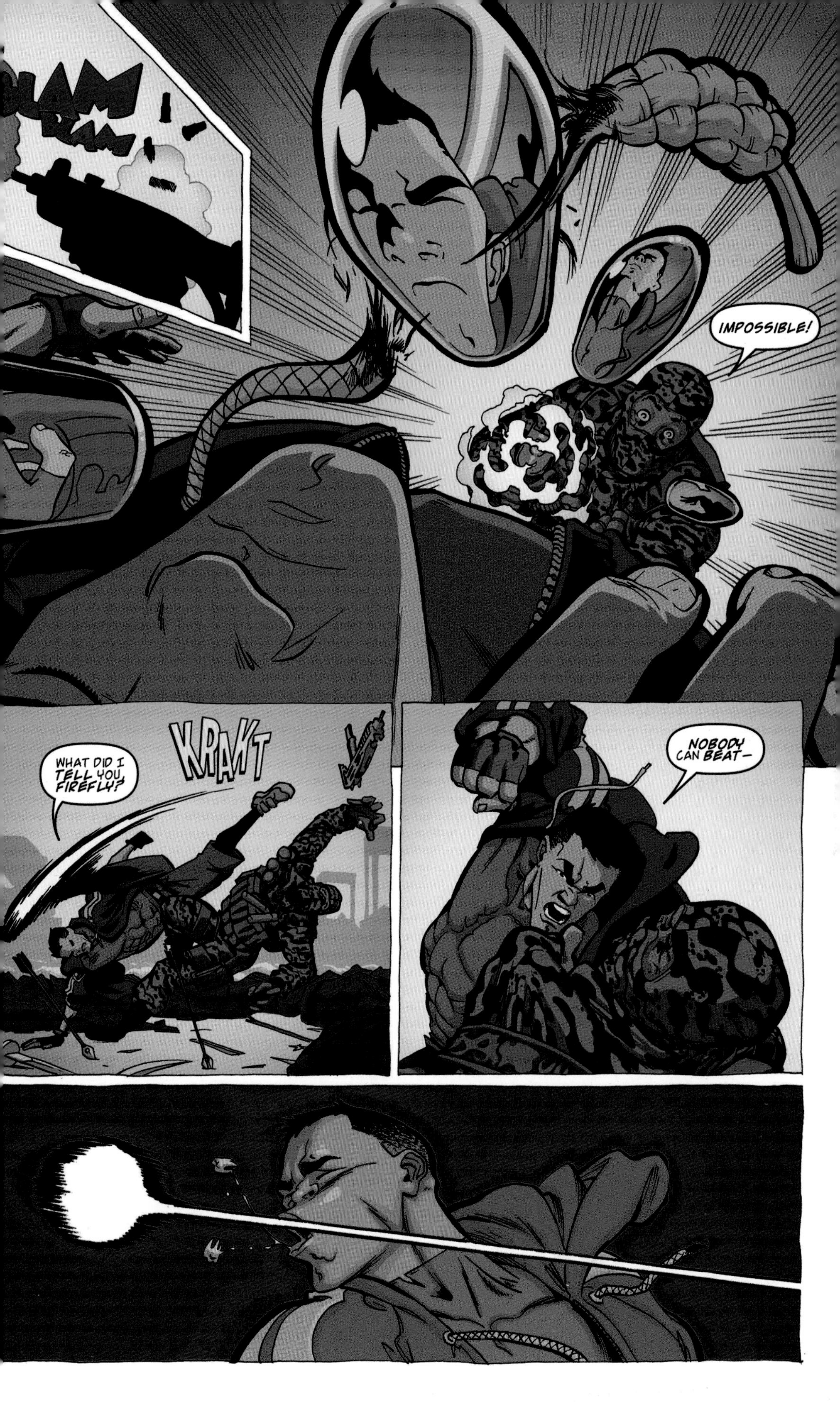
BLAM
BLAM
IMPOSSIBLE!
KRAKT
WHAT DID I TELL YOU, FIREFLY?
NOBODY CAN BEAT—

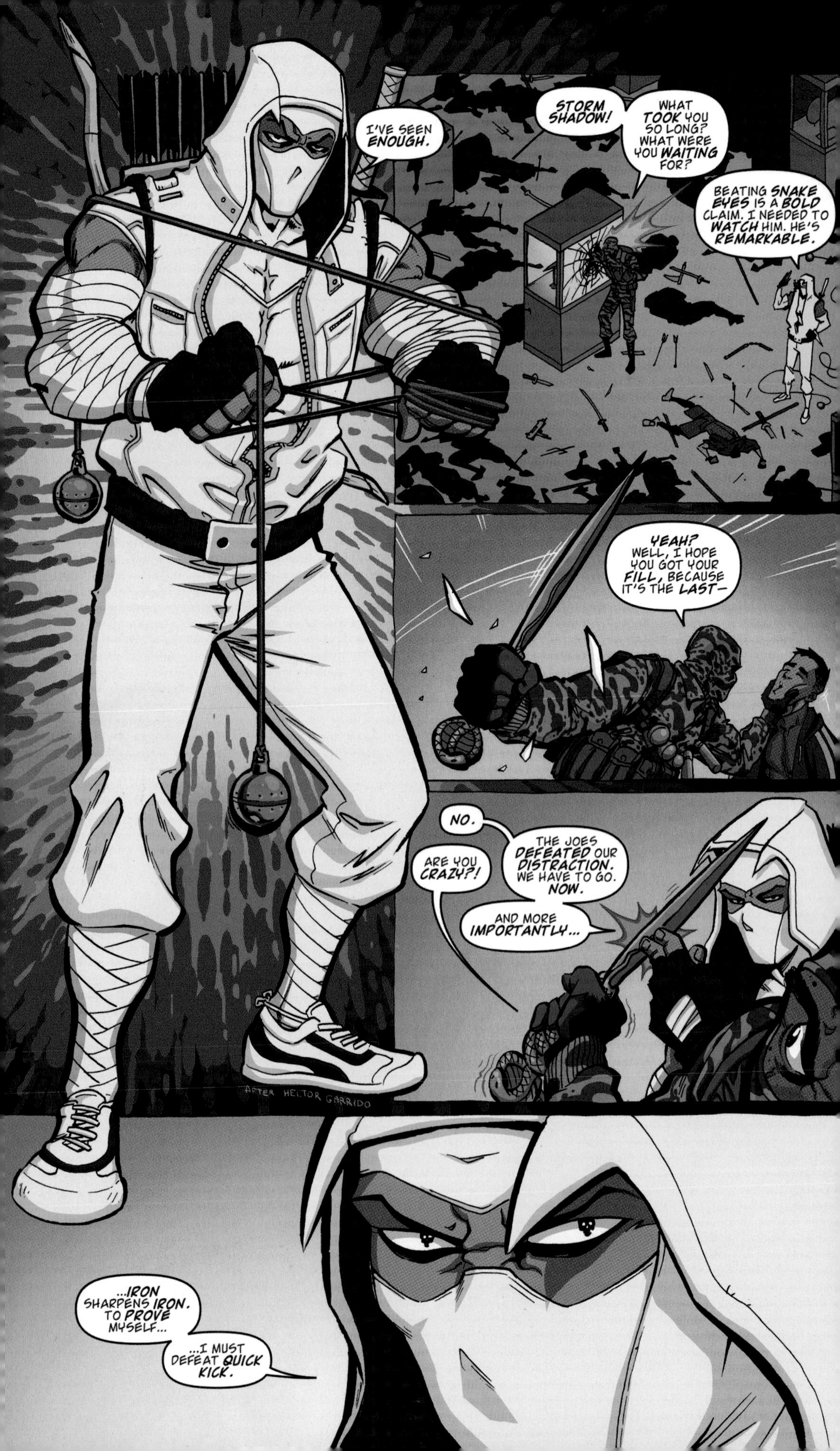
I'VE SEEN ENOUGH.
STORM SHADOW!
WHAT TOOK YOU SO LONG? WHAT WERE YOU WAITING FOR?
BEATING SNAKE EYES IS A BOLD CLAIM. I NEEDED TO WATCH HIM. HE'S REMARKABLE.
YEAH? WELL, I HOPE YOU GOT YOUR FILL, BECAUSE IT'S THE LAST—
NO.
THE JOES DEFEATED OUR DISTRACTION. WE HAVE TO GO. NOW.
ARE YOU CRAZY?!
AND MORE IMPORTANTLY...
...IRON SHARPENS IRON. TO PROVE MYSELF...
...I MUST DEFEAT QUICK KICK.
AFTER HECTOR GARRIDO

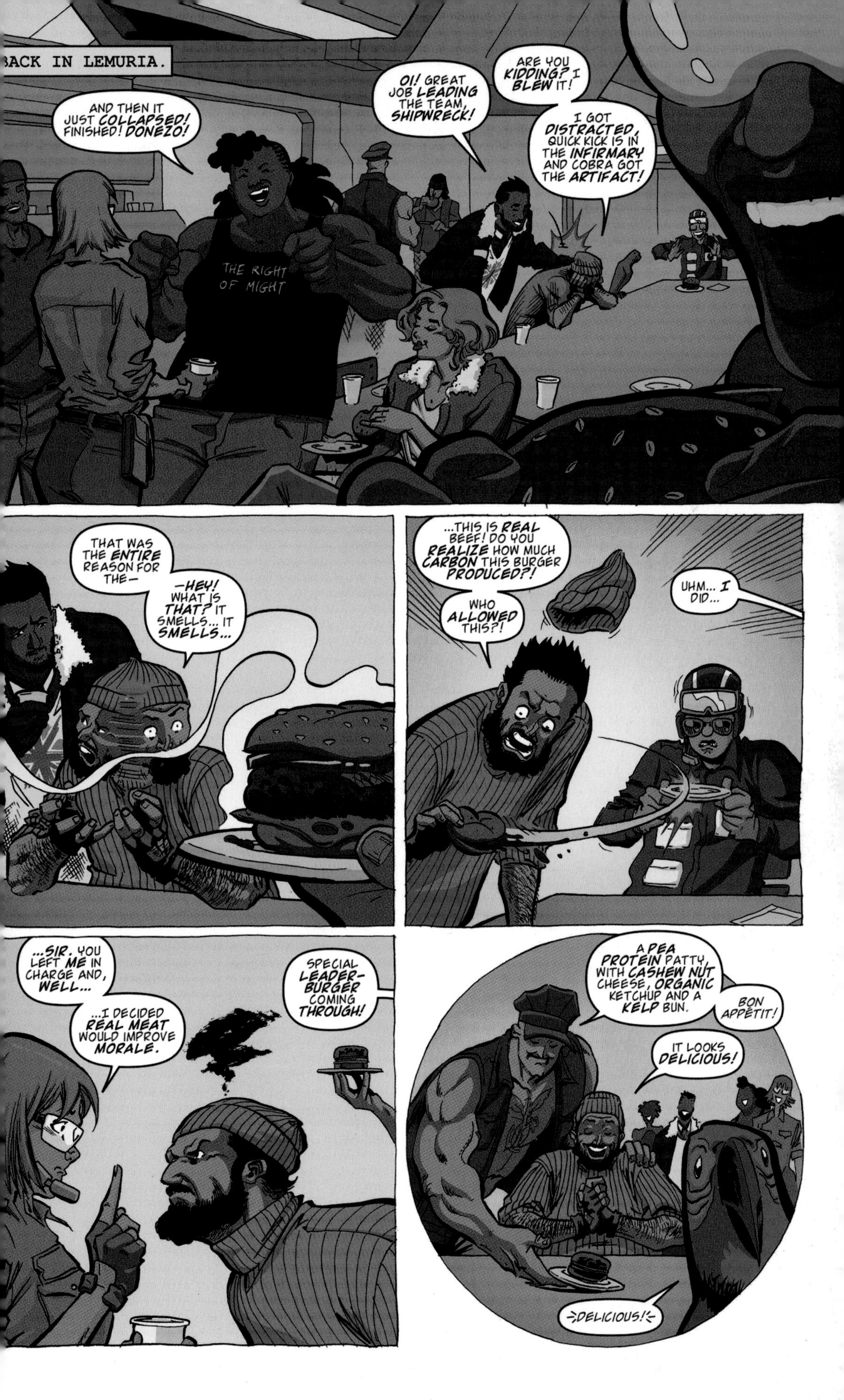
BACK IN LEMURIA.
AND THEN IT JUST COLLAPSED! FINISHED! DONEZO!
OI! GREAT JOB LEADING THE TEAM, SHIPWRECK!
ARE YOU KIDDING? I BLEW IT!
I GOT DISTRACTED, QUICK KICK IS IN THE INFIRMARY AND COBRA GOT THE ARTIFACT!
THE RIGHT OF MIGHT
THAT WAS THE ENTIRE REASON FOR THE—
—HEY! WHAT IS THAT? IT SMELLS... IT SMELLS...
...THIS IS REAL BEEF! DO YOU REALIZE HOW MUCH CARBON THIS BURGER PRODUCED?!
WHO ALLOWED THIS?!
UHM... I DID...
...SIR. YOU LEFT ME IN CHARGE AND, WELL...
...I DECIDED REAL MEAT WOULD IMPROVE MORALE.
SPECIAL LEADER-BURGER COMING THROUGH!
A PEA PROTEIN PATTY WITH CASHEW NUT CHEESE, ORGANIC KETCHUP AND A KELP BUN.
BON APPÉTIT!
IT LOOKS DELICIOUS!
DELICIOUS!

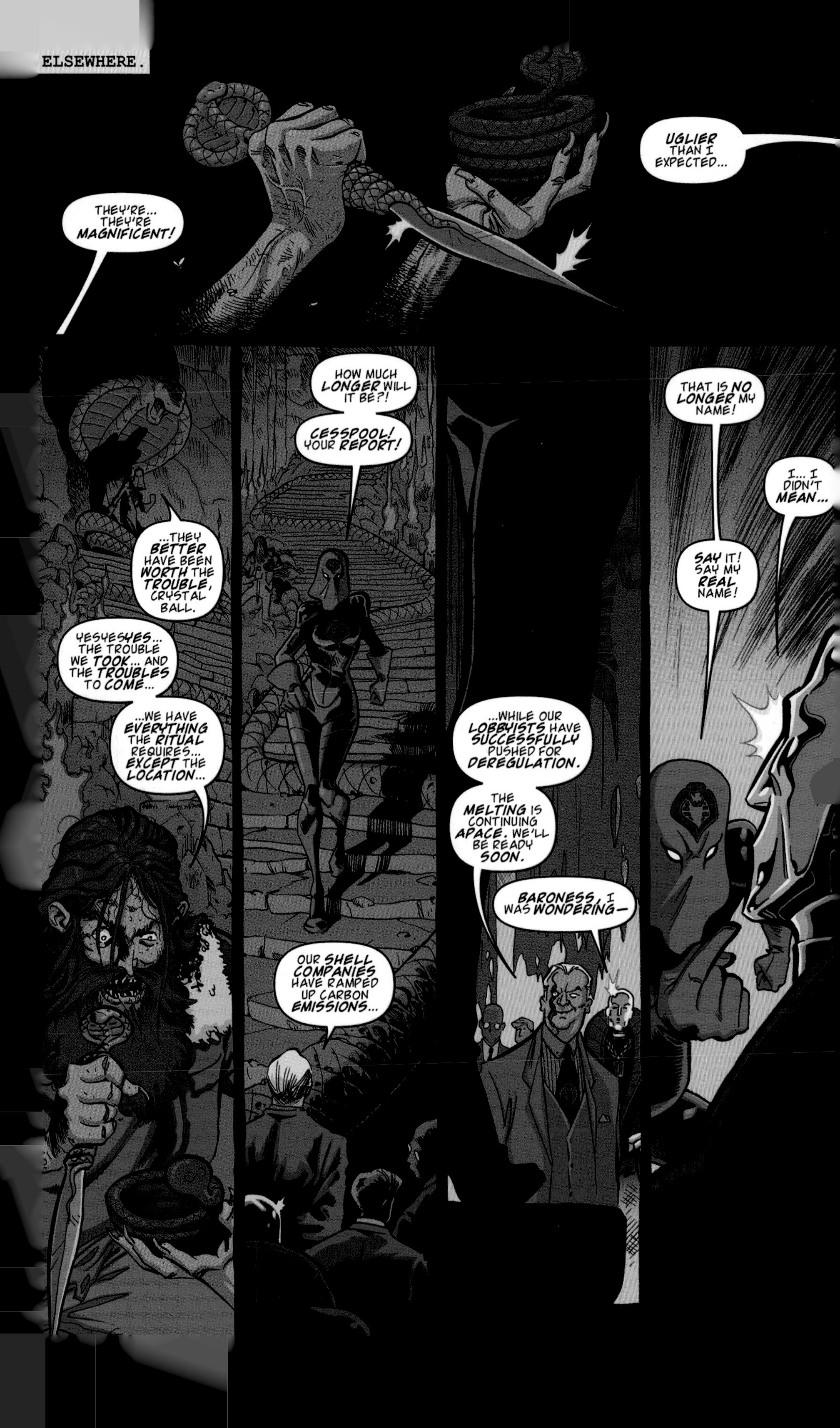

ELSEWHERE.
THEY'RE... THEY'RE MAGNIFICENT!
UGLIER THAN I EXPECTED...
...THEY BETTER HAVE BEEN WORTH THE TROUBLE, CRYSTAL BALL.
YESYESYES... THE TROUBLE WE TOOK... AND THE TROUBLES TO COME...
...WE HAVE EVERYTHING THE RITUAL REQUIRES... EXCEPT THE LOCATION...
HOW MUCH LONGER WILL IT BE?!
CESSPOOL! YOUR REPORT!
OUR SHELL COMPANIES HAVE RAMPED UP CARBON EMISSIONS...
...WHILE OUR LOBBYISTS HAVE SUCCESSFULLY PUSHED FOR DEREGULATION.
THE MELTING IS CONTINUING APACE. WE'LL BE READY SOON.
BARONESS, I WAS WONDERING—
THAT IS NO LONGER MY NAME!
SAY IT! SAY MY REAL NAME!
I... I DIDN'T MEAN...

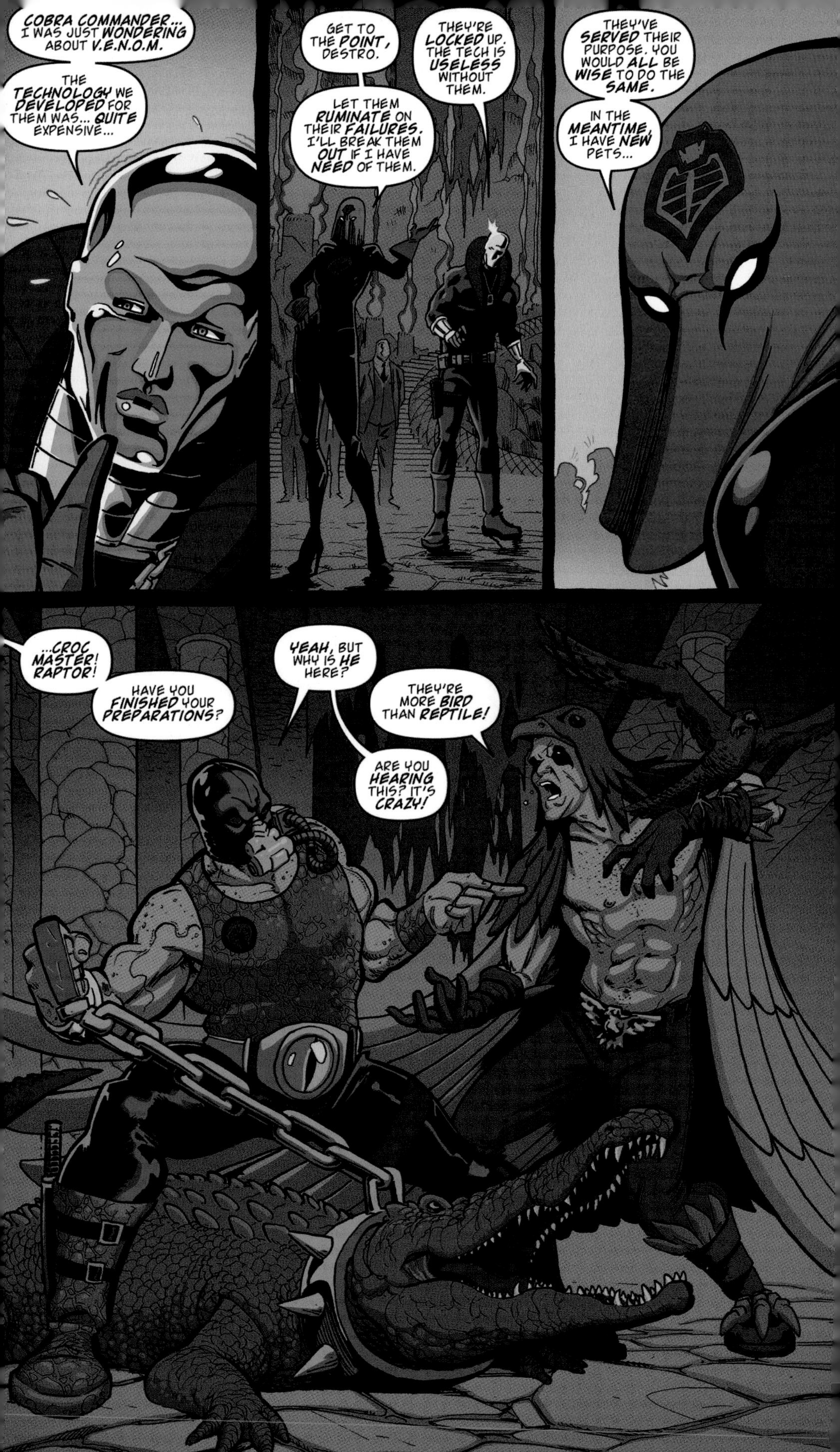
COBRA COMMANDER... I WAS JUST WONDERING ABOUT V.E.N.O.M.
THE TECHNOLOGY WE DEVELOPED FOR THEM WAS... QUITE EXPENSIVE...
GET TO THE POINT, DESTRO.
LET THEM RUMINATE ON THEIR FAILURES. I'LL BREAK THEM OUT IF I HAVE NEED OF THEM.
THEY'RE LOCKED UP. THE TECH IS USELESS WITHOUT THEM.
THEY'VE SERVED THEIR PURPOSE. YOU WOULD ALL BE WISE TO DO THE SAME.
IN THE MEANTIME, I HAVE NEW PETS...
...CROC MASTER! RAPTOR!
HAVE YOU FINISHED YOUR PREPARATIONS?
YEAH, BUT WHY IS HE HERE?
ARE YOU HEARING THIS? IT'S CRAZY!
THEY'RE MORE BIRD THAN REPTILE!

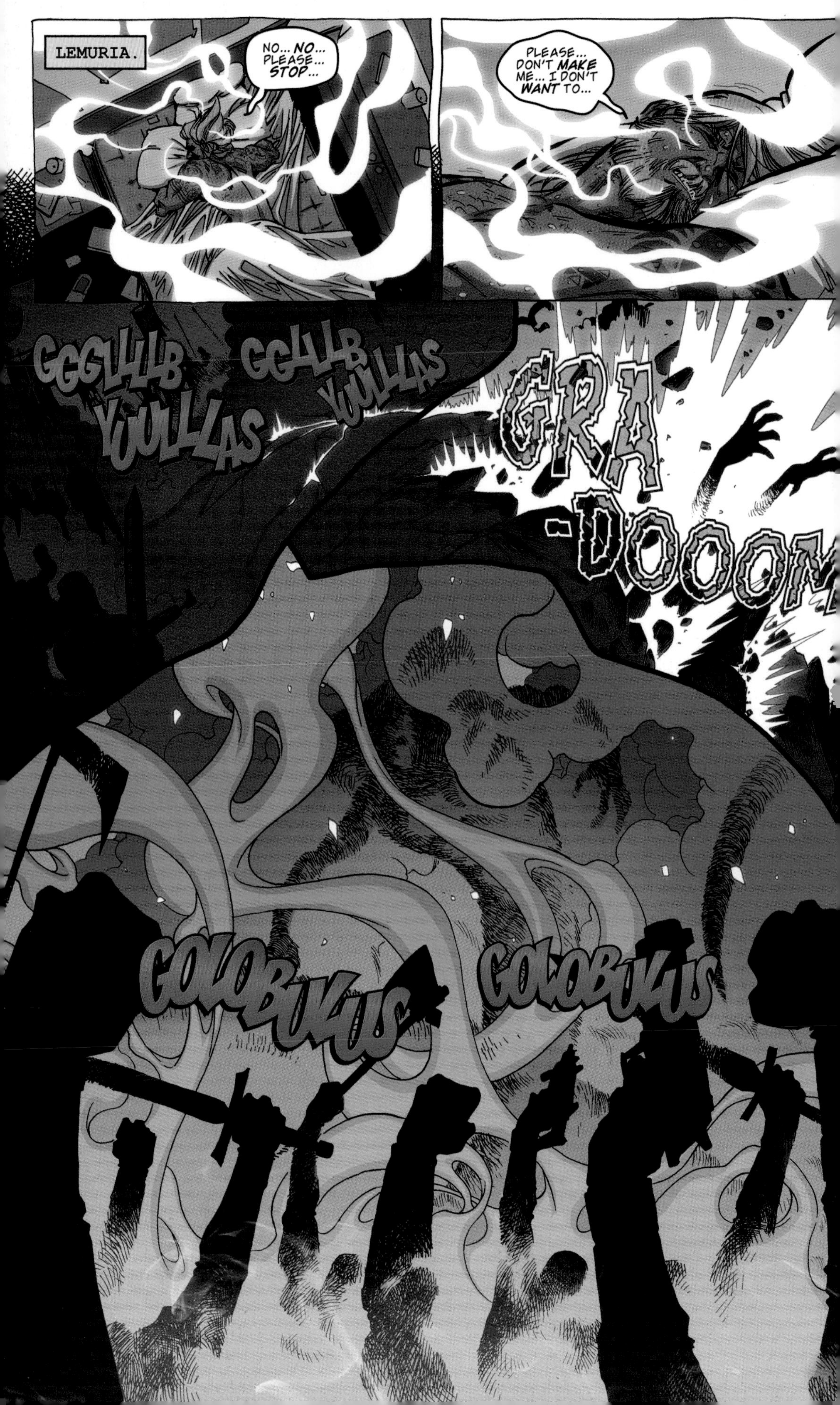
LEMURIA.
NO... NO... PLEASE... STOP...
PLEASE... DON'T MAKE ME... I DON'T WANT TO...
GGGLLLLB YUULLLAS
GGLLLB YUULLLAS
GRA-DOOOM
GOLOBUKUS
GOLOBUKUS

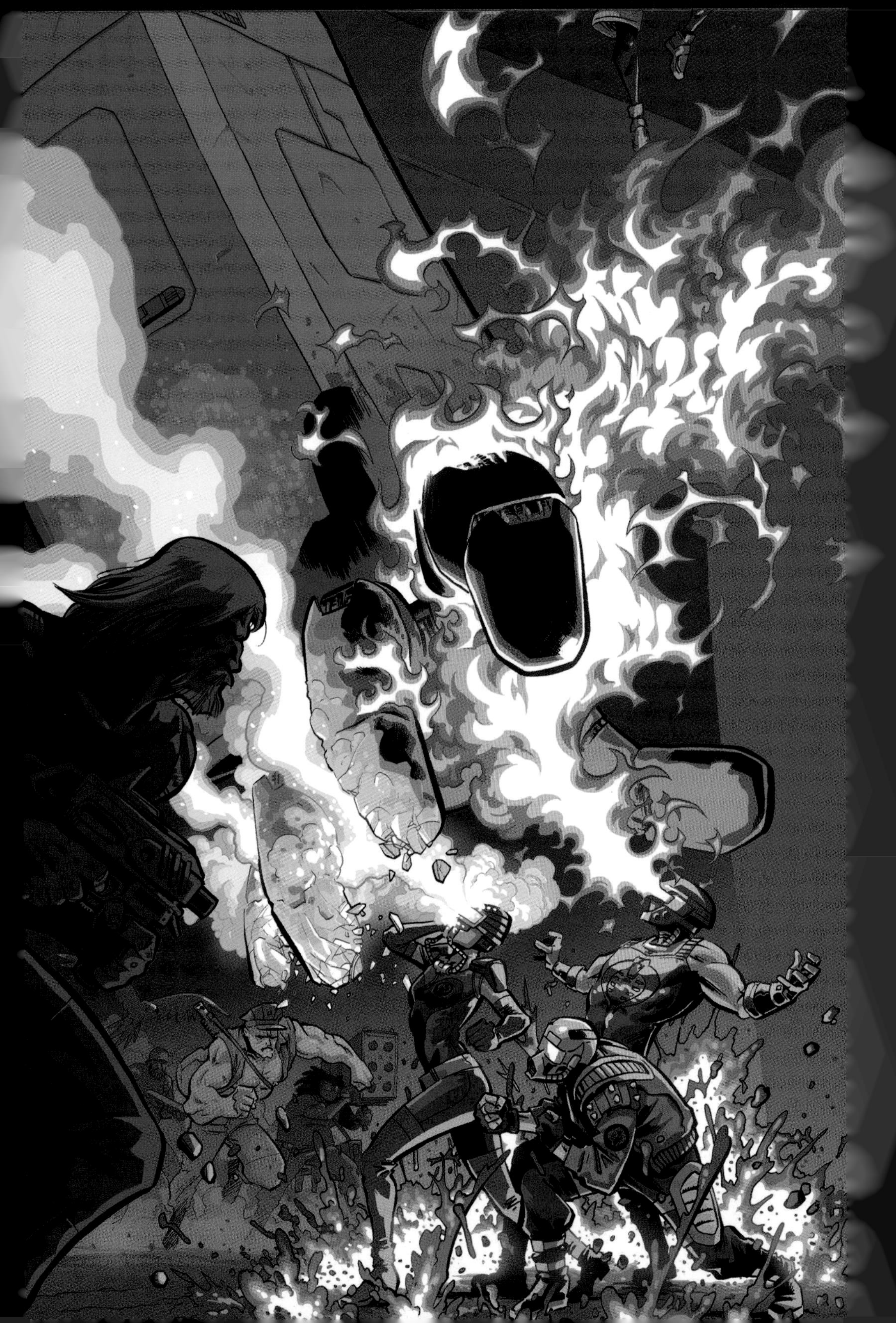

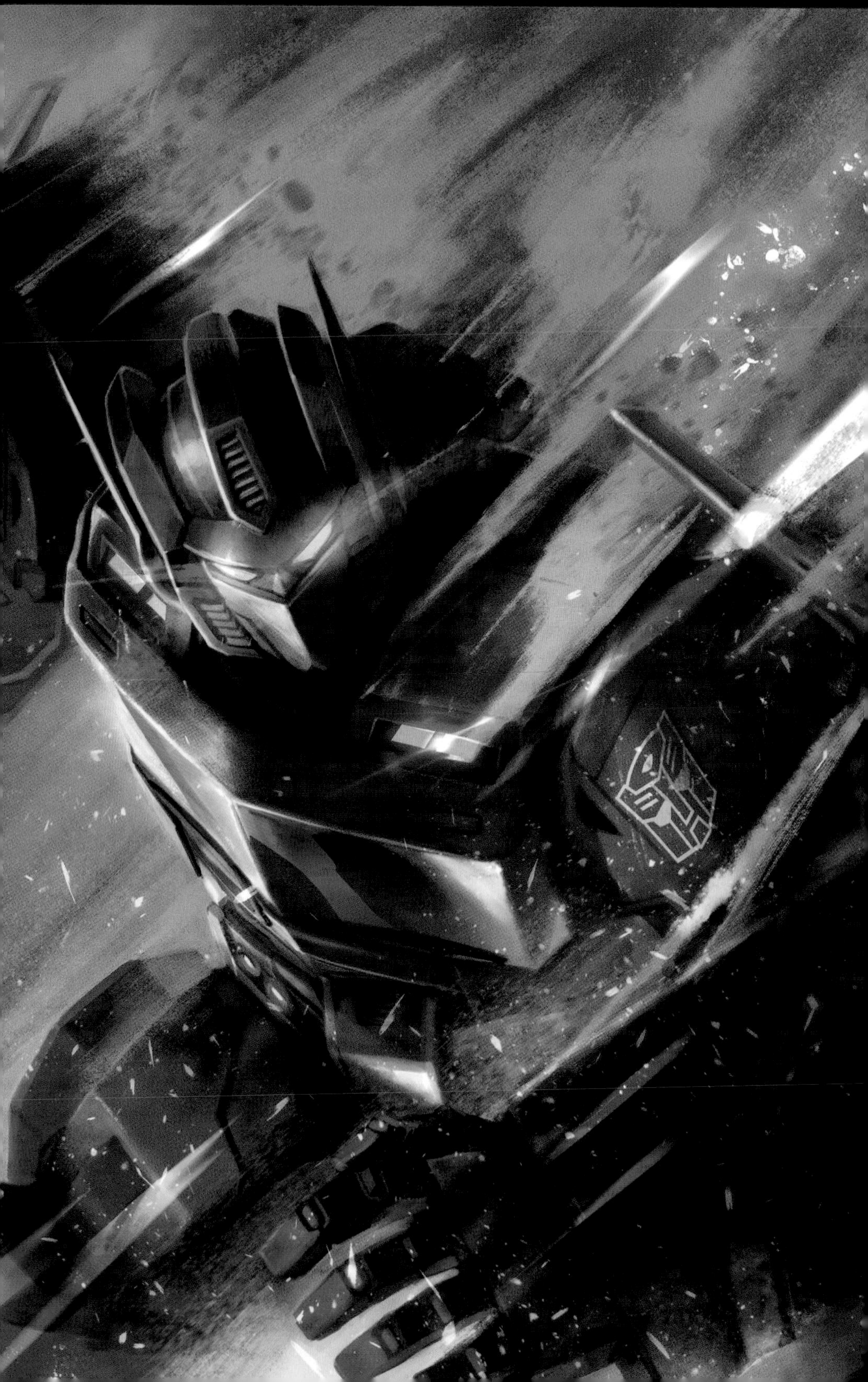

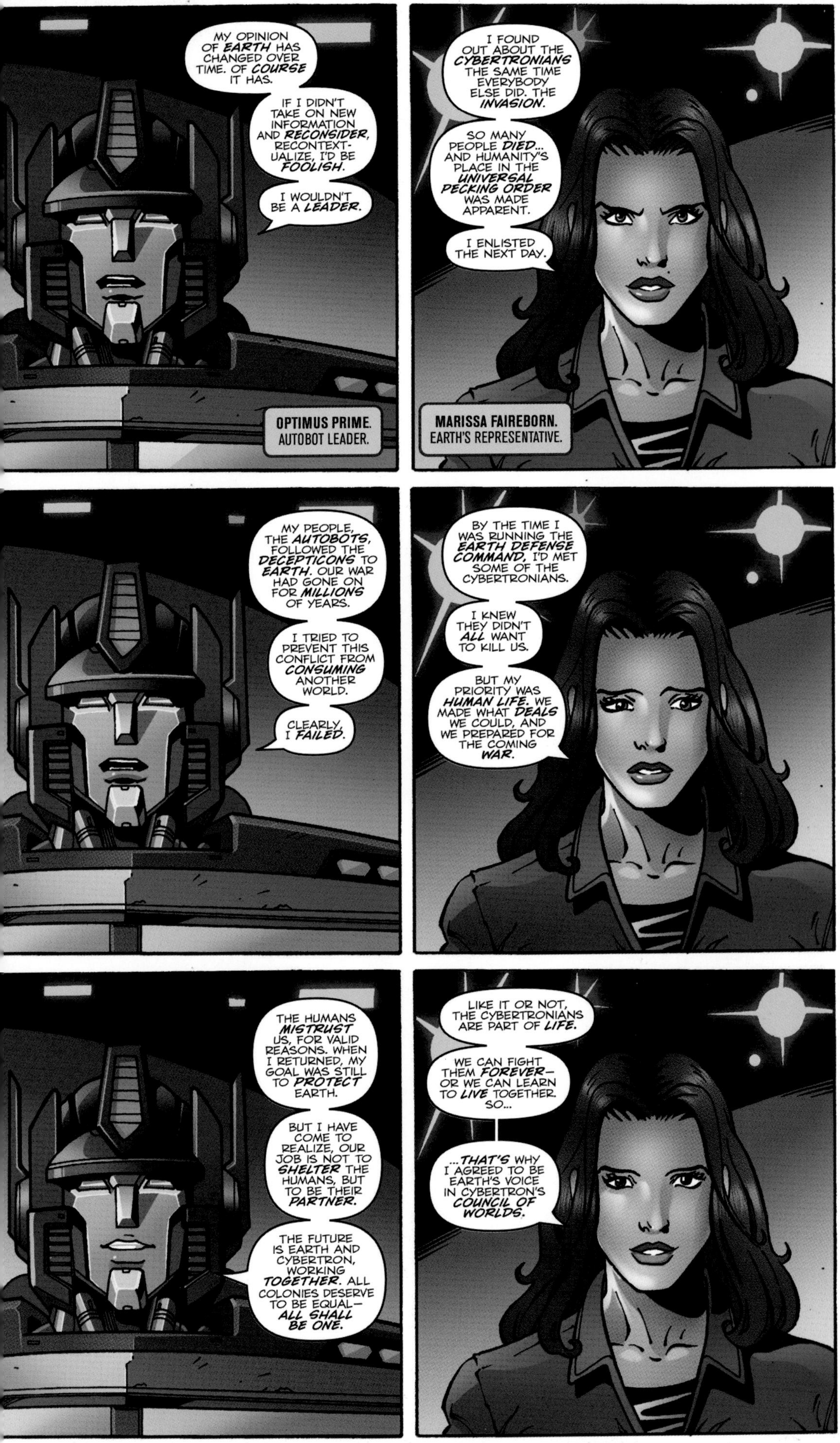
MY OPINION OF EARTH HAS CHANGED OVER TIME. OF COURSE IT HAS.
IF I DIDN'T TAKE ON NEW INFORMATION AND RECONSIDER, RECONTEXT-UALIZE, I'D BE FOOLISH.
I WOULDN'T BE A LEADER.
OPTIMUS PRIME. AUTOBOT LEADER.
I FOUND OUT ABOUT THE CYBERTRONIANS THE SAME TIME EVERYBODY ELSE DID. THE INVASION.
SO MANY PEOPLE DIED... AND HUMANITY'S PLACE IN THE UNIVERSAL PECKING ORDER WAS MADE APPARENT.
I ENLISTED THE NEXT DAY.
MARISSA FAIREBORN. EARTH'S REPRESENTATIVE.
MY PEOPLE, THE AUTOBOTS, FOLLOWED THE DECEPTICONS TO EARTH. OUR WAR HAD GONE ON FOR MILLIONS OF YEARS.
I TRIED TO PREVENT THIS CONFLICT FROM CONSUMING ANOTHER WORLD.
CLEARLY, I FAILED.
BY THE TIME I WAS RUNNING THE EARTH DEFENSE COMMAND, I'D MET SOME OF THE CYBERTRONIANS.
I KNEW THEY DIDN'T ALL WANT TO KILL US.
BUT MY PRIORITY WAS HUMAN LIFE. WE MADE WHAT DEALS WE COULD, AND WE PREPARED FOR THE COMING WAR.
THE HUMANS MISTRUST US, FOR VALID REASONS. WHEN I RETURNED, MY GOAL WAS STILL TO PROTECT EARTH.
BUT I HAVE COME TO REALIZE, OUR JOB IS NOT TO SHELTER THE HUMANS, BUT TO BE THEIR PARTNER.
THE FUTURE IS EARTH AND CYBERTRON, WORKING TOGETHER. ALL COLONIES DESERVE TO BE EQUAL— ALL SHALL BE ONE.
LIKE IT OR NOT, THE CYBERTRONIANS ARE PART OF LIFE.
WE CAN FIGHT THEM FOREVER— OR WE CAN LEARN TO LIVE TOGETHER. SO...
...THAT'S WHY I AGREED TO BE EARTH'S VOICE IN CYBERTRON'S COUNCIL OF WORLDS.

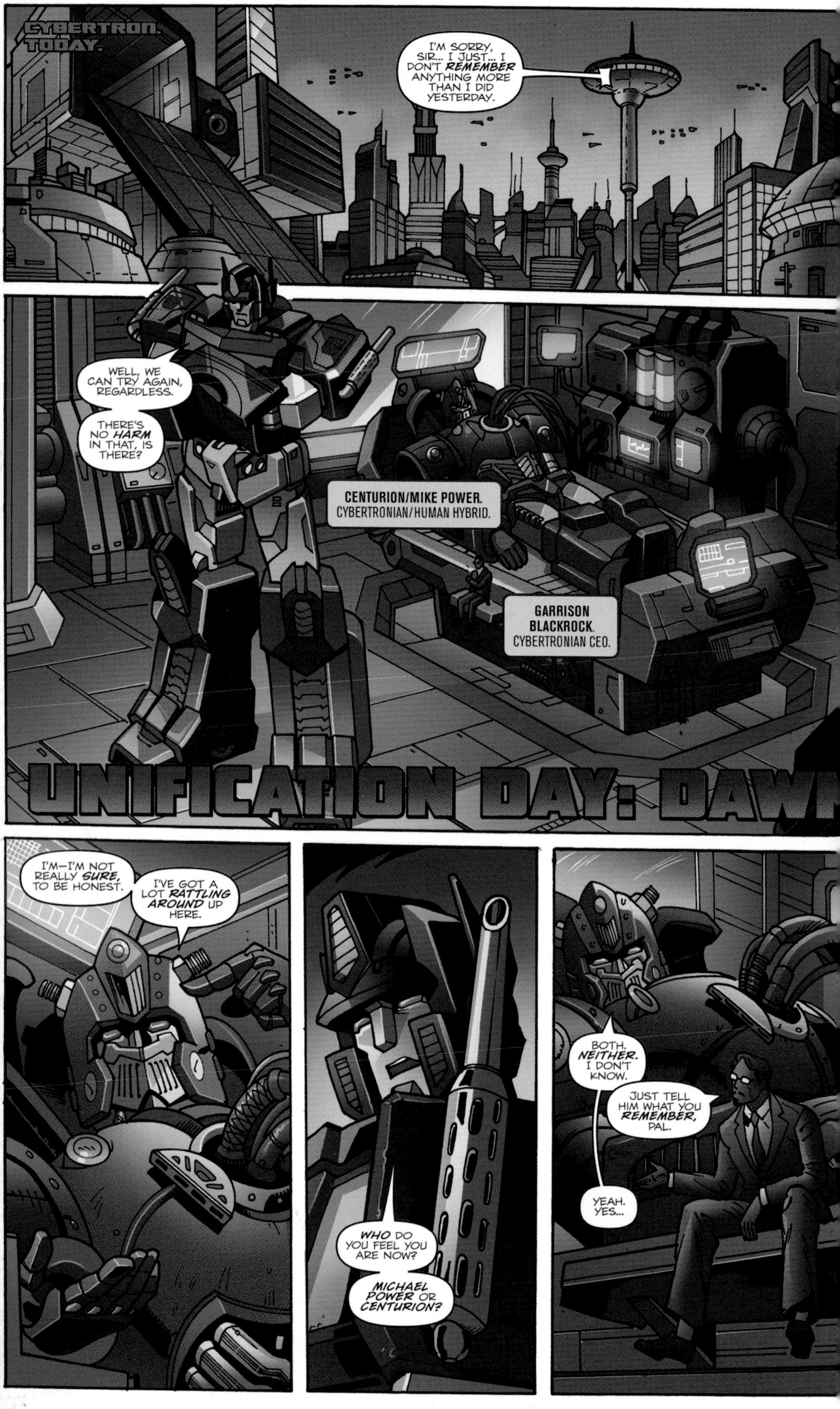
CYBERTRON. TODAY.
I'M SORRY, SIR... I JUST... I DON'T REMEMBER ANYTHING MORE THAN I DID YESTERDAY.
WELL, WE CAN TRY AGAIN, REGARDLESS.
THERE'S NO HARM IN THAT, IS THERE?
CENTURION/MIKE POWER. CYBERTRONIAN/HUMAN HYBRID.
GARRISON BLACKROCK. CYBERTRONIAN CEO.
UNIFICATION DAY: DAWN
I'M—I'M NOT REALLY SURE, TO BE HONEST.
I'VE GOT A LOT RATTLING AROUND UP HERE.
WHO DO YOU FEEL YOU ARE NOW?
MICHAEL POWER OR CENTURION?
BOTH. NEITHER. I DON'T KNOW.
JUST TELL HIM WHAT YOU REMEMBER, PAL.
YEAH. YES...

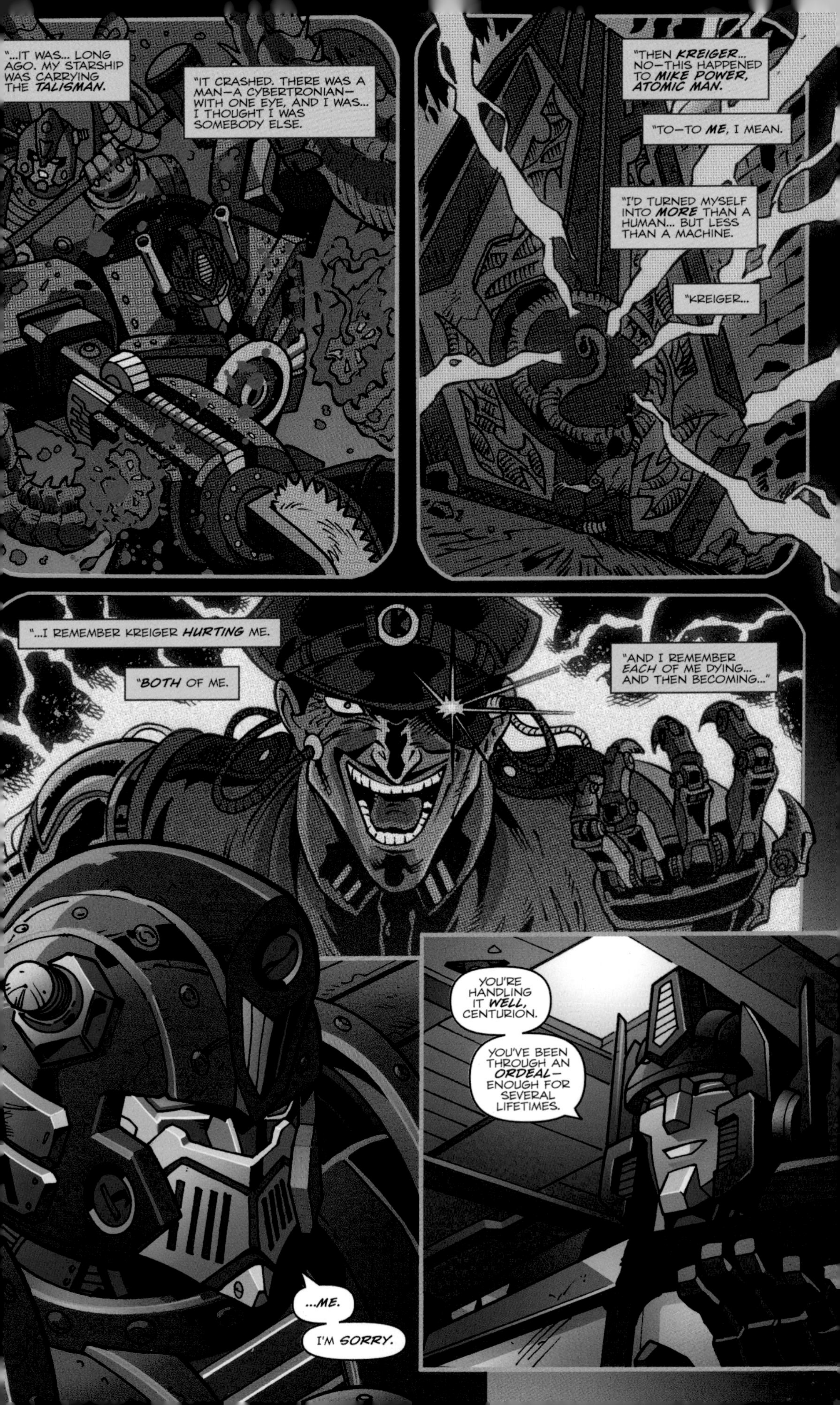
"...IT WAS... LONG AGO. MY STARSHIP WAS CARRYING THE TALISMAN.
"IT CRASHED. THERE WAS A MAN—A CYBERTRONIAN—WITH ONE EYE, AND I WAS... I THOUGHT I WAS SOMEBODY ELSE.
"THEN KREIGER... NO—THIS HAPPENED TO MIKE POWER, ATOMIC MAN.
"TO—TO ME, I MEAN.
"I'D TURNED MYSELF INTO MORE THAN A HUMAN... BUT LESS THAN A MACHINE.
"KREIGER...
"...I REMEMBER KREIGER HURTING ME.
"BOTH OF ME.
"AND I REMEMBER EACH OF ME DYING... AND THEN BECOMING..."
YOU'RE HANDLING IT WELL, CENTURION.
YOU'VE BEEN THROUGH AN ORDEAL—ENOUGH FOR SEVERAL LIFETIMES.
...ME.
I'M SORRY.

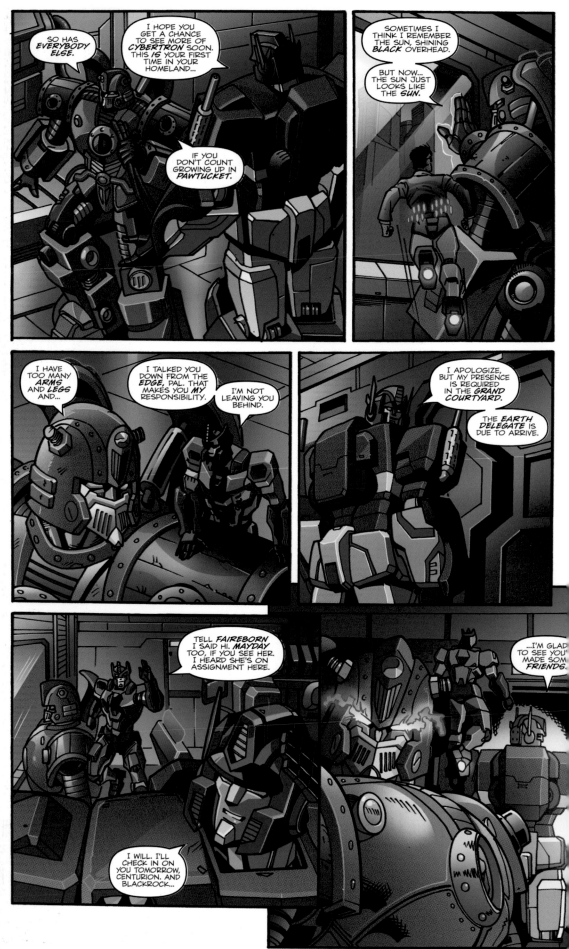

SO HAS *EVERYBODY ELSE.*

I HOPE YOU GET A CHANCE TO SEE MORE OF *CYBERTRON* SOON. THIS *IS* YOUR FIRST TIME IN YOUR HOMELAND...

IF YOU DON'T COUNT GROWING UP IN *PAWTUCKET.*

SOMETIMES I THINK I REMEMBER THE SUN, SHINING *BLACK* OVERHEAD.

BUT NOW... THE SUN JUST LOOKS LIKE THE *SUN.*

I HAVE TOO MANY *ARMS* AND *LEGS* AND...

I TALKED YOU DOWN FROM THE *EDGE,* PAL. THAT MAKES YOU *MY* RESPONSIBILITY.

I'M NOT LEAVING YOU BEHIND.

I APOLOGIZE, BUT MY PRESENCE IS REQUIRED IN THE *GRAND COURTYARD.*

THE *EARTH DELEGATE* IS DUE TO ARRIVE.

TELL *FAIREBORN* I SAID HI. *MAYDAY* TOO, IF YOU SEE HER. I HEARD SHE'S ON ASSIGNMENT HERE.

...I'M GLAD TO SEE YOU MADE SOM *FRIENDS.*

I WILL. I'LL CHECK IN ON YOU TOMORROW, *CENTURION.* AND *BLACKROCK...*

96

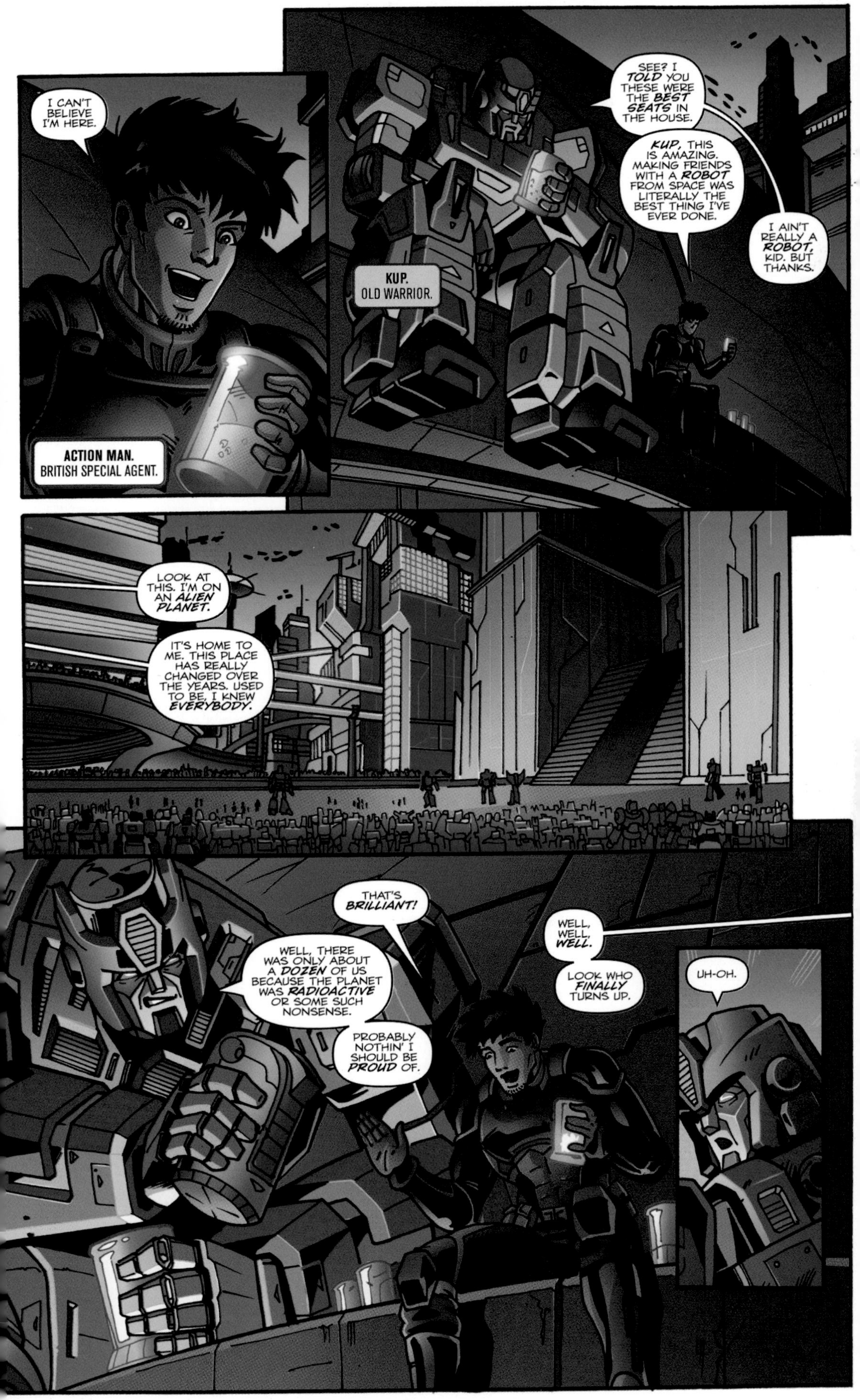
I CAN'T BELIEVE I'M HERE.
ACTION MAN. BRITISH SPECIAL AGENT.
SEE? I TOLD YOU THESE WERE THE BEST SEATS IN THE HOUSE.
KUP, THIS IS AMAZING. MAKING FRIENDS WITH A ROBOT FROM SPACE WAS LITERALLY THE BEST THING I'VE EVER DONE.
I AIN'T REALLY A ROBOT, KID. BUT THANKS.
KUP. OLD WARRIOR.
LOOK AT THIS. I'M ON AN ALIEN PLANET.
IT'S HOME TO ME. THIS PLACE HAS REALLY CHANGED OVER THE YEARS. USED TO BE, I KNEW EVERYBODY.
WELL, THERE WAS ONLY ABOUT A DOZEN OF US BECAUSE THE PLANET WAS RADIOACTIVE OR SOME SUCH NONSENSE.
THAT'S BRILLIANT!
PROBABLY NOTHIN' I SHOULD BE PROUD OF.
WELL, WELL, WELL.
LOOK WHO FINALLY TURNS UP.
UH-OH.

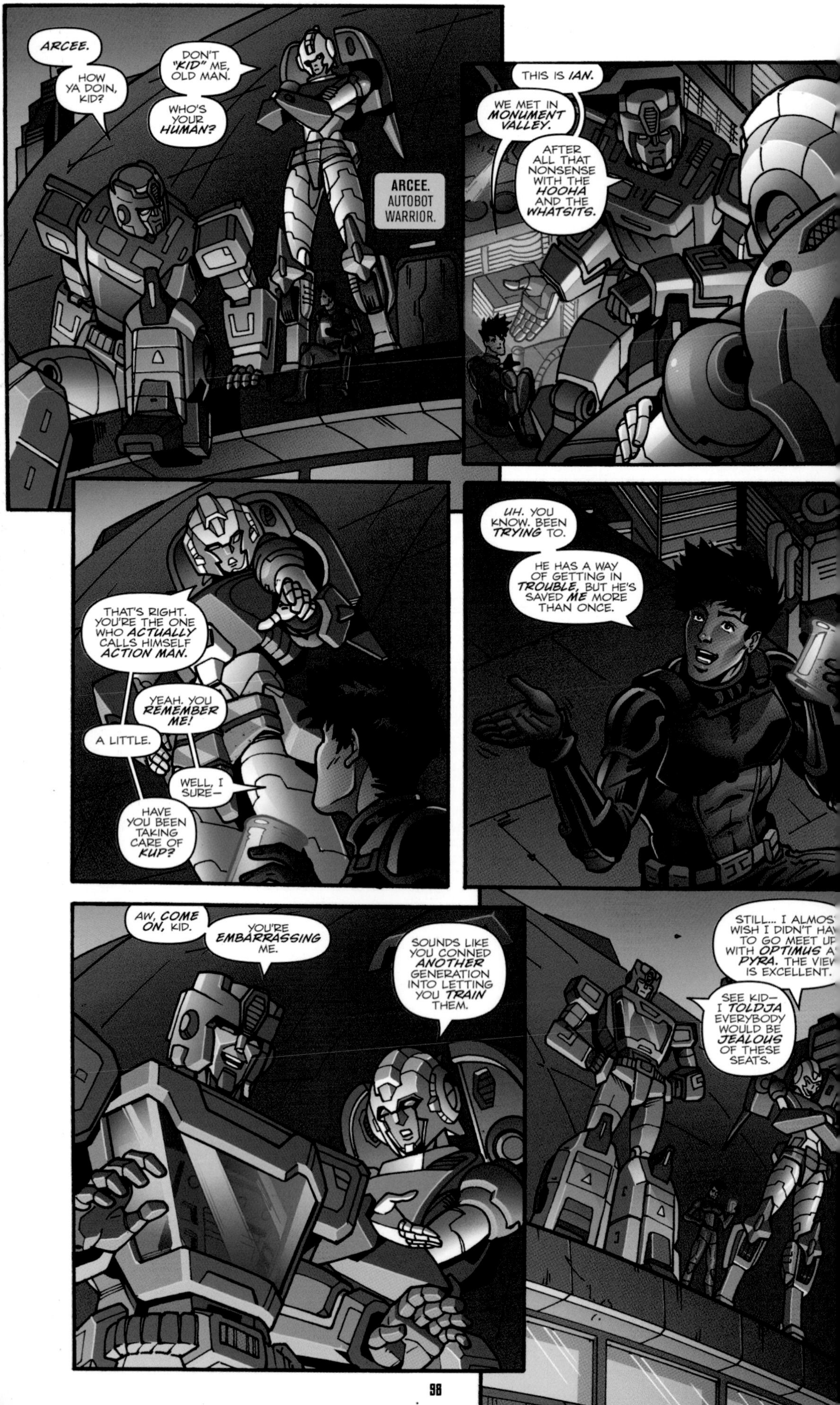
ARCEE.
HOW YA DOIN, KID?
DON'T "KID" ME, OLD MAN.
WHO'S YOUR HUMAN?
ARCEE. AUTOBOT WARRIOR.
THIS IS IAN.
WE MET IN MONUMENT VALLEY.
AFTER ALL THAT NONSENSE WITH THE HOOHA AND THE WHATSITS.
THAT'S RIGHT. YOU'RE THE ONE WHO ACTUALLY CALLS HIMSELF ACTION MAN.
YEAH. YOU REMEMBER ME!
A LITTLE.
WELL, I SURE—
HAVE YOU BEEN TAKING CARE OF KUP?
UH. YOU KNOW. BEEN TRYING TO.
HE HAS A WAY OF GETTING IN TROUBLE, BUT HE'S SAVED ME MORE THAN ONCE.
AW, COME ON, KID.
YOU'RE EMBARRASSING ME.
SOUNDS LIKE YOU CONNED ANOTHER GENERATION INTO LETTING YOU TRAIN THEM.
SEE KID— I TOLDJA EVERYBODY WOULD BE JEALOUS OF THESE SEATS.

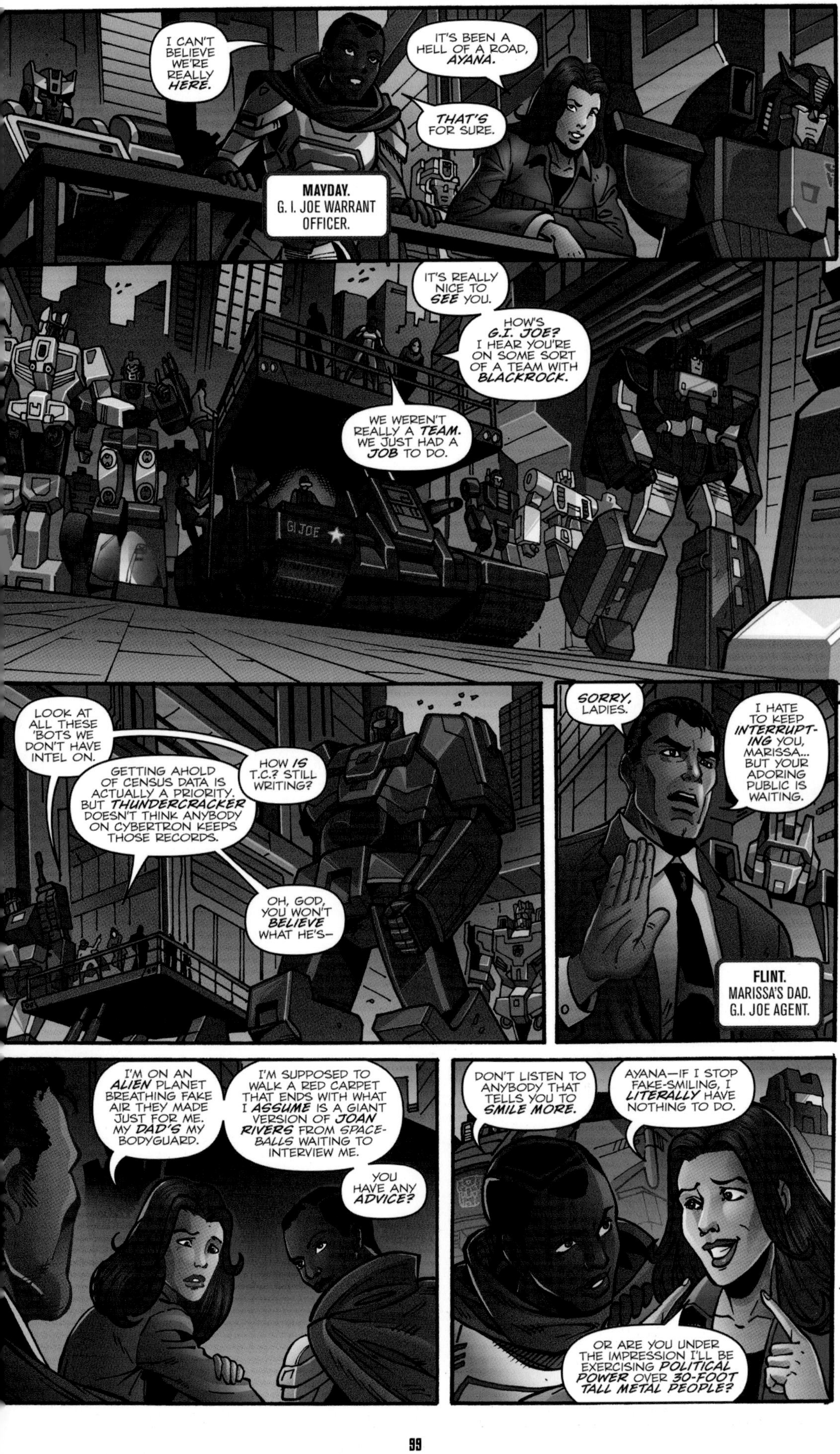

I CAN'T BELIEVE WE'RE REALLY HERE.
IT'S BEEN A HELL OF A ROAD, AYANA.
THAT'S FOR SURE.
MAYDAY. G. I. JOE WARRANT OFFICER.
IT'S REALLY NICE TO SEE YOU.
HOW'S G.I. JOE? I HEAR YOU'RE ON SOME SORT OF A TEAM WITH BLACKROCK.
WE WEREN'T REALLY A TEAM. WE JUST HAD A JOB TO DO.
GI JOE
LOOK AT ALL THESE 'BOTS WE DON'T HAVE INTEL ON.
GETTING AHOLD OF CENSUS DATA IS ACTUALLY A PRIORITY. BUT THUNDERCRACKER DOESN'T THINK ANYBODY ON CYBERTRON KEEPS THOSE RECORDS.
HOW IS T.C.? STILL WRITING?
OH, GOD, YOU WON'T BELIEVE WHAT HE'S—
SORRY, LADIES.
I HATE TO KEEP INTERRUPTING YOU, MARISSA... BUT YOUR ADORING PUBLIC IS WAITING.
FLINT. MARISSA'S DAD. G.I. JOE AGENT.
I'M ON AN ALIEN PLANET BREATHING FAKE AIR THEY MADE JUST FOR ME. MY DAD'S MY BODYGUARD.
I'M SUPPOSED TO WALK A RED CARPET THAT ENDS WITH WHAT I ASSUME IS A GIANT VERSION OF JOAN RIVERS FROM SPACE-BALLS WAITING TO INTERVIEW ME.
YOU HAVE ANY ADVICE?
DON'T LISTEN TO ANYBODY THAT TELLS YOU TO SMILE MORE.
AYANA—IF I STOP FAKE-SMILING, I LITERALLY HAVE NOTHING TO DO.
OR ARE YOU UNDER THE IMPRESSION I'LL BE EXERCISING POLITICAL POWER OVER 30-FOOT TALL METAL PEOPLE?

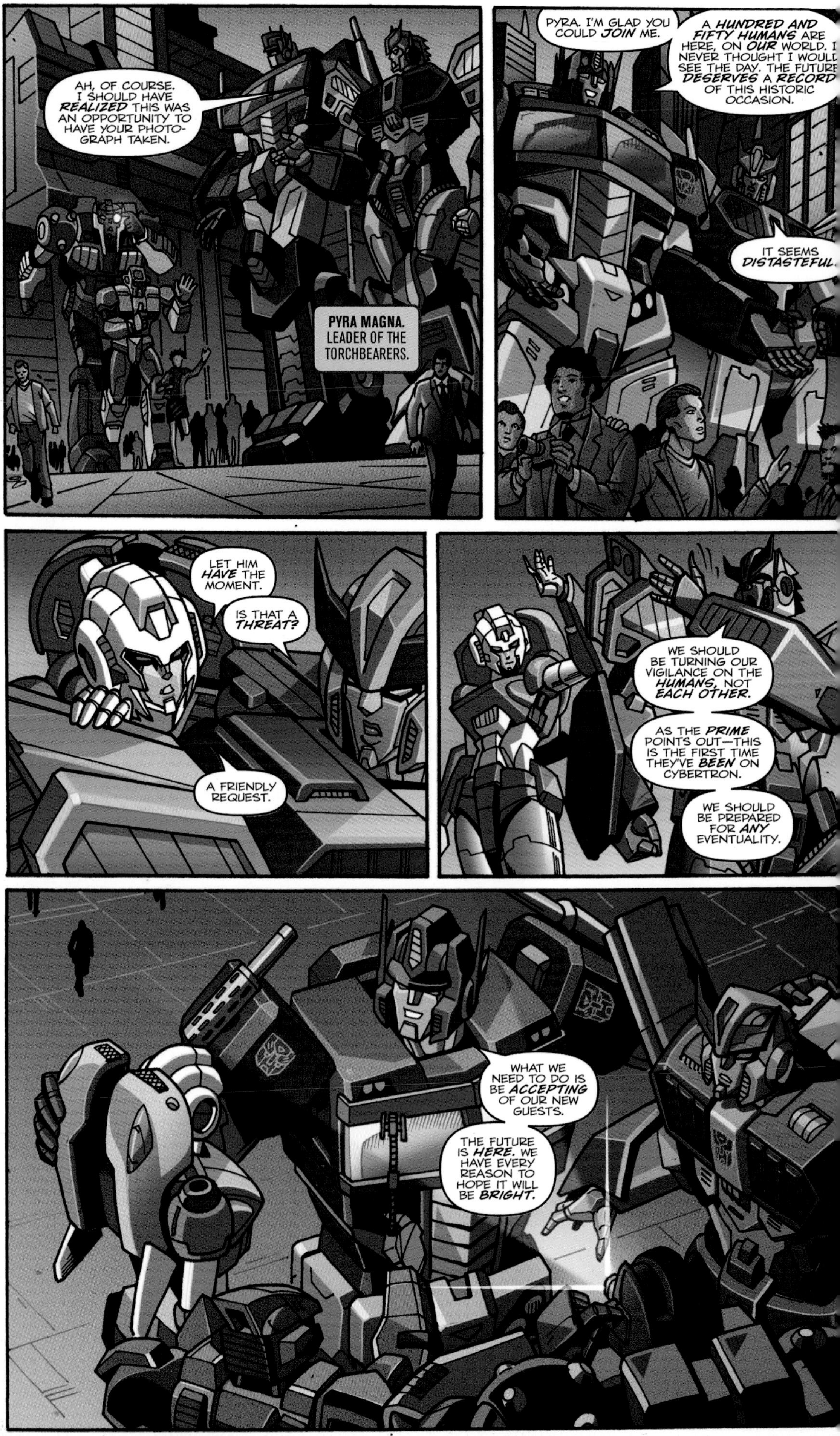
AH, OF COURSE. I SHOULD HAVE REALIZED THIS WAS AN OPPORTUNITY TO HAVE YOUR PHOTO-GRAPH TAKEN.
PYRA MAGNA. LEADER OF THE TORCHBEARERS.
PYRA. I'M GLAD YOU COULD JOIN ME.
A HUNDRED AND FIFTY HUMANS ARE HERE, ON OUR WORLD. I NEVER THOUGHT I WOULD SEE THE DAY. THE FUTURE DESERVES A RECORD OF THIS HISTORIC OCCASION.
IT SEEMS DISTASTEFUL.
LET HIM HAVE THE MOMENT.
IS THAT A THREAT?
A FRIENDLY REQUEST.
WE SHOULD BE TURNING OUR VIGILANCE ON THE HUMANS, NOT EACH OTHER.
AS THE PRIME POINTS OUT—THIS IS THE FIRST TIME THEY'VE BEEN ON CYBERTRON.
WE SHOULD BE PREPARED FOR ANY EVENTUALITY.
WHAT WE NEED TO DO IS BE ACCEPTING OF OUR NEW GUESTS.
THE FUTURE IS HERE. WE HAVE EVERY REASON TO HOPE IT WILL BE BRIGHT.

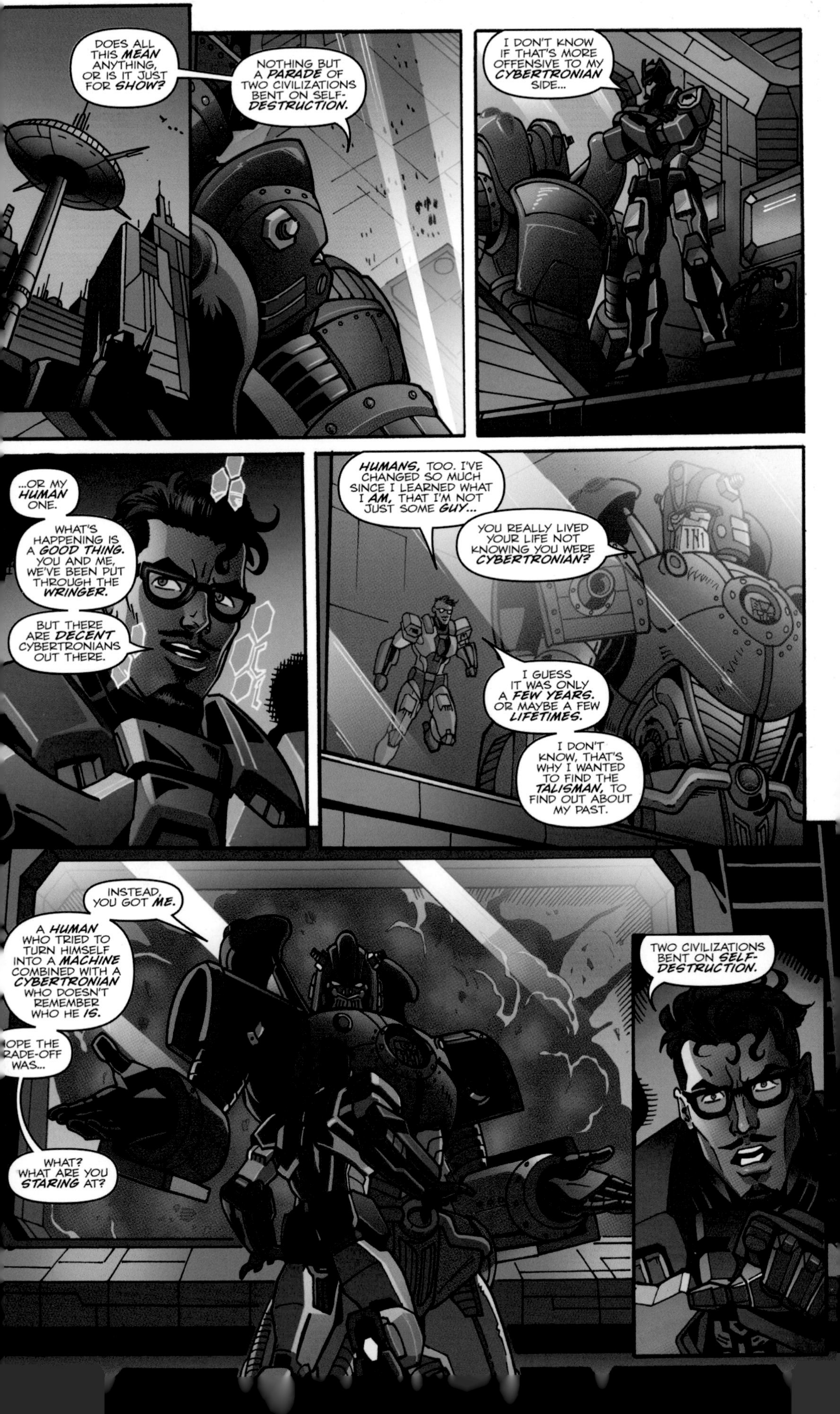
DOES ALL THIS MEAN ANYTHING, OR IS IT JUST FOR SHOW?
NOTHING BUT A PARADE OF TWO CIVILIZATIONS BENT ON SELF-DESTRUCTION.
I DON'T KNOW IF THAT'S MORE OFFENSIVE TO MY CYBERTRONIAN SIDE...
...OR MY HUMAN ONE.
WHAT'S HAPPENING IS A GOOD THING. YOU AND ME, WE'VE BEEN PUT THROUGH THE WRINGER.
BUT THERE ARE DECENT CYBERTRONIANS OUT THERE.
HUMANS, TOO. I'VE CHANGED SO MUCH SINCE I LEARNED WHAT I AM, THAT I'M NOT JUST SOME GUY...
YOU REALLY LIVED YOUR LIFE NOT KNOWING YOU WERE CYBERTRONIAN?
I GUESS IT WAS ONLY A FEW YEARS. OR MAYBE A FEW LIFETIMES.
I DON'T KNOW, THAT'S WHY I WANTED TO FIND THE TALISMAN, TO FIND OUT ABOUT MY PAST.
INSTEAD, YOU GOT ME.
A HUMAN WHO TRIED TO TURN HIMSELF INTO A MACHINE COMBINED WITH A CYBERTRONIAN WHO DOESN'T REMEMBER WHO HE IS.
OPE THE RADE-OFF WAS...
WHAT? WHAT ARE YOU STARING AT?
TWO CIVILIZATIONS BENT ON SELF-DESTRUCTION.

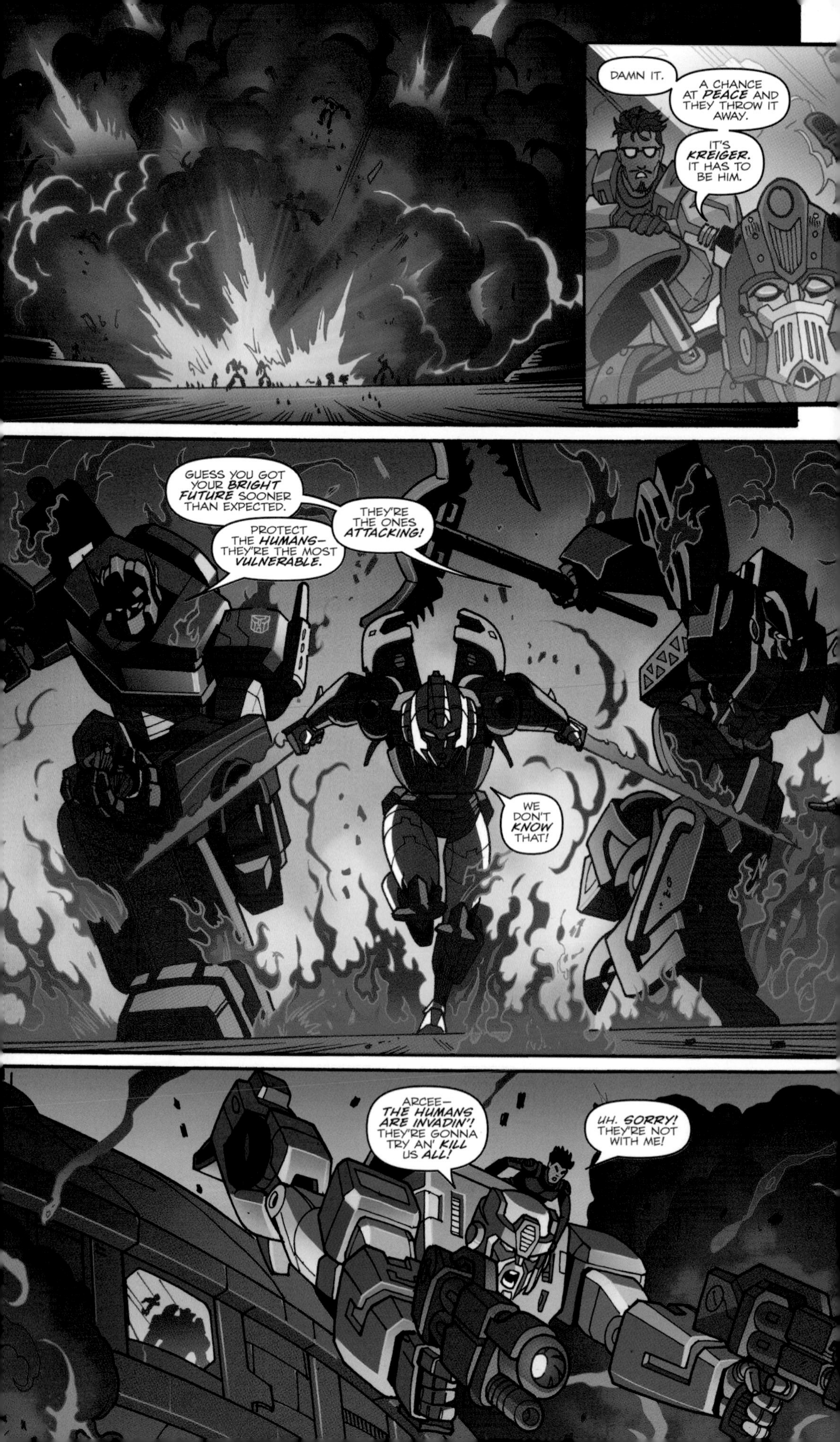
DAMN IT.
A CHANCE AT PEACE AND THEY THROW IT AWAY.
IT'S KREIGER. IT HAS TO BE HIM.
GUESS YOU GOT YOUR BRIGHT FUTURE SOONER THAN EXPECTED.
PROTECT THE HUMANS— THEY'RE THE MOST VULNERABLE.
THEY'RE THE ONES ATTACKING!
WE DON'T KNOW THAT!
ARCEE— THE HUMANS ARE INVADIN'! THEY'RE GONNA TRY AN' KILL US ALL!
UH. SORRY! THEY'RE NOT WITH ME!

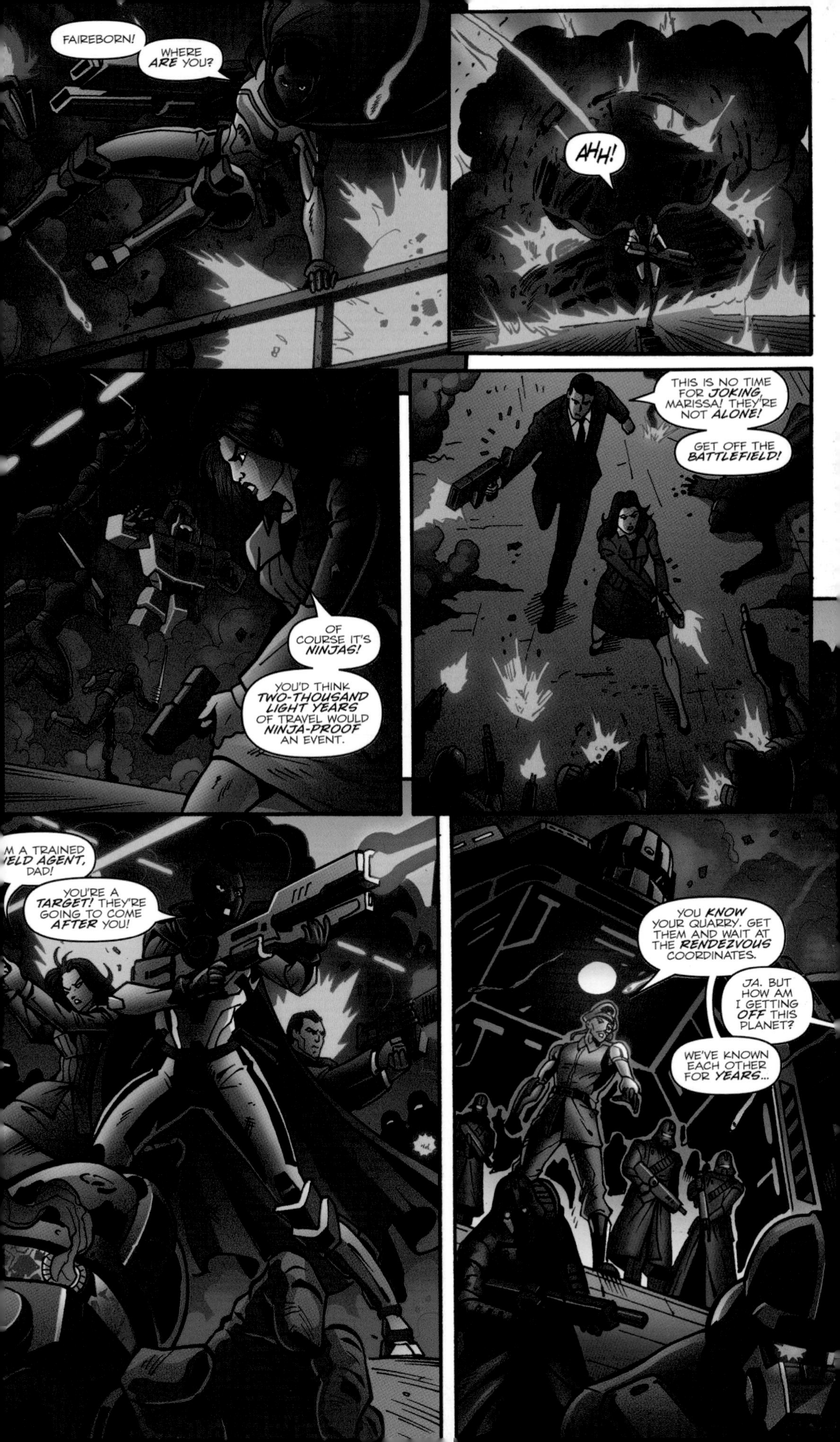
FAIREBORN!
WHERE ARE YOU?
AHH!
OF COURSE IT'S NINJAS!
YOU'D THINK TWO-THOUSAND LIGHT YEARS OF TRAVEL WOULD NINJA-PROOF AN EVENT.
THIS IS NO TIME FOR JOKING, MARISSA! THEY'RE NOT ALONE!
GET OFF THE BATTLEFIELD!
M A TRAINED IELD AGENT, DAD!
YOU'RE A TARGET! THEY'RE GOING TO COME AFTER YOU!
YOU KNOW YOUR QUARRY. GET THEM AND WAIT AT THE RENDEZVOUS COORDINATES.
JA. BUT HOW AM I GETTING OFF THIS PLANET?
WE'VE KNOWN EACH OTHER FOR YEARS...

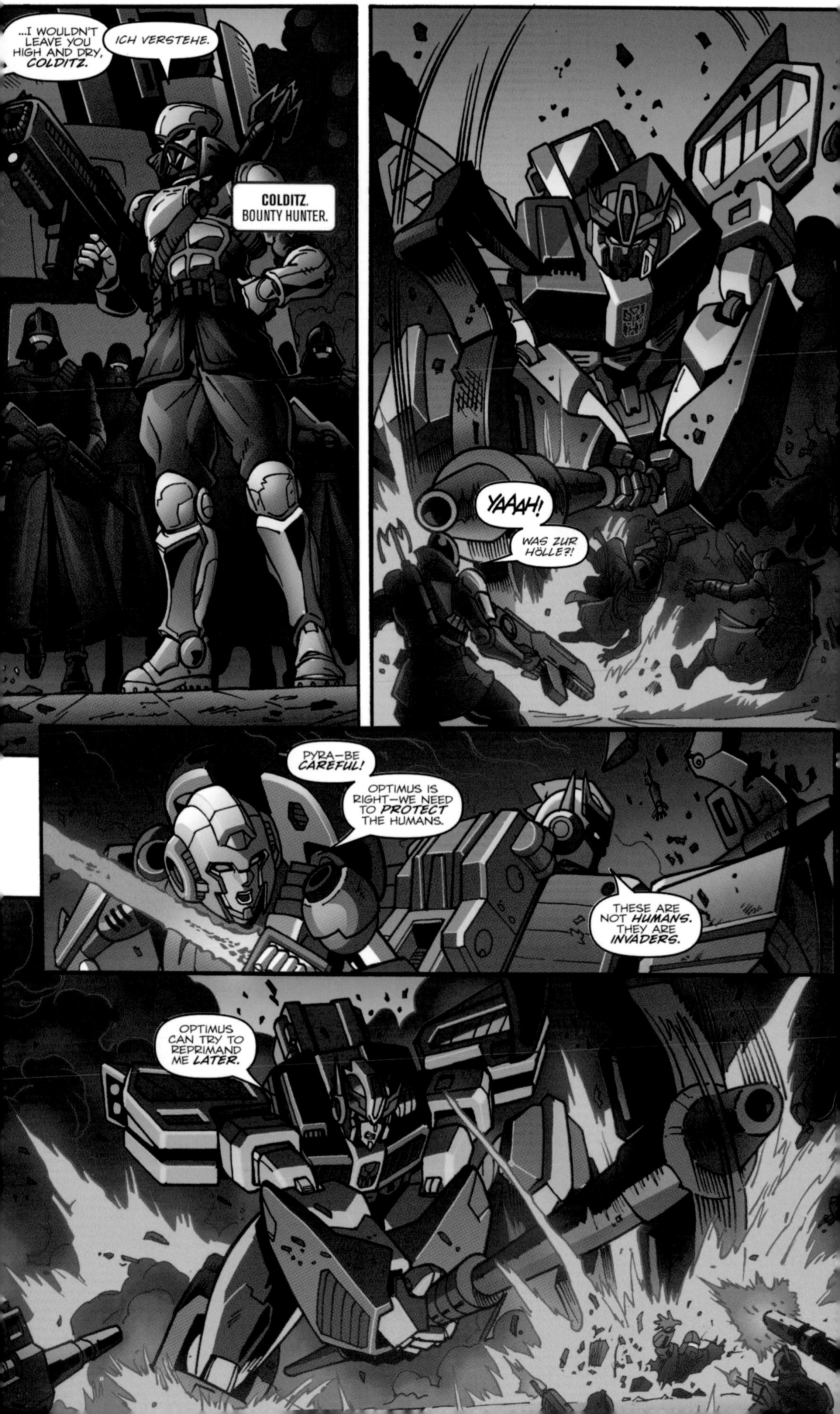
...I WOULDN'T LEAVE YOU HIGH AND DRY, COLDITZ.
ICH VERSTEHE.
COLDITZ. BOUNTY HUNTER.
YAAAH!
WAS ZUR HÖLLE?!
PYRA—BE CAREFUL!
OPTIMUS IS RIGHT—WE NEED TO PROTECT THE HUMANS.
THESE ARE NOT HUMANS. THEY ARE INVADERS.
OPTIMUS CAN TRY TO REPRIMAND ME LATER.

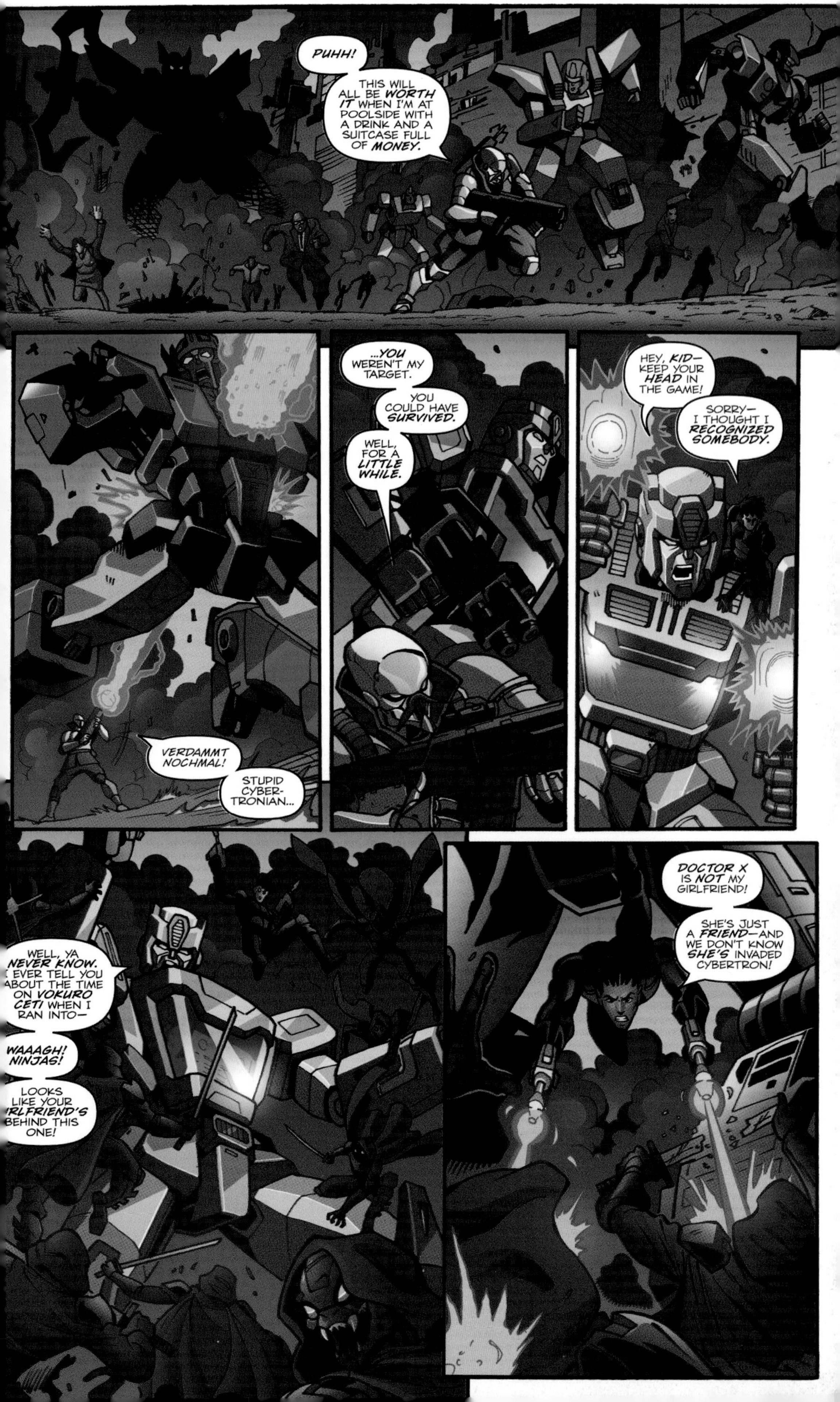
PUHH!
THIS WILL ALL BE WORTH IT WHEN I'M AT POOLSIDE WITH A DRINK AND A SUITCASE FULL OF MONEY.
VERDAMMT NOCHMAL!
STUPID CYBER-TRONIAN...
...YOU WEREN'T MY TARGET.
YOU COULD HAVE SURVIVED.
WELL, FOR A LITTLE WHILE.
HEY, KID-- KEEP YOUR HEAD IN THE GAME!
SORRY-- I THOUGHT I RECOGNIZED SOMEBODY.
WELL, YA NEVER KNOW.
ABOUT THE TIME ON VOKURO CETI WHEN I RAN INTO--
WAAAGH! NINJAS!
LOOKS LIKE YOUR
BEHIND THIS ONE!
DOCTOR X IS NOT MY GIRLFRIEND!
SHE'S JUST A FRIEND--AND WE DON'T KNOW SHE'S INVADED CYBERTRON!

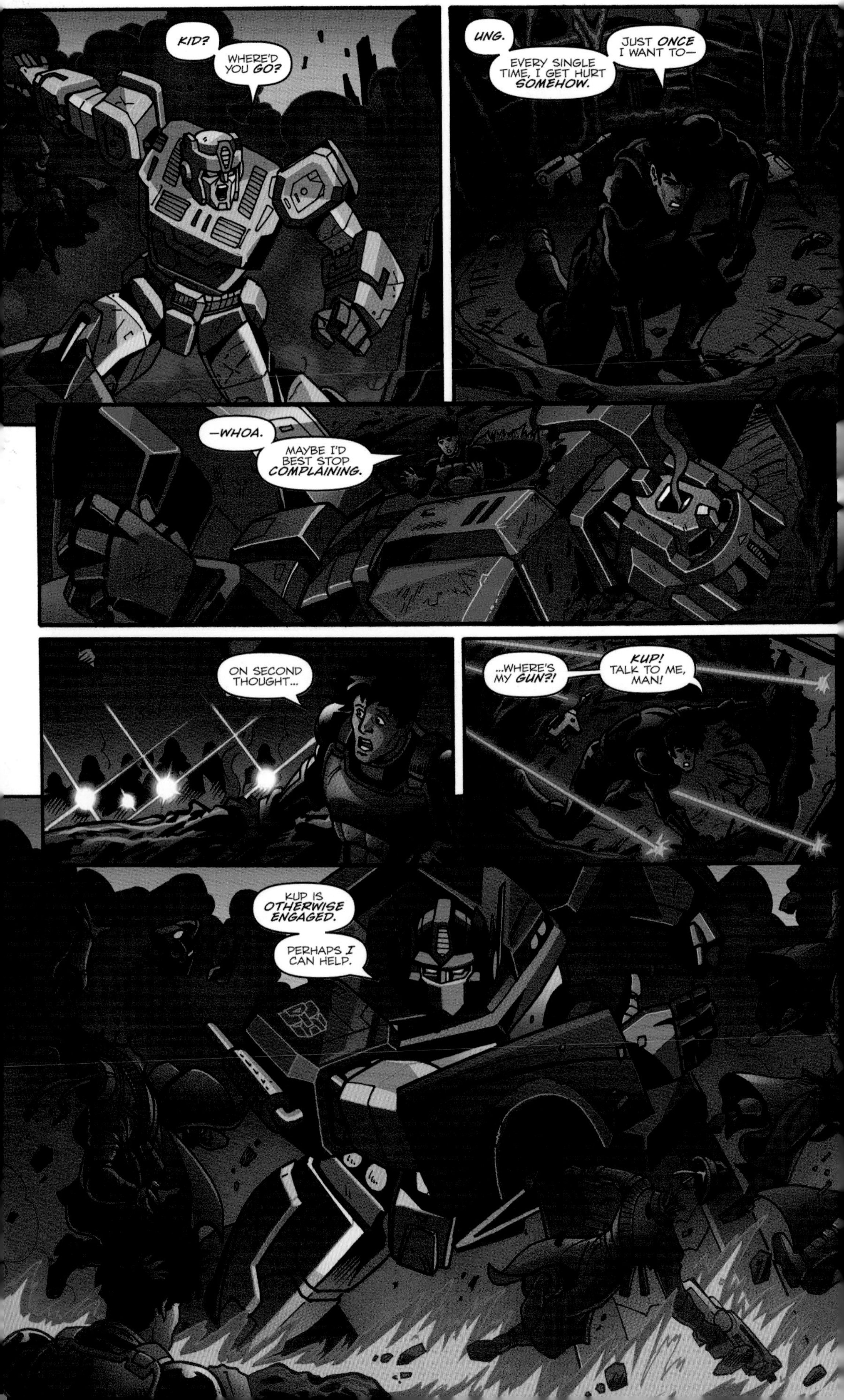
KID?
WHERE'D YOU GO?
UNG.
EVERY SINGLE TIME, I GET HURT SOMEHOW.
JUST ONCE I WANT TO—
—WHOA.
MAYBE I'D BEST STOP COMPLAINING.
ON SECOND THOUGHT...
KUP! TALK TO ME, MAN!
...WHERE'S MY GUN?!
KUP IS OTHERWISE ENGAGED.
PERHAPS I CAN HELP.

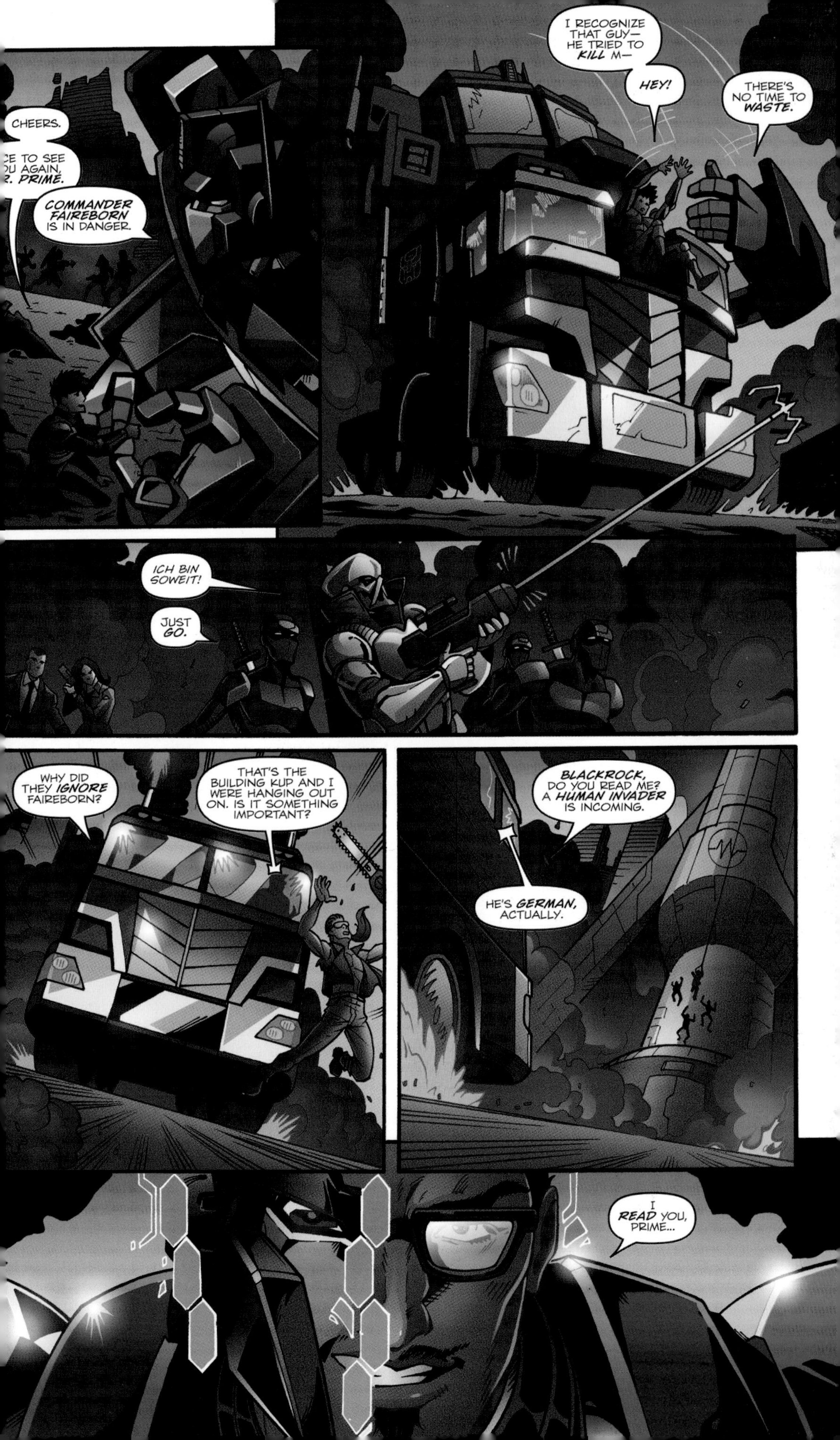

CHEERS.
CE TO SEE
OU AGAIN,
R. PRIME.
COMMANDER FAIREBORN IS IN DANGER.
I RECOGNIZE THAT GUY— HE TRIED TO KILL M—
HEY!
THERE'S NO TIME TO WASTE.
ICH BIN SOWEIT!
JUST GO.
WHY DID THEY IGNORE FAIREBORN?
THAT'S THE BUILDING KUP AND I WERE HANGING OUT ON. IS IT SOMETHING IMPORTANT?
BLACKROCK, DO YOU READ ME? A HUMAN INVADER IS INCOMING.
HE'S GERMAN, ACTUALLY.
I READ YOU, PRIME...

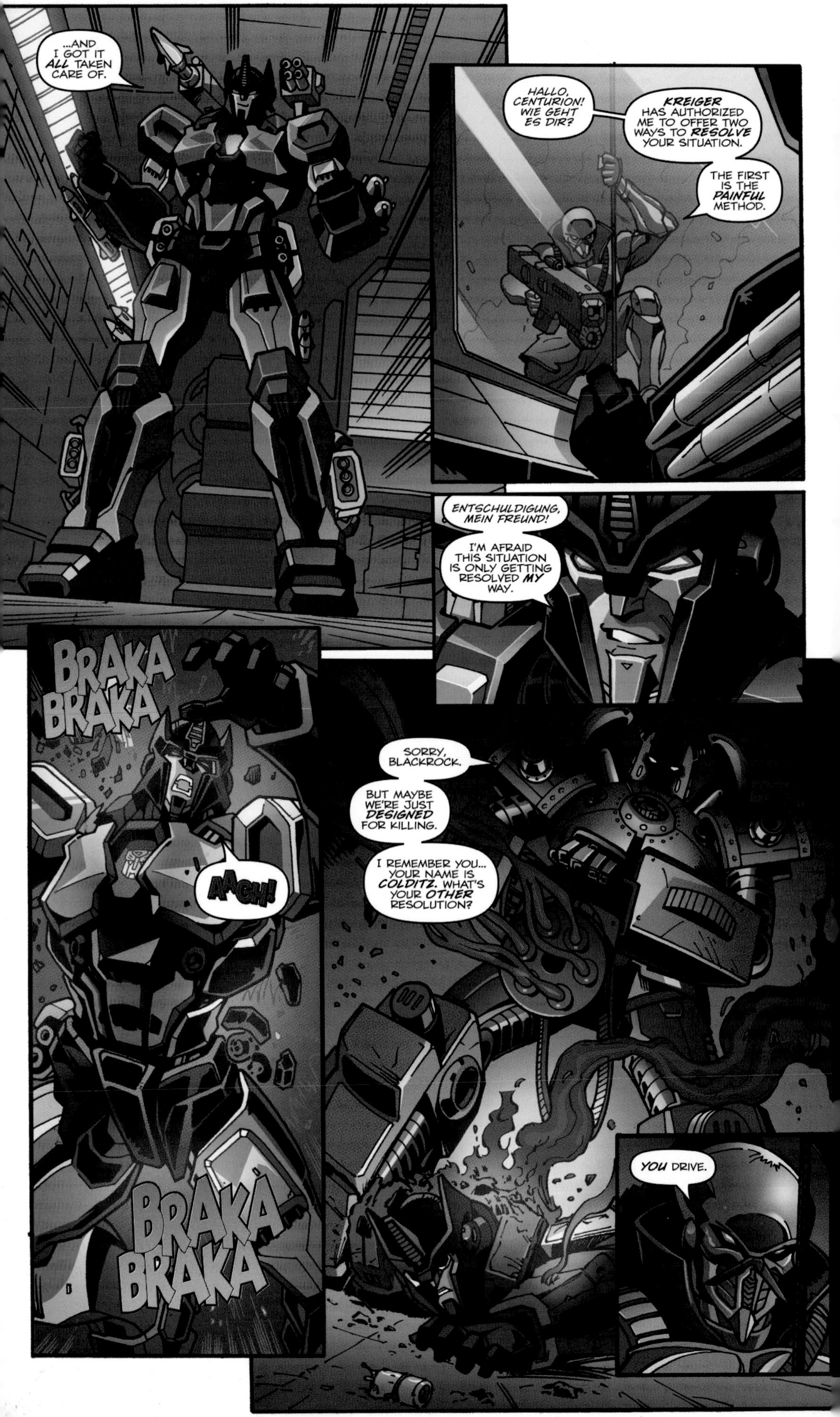
...AND I GOT IT ALL TAKEN CARE OF.
HALLO, CENTURION! WIE GEHT ES DIR?
KREIGER HAS AUTHORIZED ME TO OFFER TWO WAYS TO RESOLVE YOUR SITUATION.
THE FIRST IS THE PAINFUL METHOD.
ENTSCHULDIGUNG, MEIN FREUND!
I'M AFRAID THIS SITUATION IS ONLY GETTING RESOLVED MY WAY.
BRAKA BRAKA
AAGH!
BRAKA BRAKA
SORRY, BLACKROCK.
BUT MAYBE WE'RE JUST DESIGNED FOR KILLING.
I REMEMBER YOU... YOUR NAME IS COLDITZ. WHAT'S YOUR OTHER RESOLUTION?
YOU DRIVE.

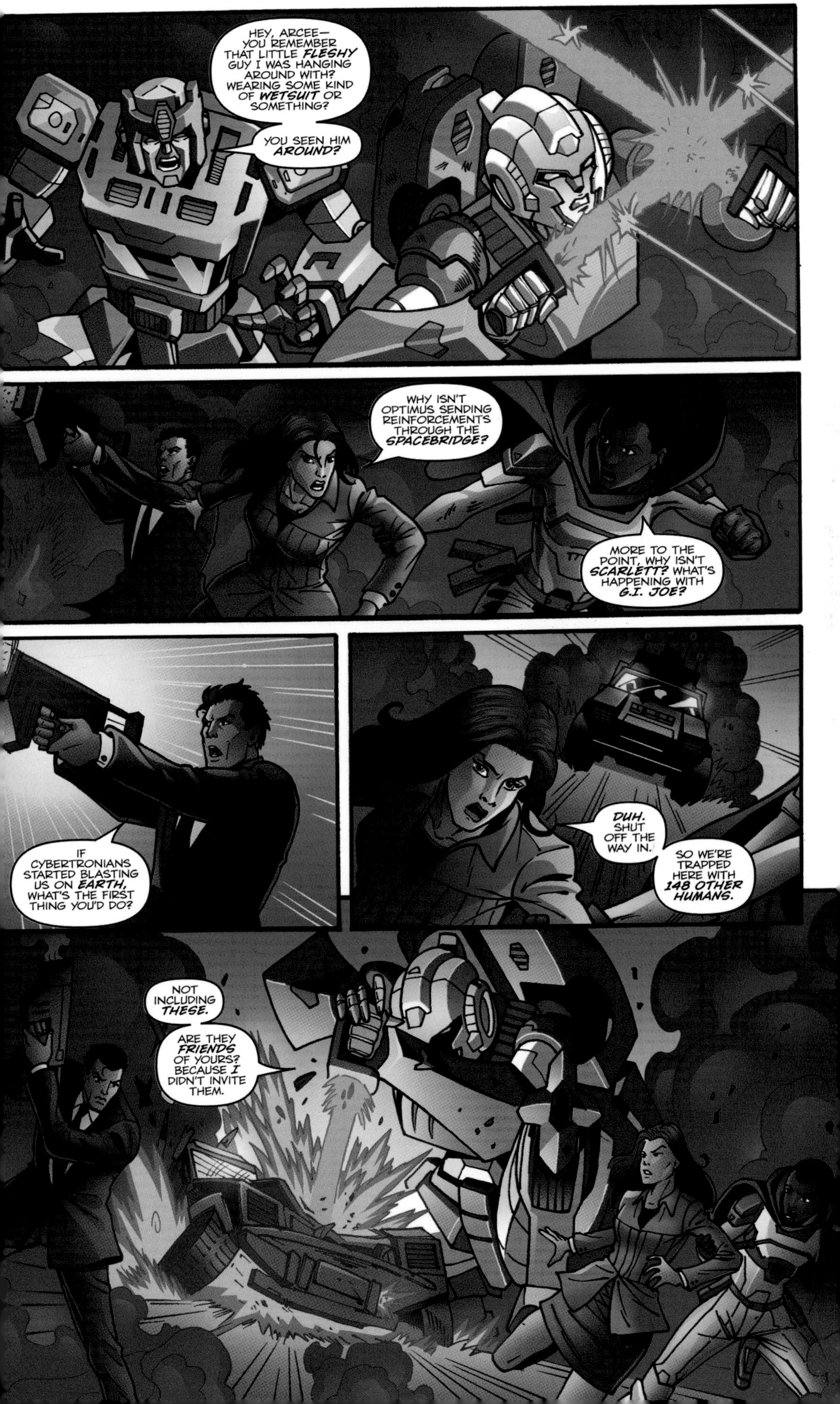
HEY, ARCEE-- YOU REMEMBER THAT LITTLE FLESHY GUY I WAS HANGING AROUND WITH? WEARING SOME KIND OF WETSUIT OR SOMETHING?
YOU SEEN HIM AROUND?
WHY ISN'T OPTIMUS SENDING REINFORCEMENTS THROUGH THE SPACEBRIDGE?
MORE TO THE POINT, WHY ISN'T SCARLETT? WHAT'S HAPPENING WITH G.I. JOE?
IF CYBERTRONIANS STARTED BLASTING US ON EARTH, WHAT'S THE FIRST THING YOU'D DO?
DUH. SHUT OFF THE WAY IN.
SO WE'RE TRAPPED HERE WITH 148 OTHER HUMANS.
NOT INCLUDING THESE.
ARE THEY FRIENDS OF YOURS? BECAUSE I DIDN'T INVITE THEM.

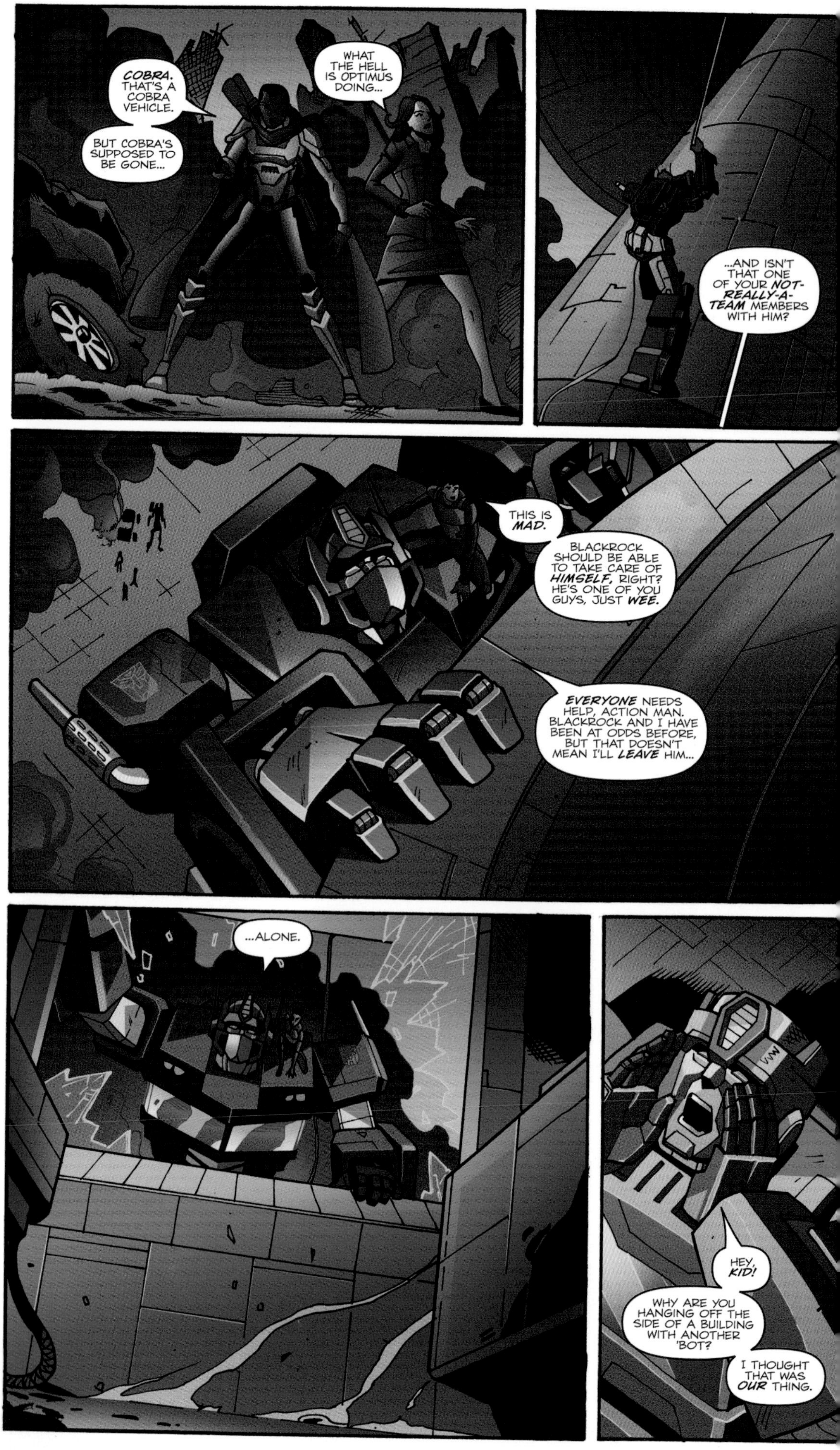

COBRA. THAT'S A COBRA VEHICLE.
BUT COBRA'S SUPPOSED TO BE GONE...
WHAT THE HELL IS OPTIMUS DOING...
...AND ISN'T THAT ONE OF YOUR NOT-REALLY-A-TEAM MEMBERS WITH HIM?
THIS IS MAD.
BLACKROCK SHOULD BE ABLE TO TAKE CARE OF HIMSELF, RIGHT? HE'S ONE OF YOU GUYS, JUST WEE.
EVERYONE NEEDS HELP, ACTION MAN. BLACKROCK AND I HAVE BEEN AT ODDS BEFORE, BUT THAT DOESN'T MEAN I'LL LEAVE HIM...
...ALONE.
HEY, KID!
WHY ARE YOU HANGING OFF THE SIDE OF A BUILDING WITH ANOTHER 'BOT?
I THOUGHT THAT WAS OUR THING.

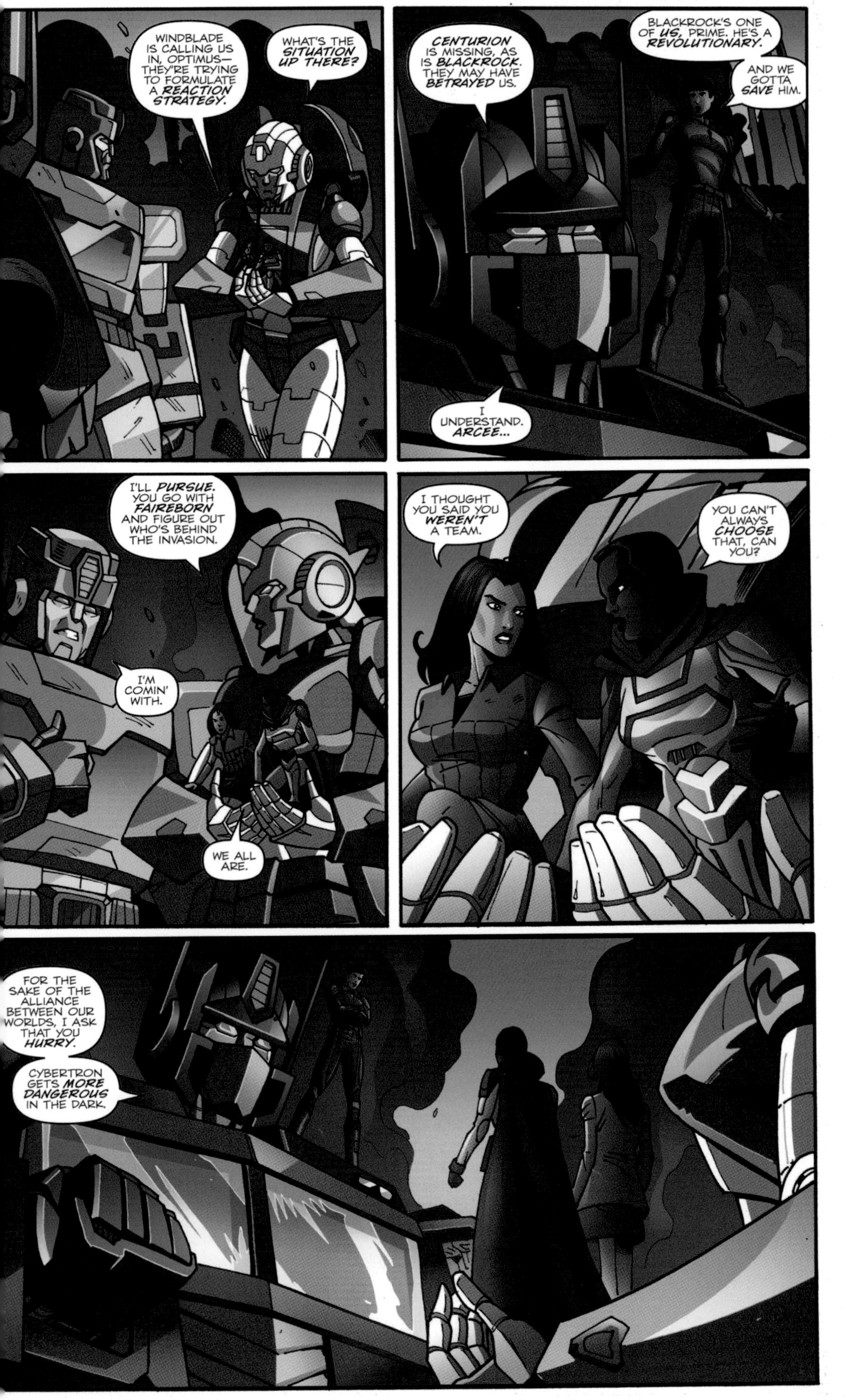
WINDBLADE IS CALLING US IN, OPTIMUS— THEY'RE TRYING TO FORMULATE A *REACTION STRATEGY*.
WHAT'S THE *SITUATION UP THERE?*
CENTURION IS MISSING, AS IS *BLACKROCK*. THEY MAY HAVE *BETRAYED* US.
BLACKROCK'S ONE OF *US*, PRIME. HE'S A *REVOLUTIONARY*.
AND WE GOTTA *SAVE* HIM.
I UNDERSTAND. *ARCEE...*
I'LL *PURSUE*. YOU GO WITH *FAIREBORN* AND FIGURE OUT WHO'S BEHIND THE INVASION.
I'M COMIN' WITH.
WE ALL ARE.
I THOUGHT YOU SAID YOU *WEREN'T* A TEAM.
YOU CAN'T ALWAYS *CHOOSE* THAT, CAN YOU?
FOR THE SAKE OF THE ALLIANCE BETWEEN OUR WORLDS, I ASK THAT YOU *HURRY*.
CYBERTRON GETS *MORE DANGEROUS* IN THE DARK.

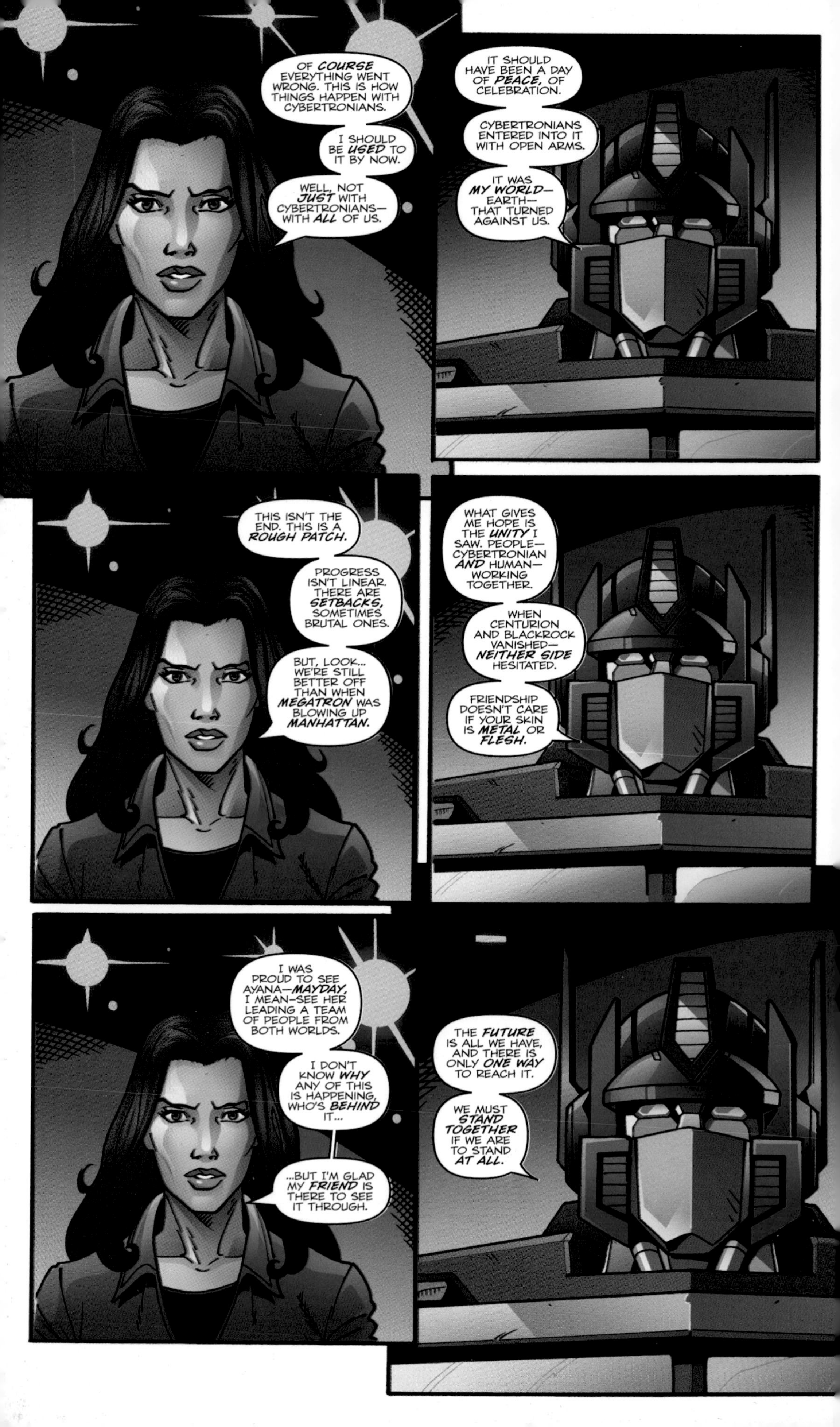

OF COURSE EVERYTHING WENT WRONG. THIS IS HOW THINGS HAPPEN WITH CYBERTRONIANS.
I SHOULD BE USED TO IT BY NOW.
WELL, NOT JUST WITH CYBERTRONIANS— WITH ALL OF US.
IT SHOULD HAVE BEEN A DAY OF PEACE, OF CELEBRATION.
CYBERTRONIANS ENTERED INTO IT WITH OPEN ARMS.
IT WAS MY WORLD— EARTH— THAT TURNED AGAINST US.
THIS ISN'T THE END. THIS IS A ROUGH PATCH.
PROGRESS ISN'T LINEAR. THERE ARE SETBACKS, SOMETIMES BRUTAL ONES.
BUT, LOOK... WE'RE STILL BETTER OFF THAN WHEN MEGATRON WAS BLOWING UP MANHATTAN.
WHAT GIVES ME HOPE IS THE UNITY I SAW. PEOPLE— CYBERTRONIAN AND HUMAN— WORKING TOGETHER.
WHEN CENTURION AND BLACKROCK VANISHED— NEITHER SIDE HESITATED.
FRIENDSHIP DOESN'T CARE IF YOUR SKIN IS METAL OR FLESH.
I WAS PROUD TO SEE AYANA—MAYDAY, I MEAN—SEE HER LEADING A TEAM OF PEOPLE FROM BOTH WORLDS.
I DON'T KNOW WHY ANY OF THIS IS HAPPENING, WHO'S BEHIND IT...
...BUT I'M GLAD MY FRIEND IS THERE TO SEE IT THROUGH.
THE FUTURE IS ALL WE HAVE, AND THERE IS ONLY ONE WAY TO REACH IT.
WE MUST STAND TOGETHER IF WE ARE TO STAND AT ALL.

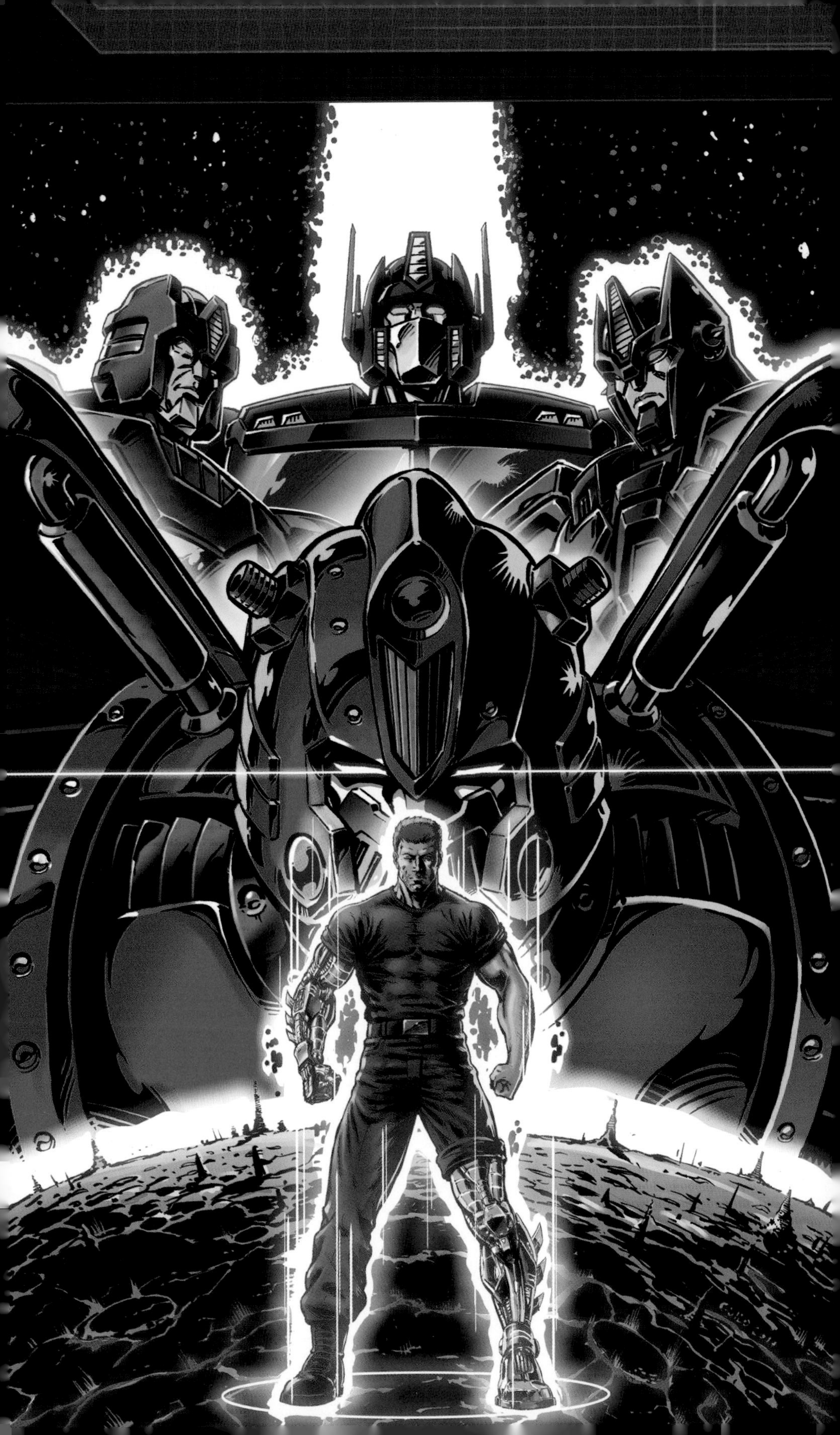

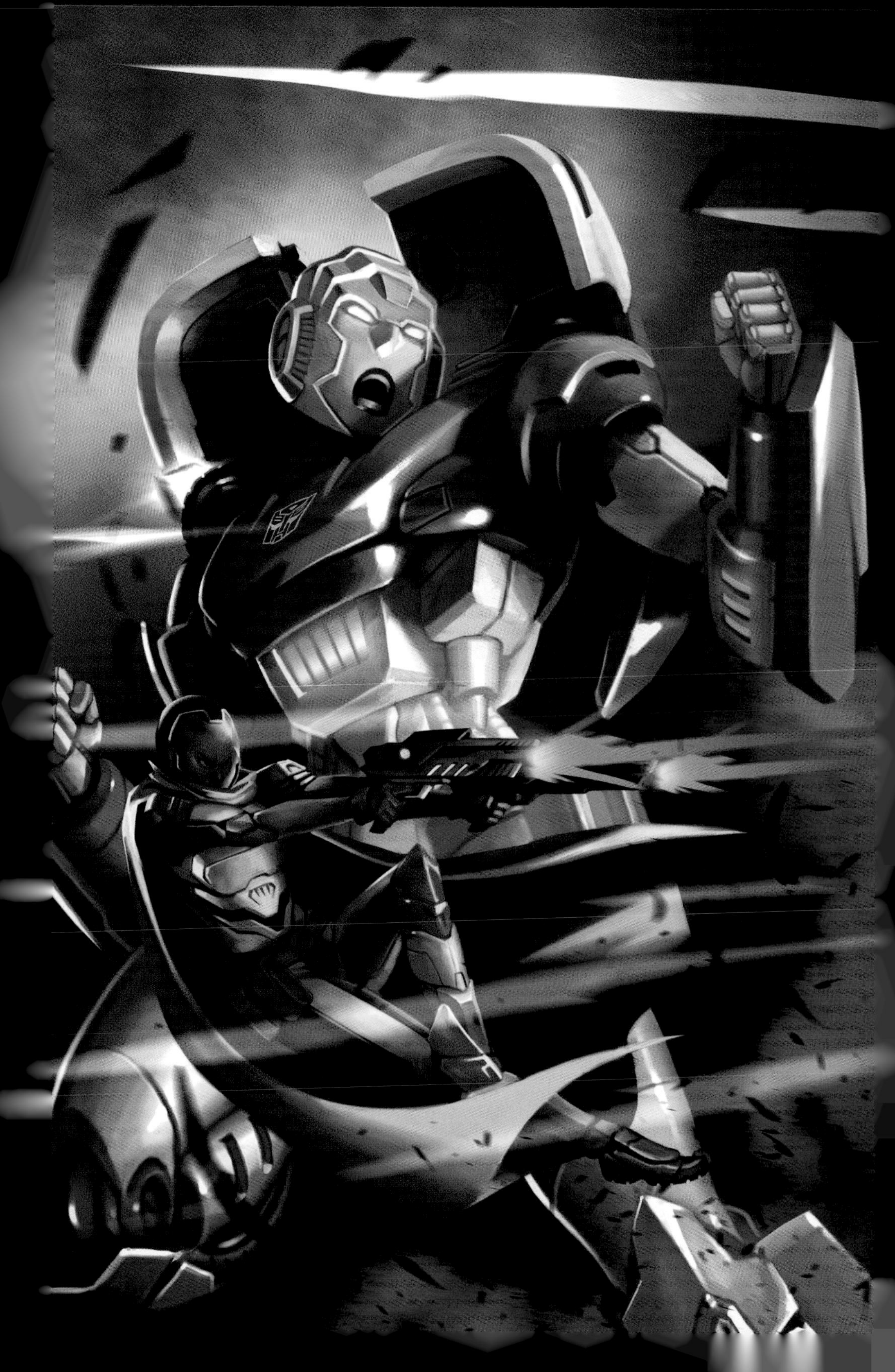

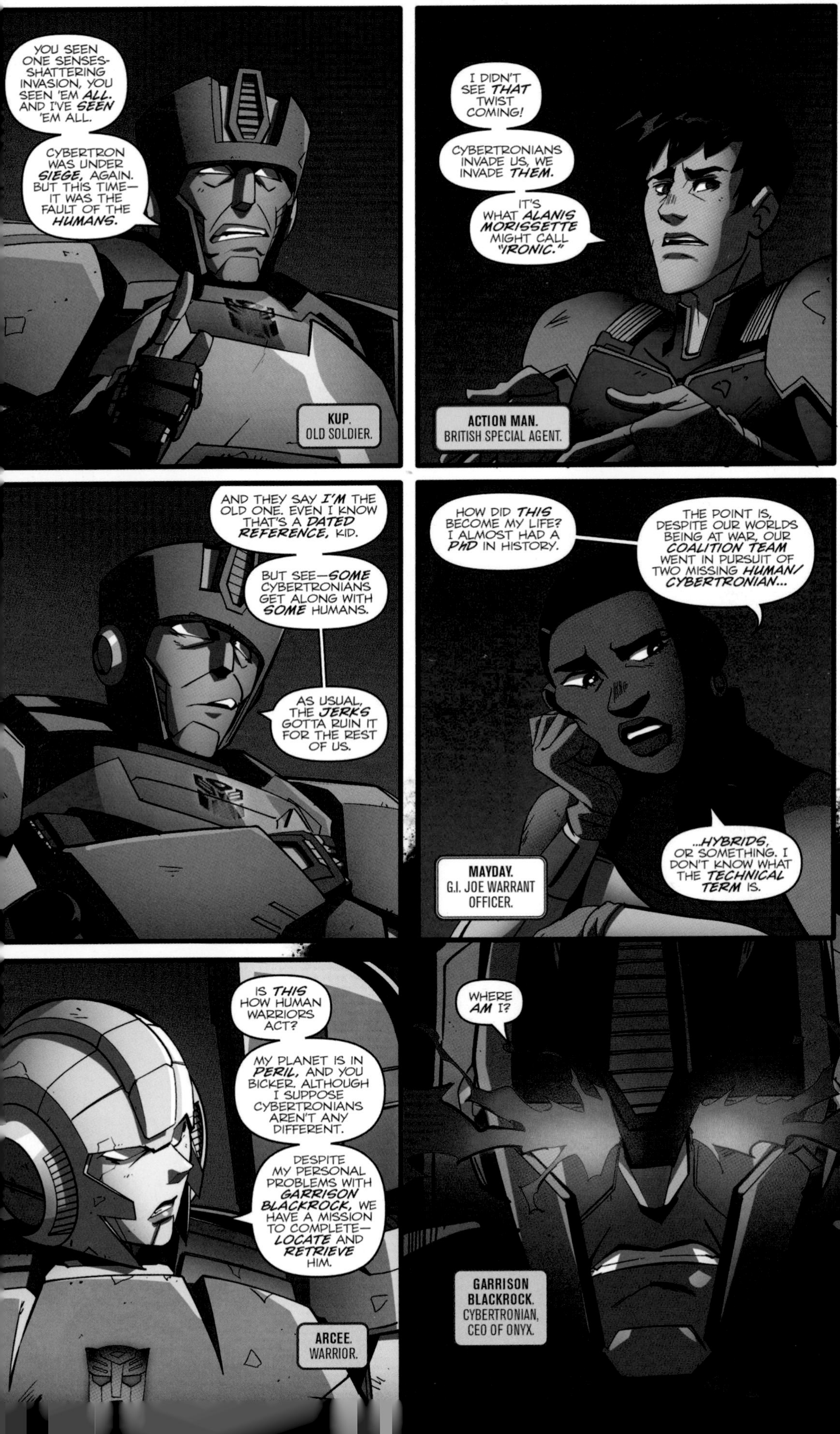
YOU SEEN ONE SENSES-SHATTERING INVASION, YOU SEEN 'EM ALL. AND I'VE SEEN 'EM ALL.
CYBERTRON WAS UNDER SIEGE, AGAIN. BUT THIS TIME— IT WAS THE FAULT OF THE HUMANS.
KUP. OLD SOLDIER.
I DIDN'T SEE THAT TWIST COMING!
CYBERTRONIANS INVADE US, WE INVADE THEM.
IT'S WHAT ALANIS MORISSETTE MIGHT CALL "IRONIC."
ACTION MAN. BRITISH SPECIAL AGENT.
AND THEY SAY I'M THE OLD ONE. EVEN I KNOW THAT'S A DATED REFERENCE, KID.
BUT SEE—SOME CYBERTRONIANS GET ALONG WITH SOME HUMANS.
AS USUAL, THE JERKS GOTTA RUIN IT FOR THE REST OF US.
HOW DID THIS BECOME MY LIFE? I ALMOST HAD A PhD IN HISTORY.
THE POINT IS, DESPITE OUR WORLDS BEING AT WAR, OUR COALITION TEAM WENT IN PURSUIT OF TWO MISSING HUMAN/ CYBERTRONIAN...
...HYBRIDS, OR SOMETHING. I DON'T KNOW WHAT THE TECHNICAL TERM IS.
MAYDAY. G.I. JOE WARRANT OFFICER.
IS THIS HOW HUMAN WARRIORS ACT?
MY PLANET IS IN PERIL, AND YOU BICKER. ALTHOUGH I SUPPOSE CYBERTRONIANS AREN'T ANY DIFFERENT.
DESPITE MY PERSONAL PROBLEMS WITH GARRISON BLACKROCK, WE HAVE A MISSION TO COMPLETE— LOCATE AND RETRIEVE HIM.
ARCEE. WARRIOR.
WHERE AM I?
GARRISON BLACKROCK. CYBERTRONIAN, CEO OF ONYX.

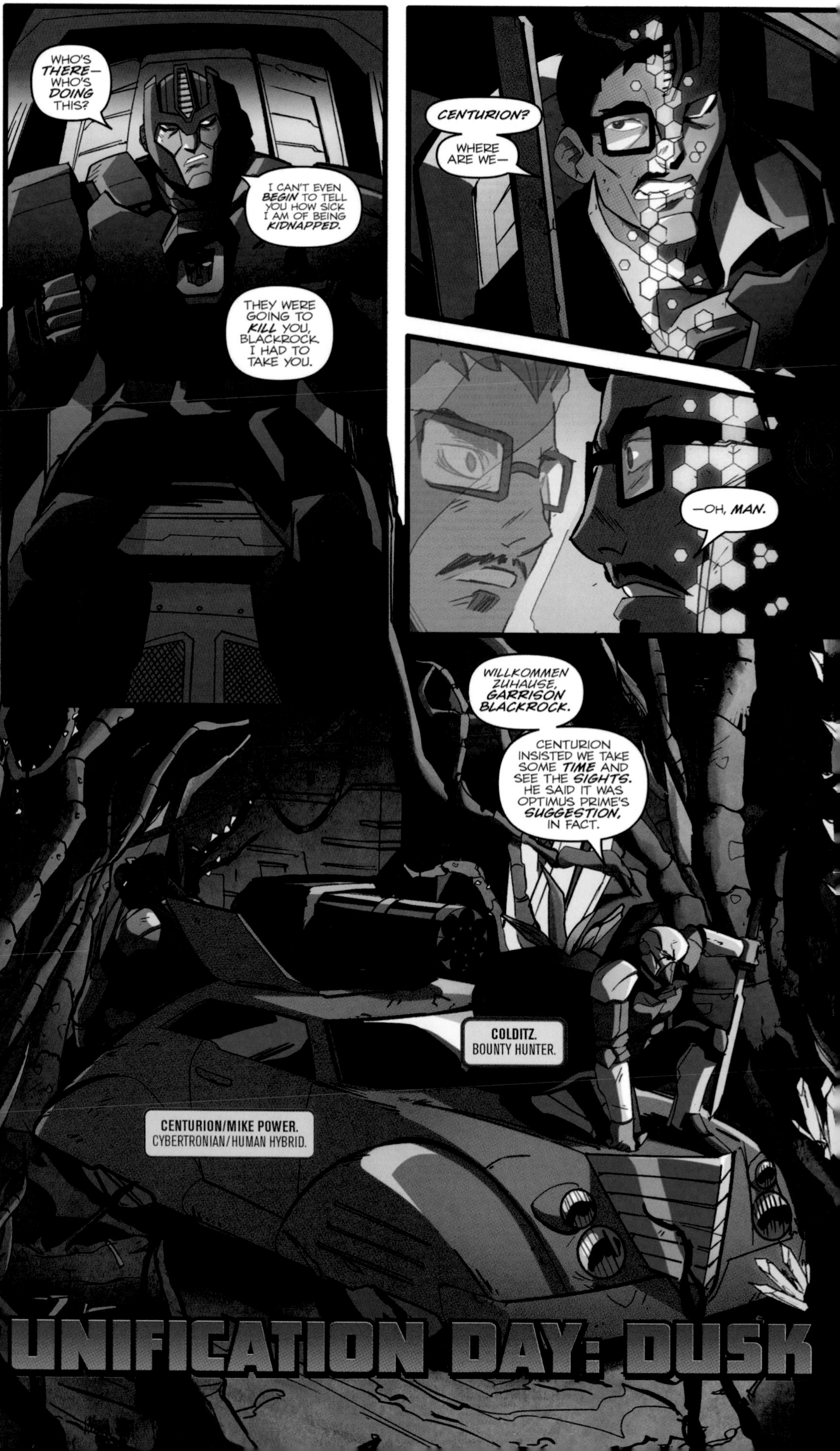
WHO'S THERE— WHO'S DOING THIS?
I CAN'T EVEN BEGIN TO TELL YOU HOW SICK I AM OF BEING KIDNAPPED.
THEY WERE GOING TO KILL YOU, BLACKROCK. I HAD TO TAKE YOU.
CENTURION?
WHERE ARE WE—
—OH, MAN.
WILLKOMMEN ZUHAUSE, GARRISON BLACKROCK.
CENTURION INSISTED WE TAKE SOME TIME AND SEE THE SIGHTS. HE SAID IT WAS OPTIMUS PRIME'S SUGGESTION, IN FACT.
COLDITZ. BOUNTY HUNTER.
CENTURION/MIKE POWER. CYBERTRONIAN/HUMAN HYBRID.
UNIFICATION DAY: DUSK

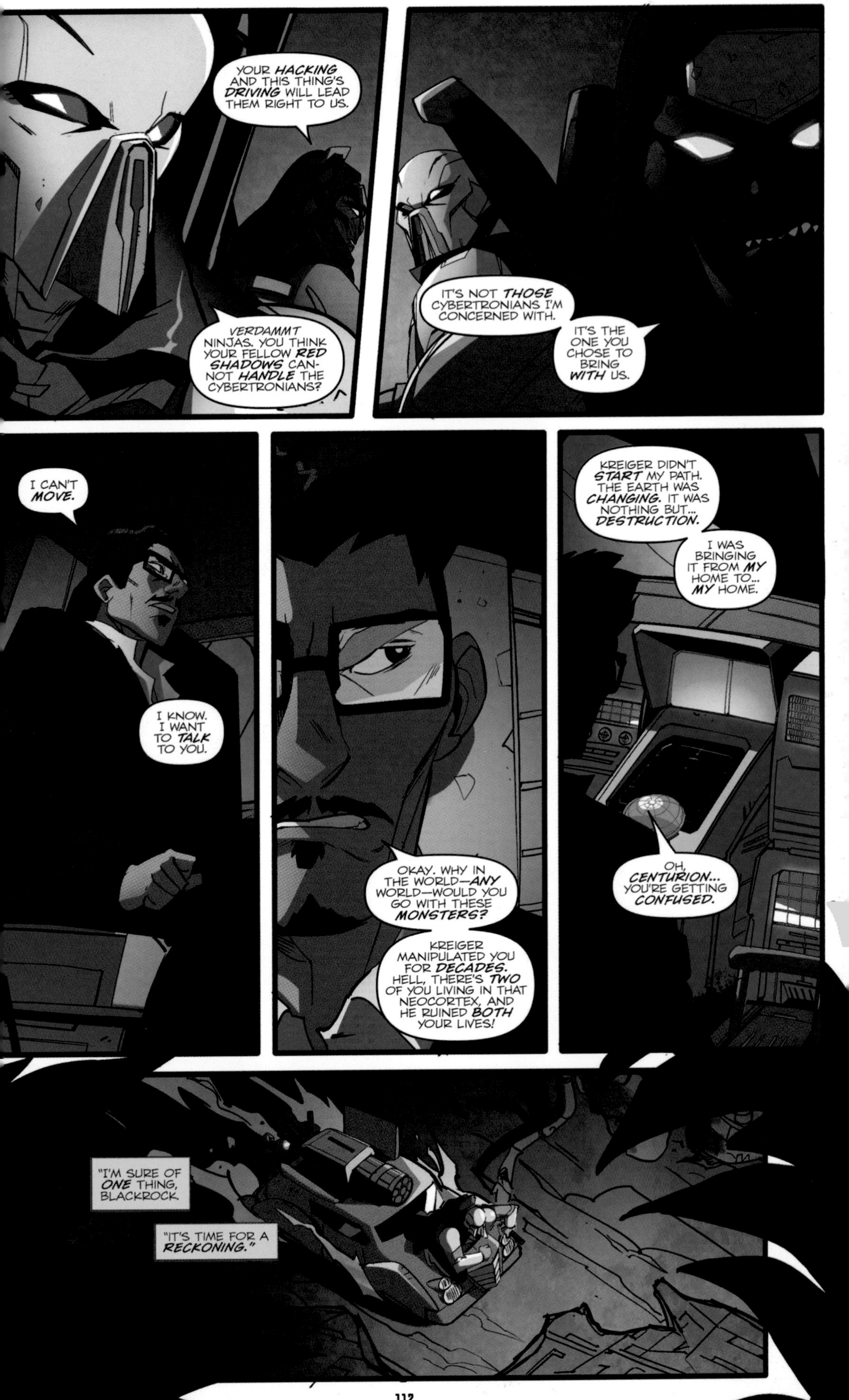
YOUR HACKING AND THIS THING'S DRIVING WILL LEAD THEM RIGHT TO US.
VERDAMMT NINJAS. YOU THINK YOUR FELLOW RED SHADOWS CAN-NOT HANDLE THE CYBERTRONIANS?
IT'S NOT THOSE CYBERTRONIANS I'M CONCERNED WITH.
IT'S THE ONE YOU CHOSE TO BRING WITH US.
I CAN'T MOVE.
I KNOW. I WANT TO TALK TO YOU.
OKAY. WHY IN THE WORLD—ANY WORLD—WOULD YOU GO WITH THESE MONSTERS?
KREIGER MANIPULATED YOU FOR DECADES. HELL, THERE'S TWO OF YOU LIVING IN THAT NEOCORTEX, AND HE RUINED BOTH YOUR LIVES!
KREIGER DIDN'T START MY PATH. THE EARTH WAS CHANGING. IT WAS NOTHING BUT... DESTRUCTION.
I WAS BRINGING IT FROM MY HOME TO... MY HOME.
OH, CENTURION... YOU'RE GETTING CONFUSED.
"I'M SURE OF ONE THING, BLACKROCK.
"IT'S TIME FOR A RECKONING."

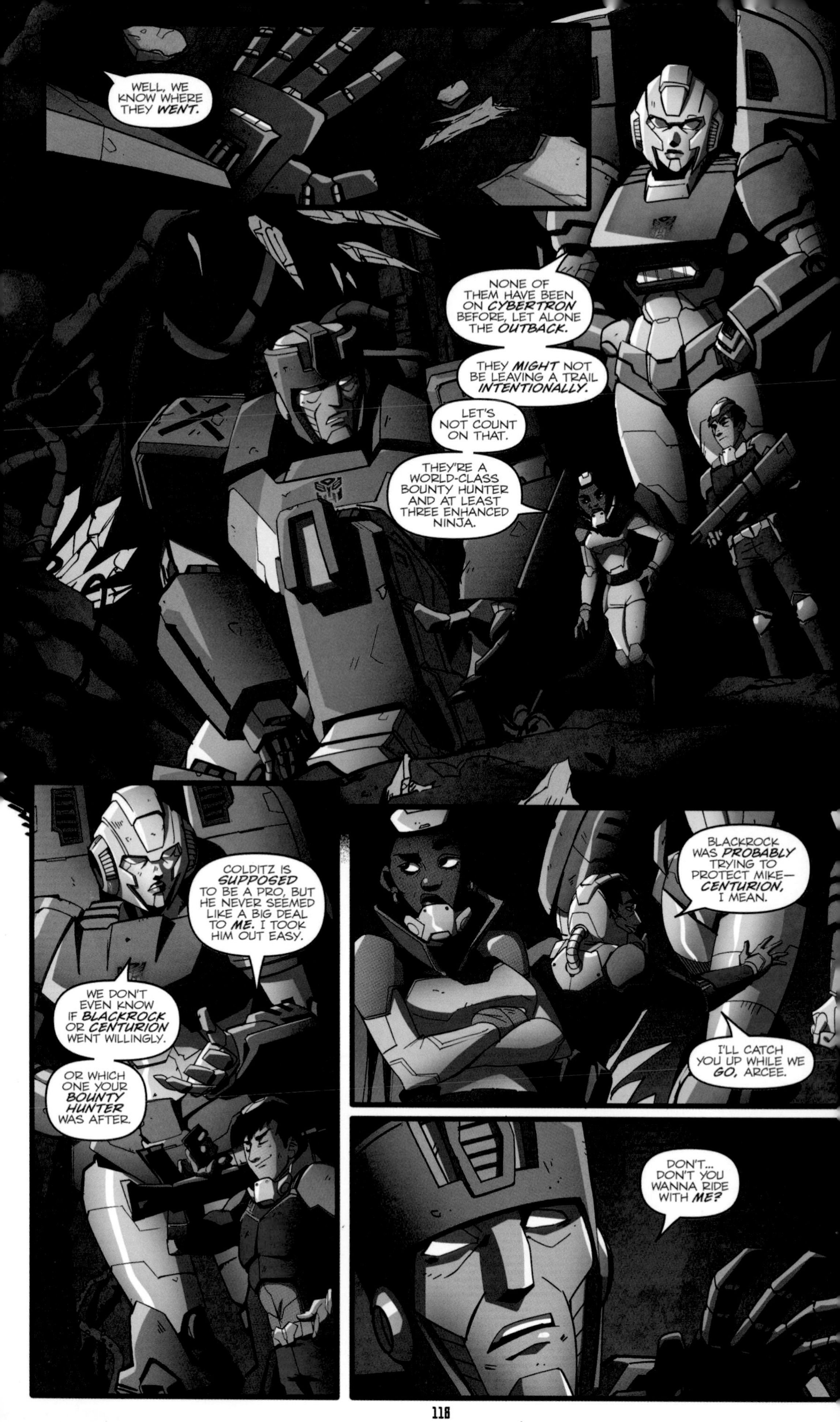
WELL, WE KNOW WHERE THEY *WENT.*
NONE OF THEM HAVE BEEN ON *CYBERTRON* BEFORE, LET ALONE THE *OUTBACK.*
THEY *MIGHT* NOT BE LEAVING A TRAIL *INTENTIONALLY.*
LET'S NOT COUNT ON THAT.
THEY'RE A WORLD-CLASS BOUNTY HUNTER AND AT LEAST THREE ENHANCED NINJA.
COLDITZ IS *SUPPOSED* TO BE A PRO, BUT HE NEVER SEEMED LIKE A BIG DEAL TO *ME.* I TOOK HIM OUT EASY.
WE DON'T EVEN KNOW IF *BLACKROCK* OR *CENTURION* WENT WILLINGLY.
OR WHICH ONE YOUR *BOUNTY HUNTER* WAS AFTER.
BLACKROCK WAS *PROBABLY* TRYING TO PROTECT MIKE— *CENTURION,* I MEAN.
I'LL CATCH YOU UP WHILE WE *GO,* ARCEE.
DON'T... DON'T YOU WANNA RIDE WITH *ME?*

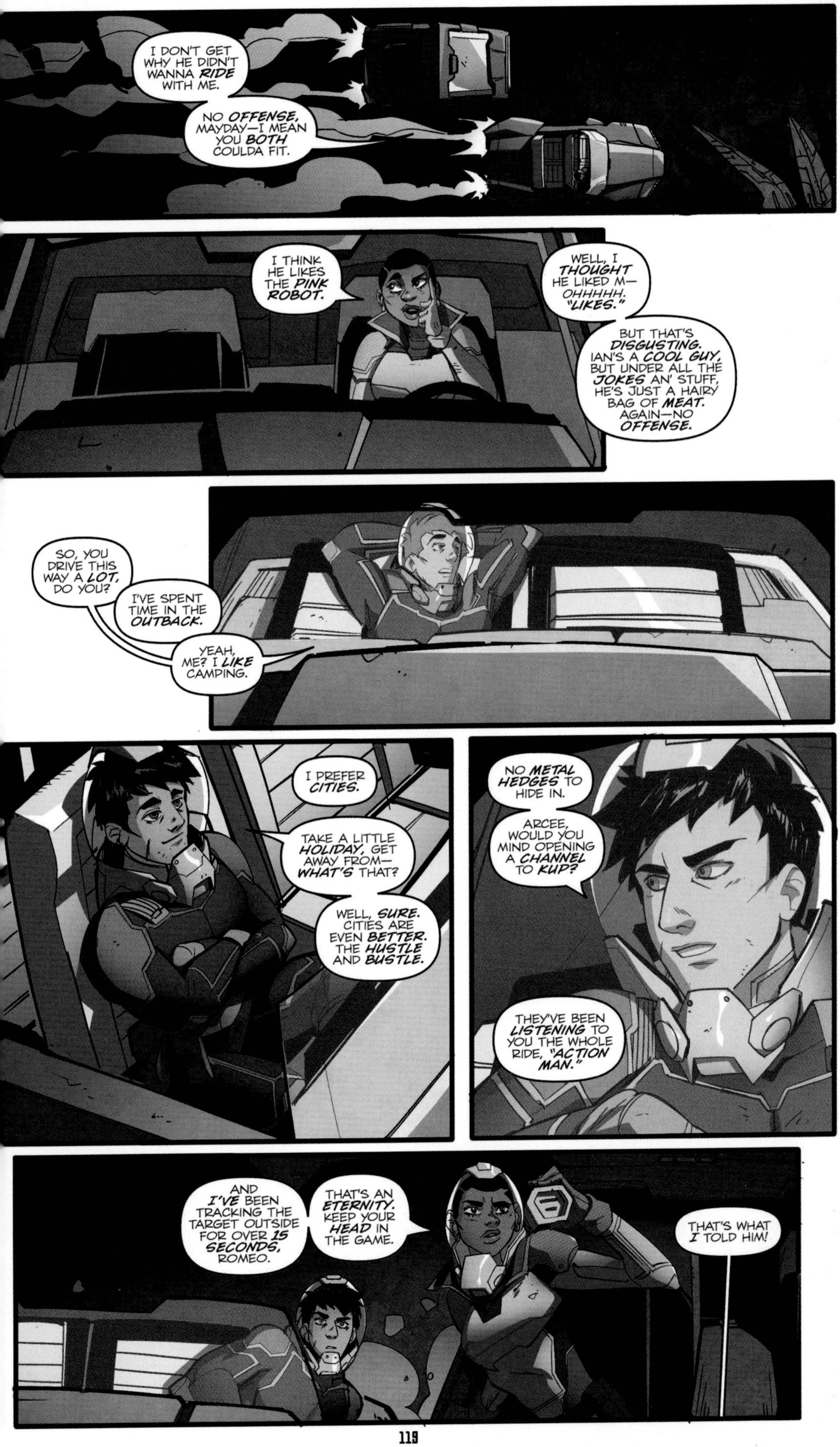
I DON'T GET WHY HE DIDN'T WANNA RIDE WITH ME.
NO OFFENSE, MAYDAY—I MEAN YOU BOTH COULDA FIT.
I THINK HE LIKES THE PINK ROBOT.
WELL, I THOUGHT HE LIKED M— OHHHHH. "LIKES."
BUT THAT'S DISGUSTING. IAN'S A COOL GUY, BUT UNDER ALL THE JOKES AN' STUFF, HE'S JUST A HAIRY BAG OF MEAT. AGAIN—NO OFFENSE.
SO, YOU DRIVE THIS WAY A LOT, DO YOU?
I'VE SPENT TIME IN THE OUTBACK.
YEAH, ME? I LIKE CAMPING.
I PREFER CITIES.
TAKE A LITTLE HOLIDAY, GET AWAY FROM— WHAT'S THAT?
WELL, SURE. CITIES ARE EVEN BETTER. THE HUSTLE AND BUSTLE.
NO METAL HEDGES TO HIDE IN.
ARCEE, WOULD YOU MIND OPENING A CHANNEL TO KUP?
THEY'VE BEEN LISTENING TO YOU THE WHOLE RIDE, "ACTION MAN."
AND I'VE BEEN TRACKING THE TARGET OUTSIDE FOR OVER 15 SECONDS, ROMEO.
THAT'S AN ETERNITY. KEEP YOUR HEAD IN THE GAME.
THAT'S WHAT I TOLD HIM!

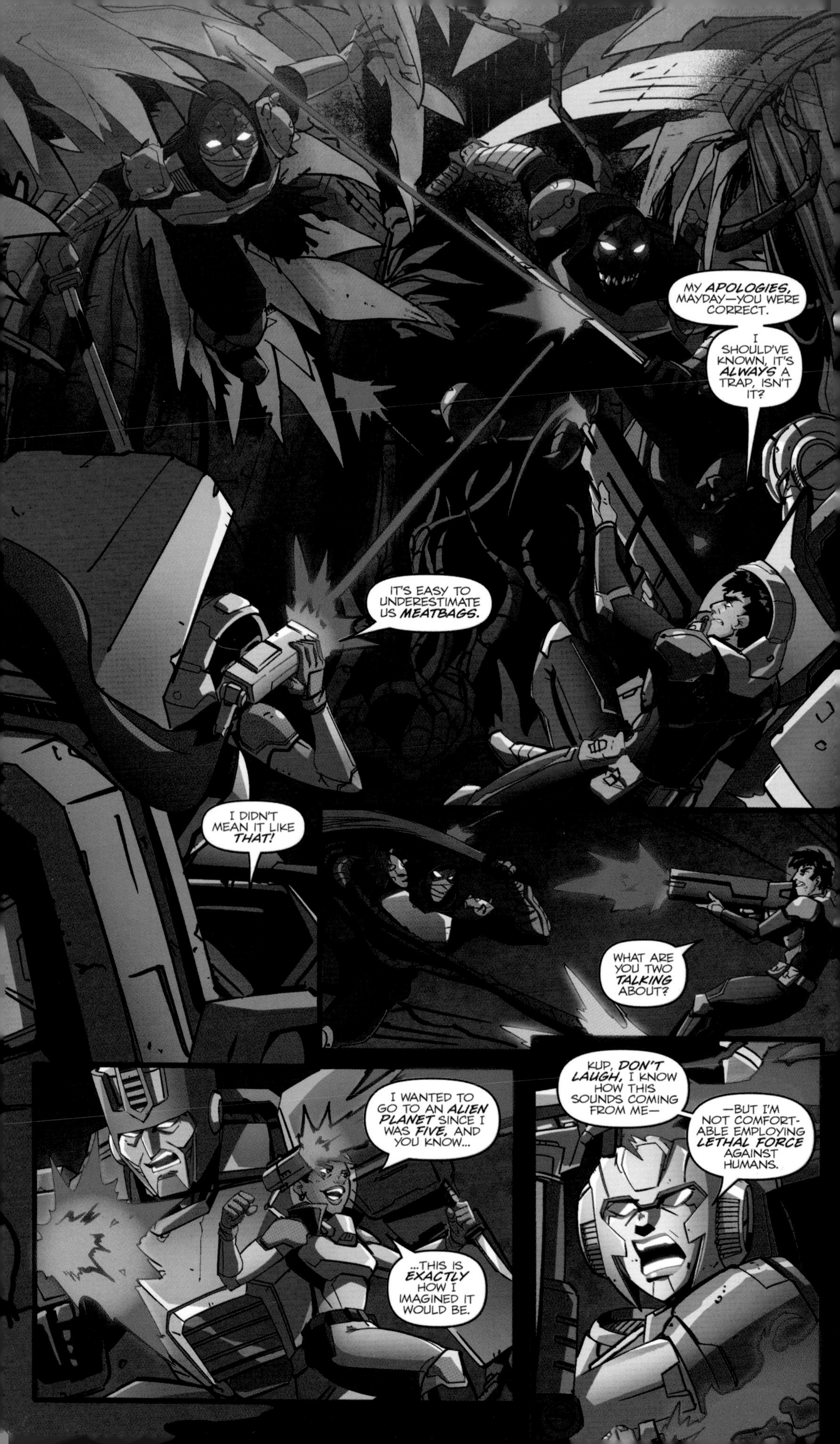

MY APOLOGIES, MAYDAY—YOU WERE CORRECT.
I SHOULD'VE KNOWN, IT'S ALWAYS A TRAP, ISN'T IT?
IT'S EASY TO UNDERESTIMATE US MEATBAGS.
I DIDN'T MEAN IT LIKE THAT!
WHAT ARE YOU TWO TALKING ABOUT?
I WANTED TO GO TO AN ALIEN PLANET SINCE I WAS FIVE, AND YOU KNOW...
...THIS IS EXACTLY HOW I IMAGINED IT WOULD BE.
KUP, DON'T LAUGH, I KNOW HOW THIS SOUNDS COMING FROM ME—
—BUT I'M NOT COMFORTABLE EMPLOYING LETHAL FORCE AGAINST HUMANS.

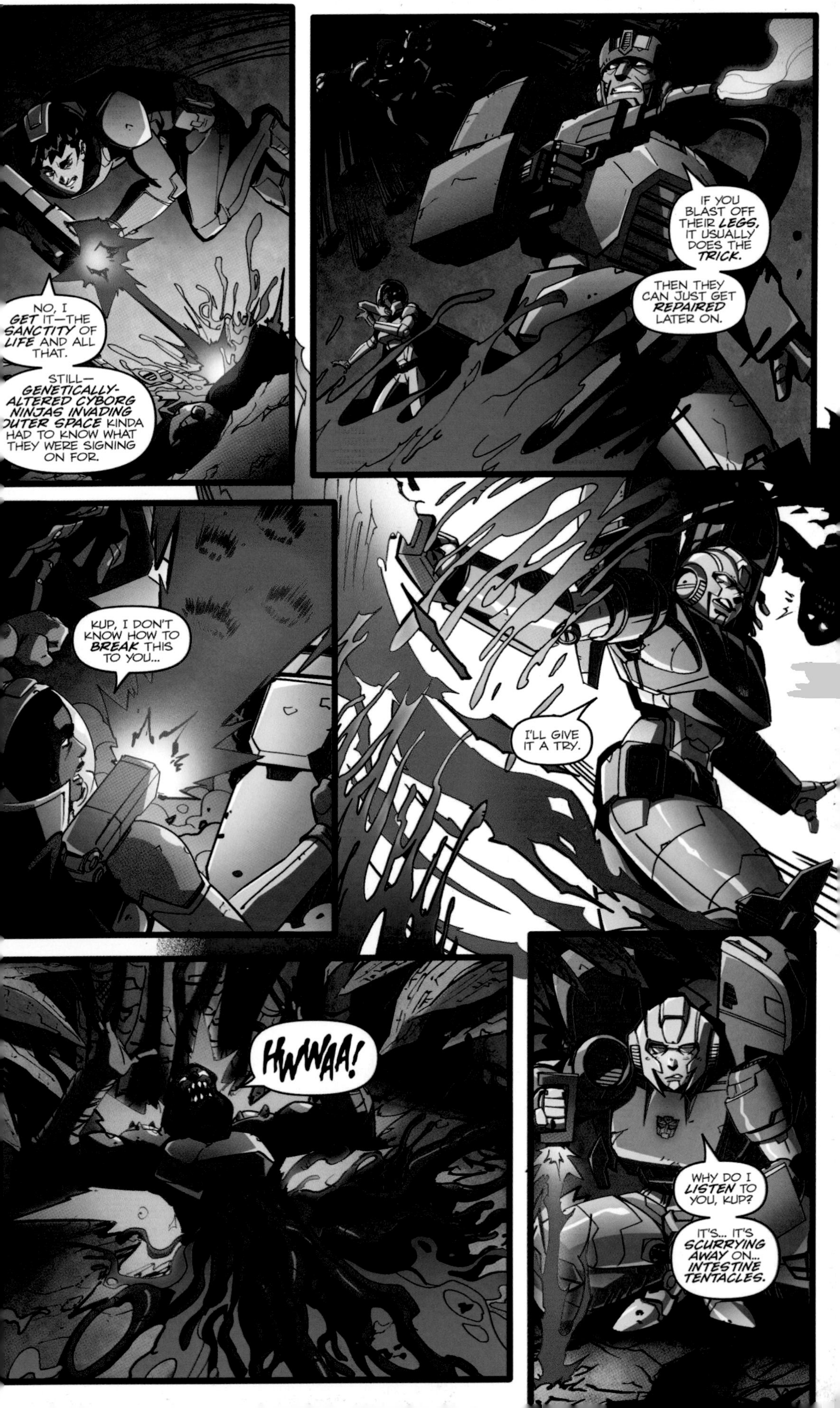
NO, I GET IT—THE SANCTITY OF LIFE AND ALL THAT.
STILL—GENETICALLY-ALTERED CYBORG NINJAS INVADING OUTER SPACE KINDA HAD TO KNOW WHAT THEY WERE SIGNING ON FOR.
IF YOU BLAST OFF THEIR LEGS, IT USUALLY DOES THE TRICK.
THEN THEY CAN JUST GET REPAIRED LATER ON.
KUP, I DON'T KNOW HOW TO BREAK THIS TO YOU...
I'LL GIVE IT A TRY.
HWWAA!
WHY DO I LISTEN TO YOU, KUP?
IT'S... IT'S SCURRYING AWAY ON... INTESTINE TENTACLES.

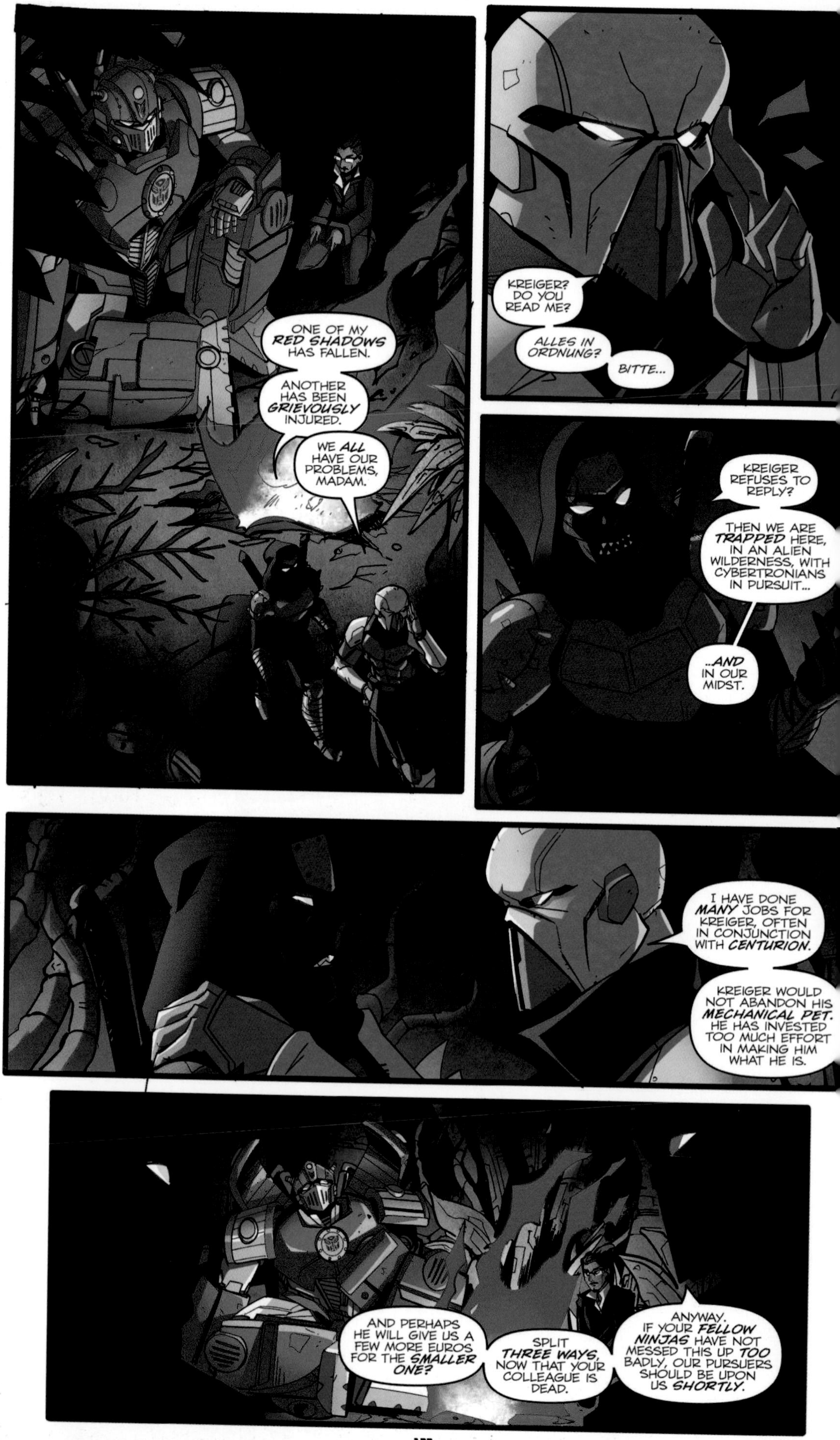
ONE OF MY RED SHADOWS HAS FALLEN.
ANOTHER HAS BEEN GRIEVOUSLY INJURED.
WE ALL HAVE OUR PROBLEMS, MADAM.
KREIGER? DO YOU READ ME?
ALLES IN ORDNUNG?
BITTE...
KREIGER REFUSES TO REPLY?
THEN WE ARE TRAPPED HERE, IN AN ALIEN WILDERNESS, WITH CYBERTRONIANS IN PURSUIT...
...AND IN OUR MIDST.
I HAVE DONE MANY JOBS FOR KREIGER, OFTEN IN CONJUNCTION WITH CENTURION.
KREIGER WOULD NOT ABANDON HIS MECHANICAL PET. HE HAS INVESTED TOO MUCH EFFORT IN MAKING HIM WHAT HE IS.
AND PERHAPS HE WILL GIVE US A FEW MORE EUROS FOR THE SMALLER ONE?
SPLIT THREE WAYS, NOW THAT YOUR COLLEAGUE IS DEAD.
ANYWAY. IF YOUR FELLOW NINJAS HAVE NOT MESSED THIS UP TOO BADLY, OUR PURSUERS SHOULD BE UPON US SHORTLY.

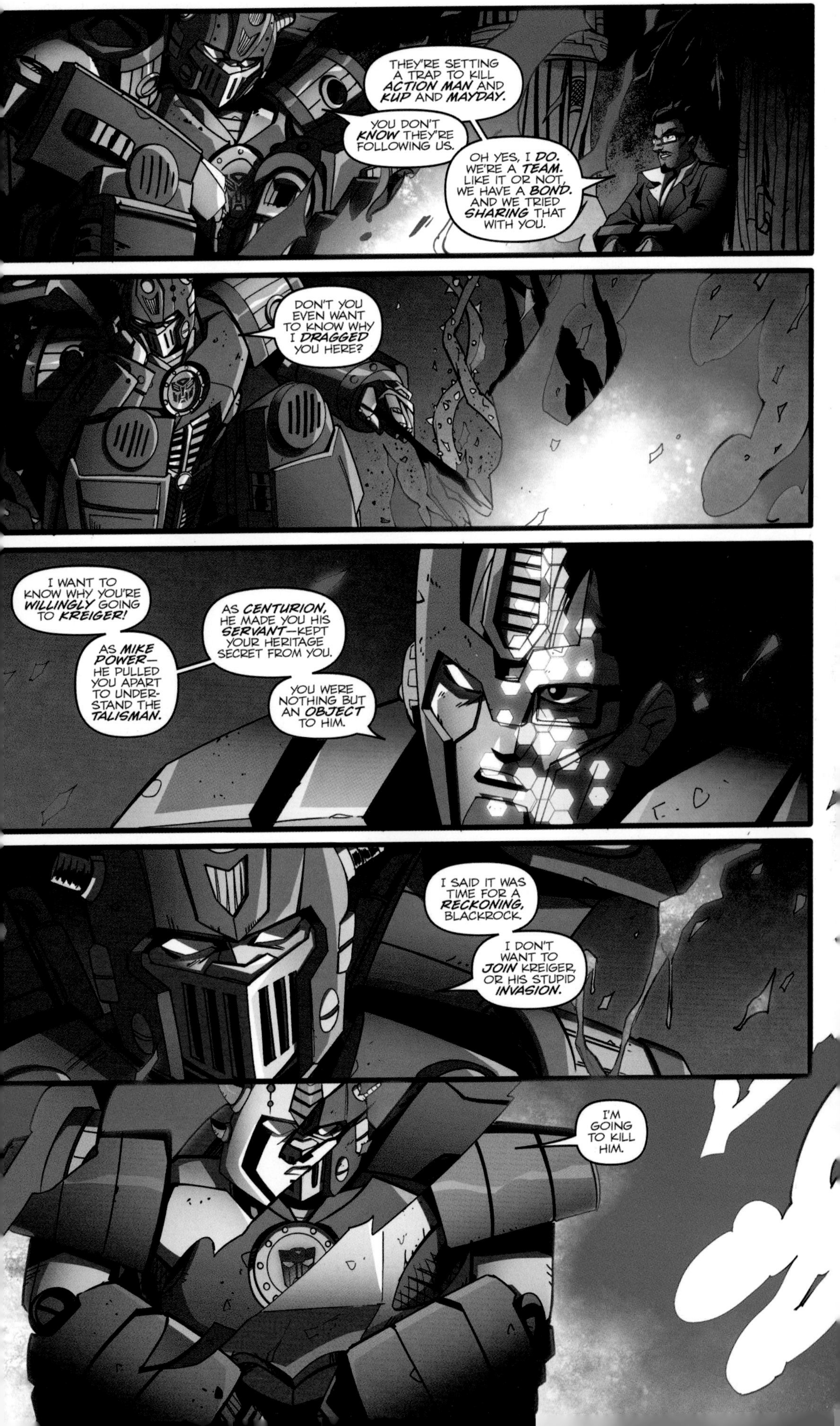
THEY'RE SETTING A TRAP TO KILL ACTION MAN AND KUP AND MAYDAY.
YOU DON'T KNOW THEY'RE FOLLOWING US.
OH YES, I DO. WE'RE A TEAM. LIKE IT OR NOT, WE HAVE A BOND. AND WE TRIED SHARING THAT WITH YOU.
DON'T YOU EVEN WANT TO KNOW WHY I DRAGGED YOU HERE?
I WANT TO KNOW WHY YOU'RE WILLINGLY GOING TO KREIGER!
AS MIKE POWER— HE PULLED YOU APART TO UNDERSTAND THE TALISMAN.
AS CENTURION, HE MADE YOU HIS SERVANT—KEPT YOUR HERITAGE SECRET FROM YOU.
YOU WERE NOTHING BUT AN OBJECT TO HIM.
I SAID IT WAS TIME FOR A RECKONING, BLACKROCK.
I DON'T WANT TO JOIN KREIGER, OR HIS STUPID INVASION.
I'M GOING TO KILL HIM.

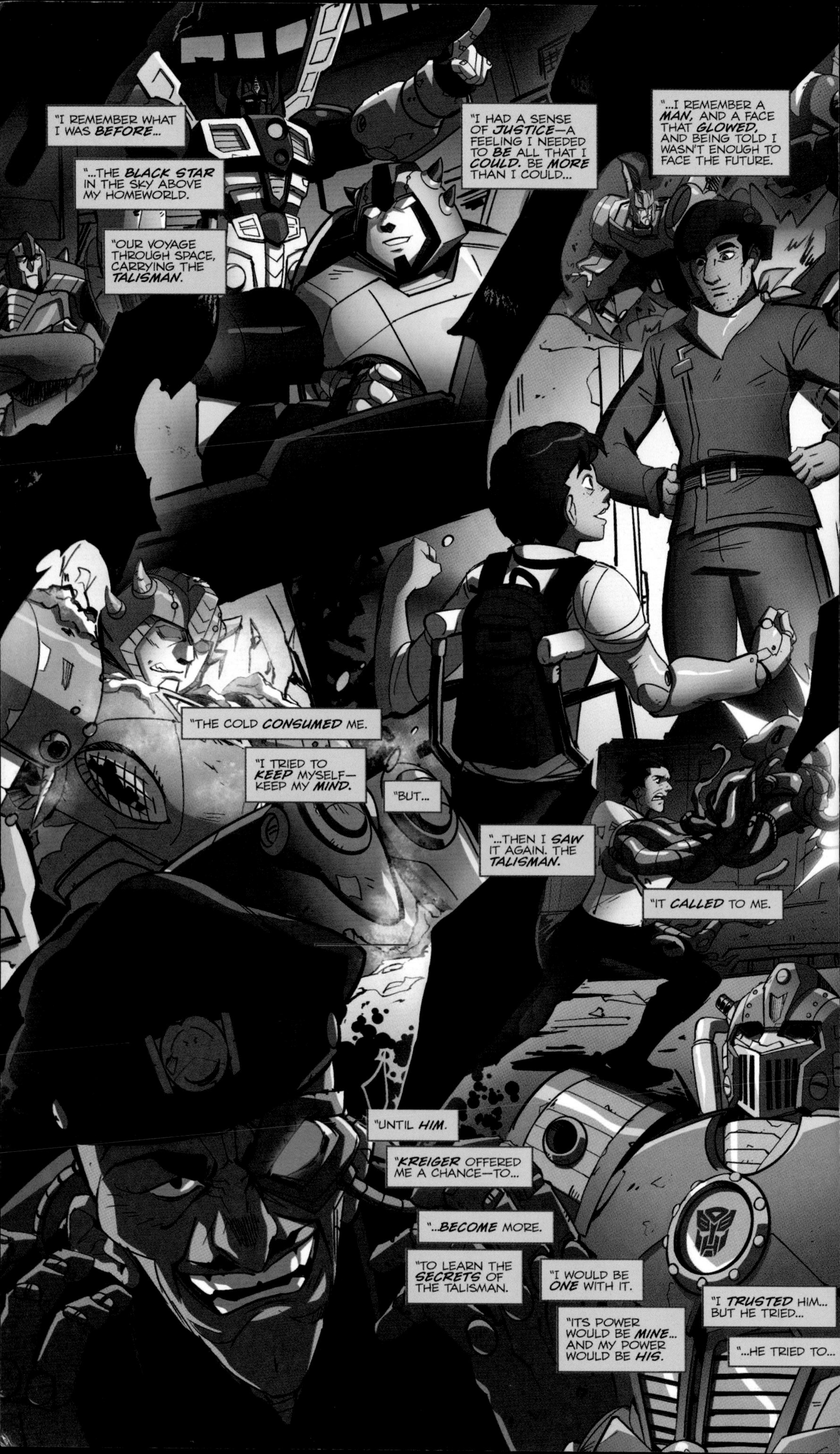
"I REMEMBER WHAT I WAS BEFORE...
"...THE BLACK STAR IN THE SKY ABOVE MY HOMEWORLD.
"OUR VOYAGE THROUGH SPACE, CARRYING THE TALISMAN.
"I HAD A SENSE OF JUSTICE—A FEELING I NEEDED TO BE ALL THAT I COULD. BE MORE THAN I COULD...
"...I REMEMBER A MAN, AND A FACE THAT GLOWED, AND BEING TOLD I WASN'T ENOUGH TO FACE THE FUTURE.
"THE COLD CONSUMED ME.
"I TRIED TO KEEP MYSELF— KEEP MY MIND.
"BUT...
"...THEN I SAW IT AGAIN. THE TALISMAN.
"IT CALLED TO ME.
"UNTIL HIM.
"KREIGER OFFERED ME A CHANCE—TO...
"...BECOME MORE.
"TO LEARN THE SECRETS OF THE TALISMAN.
"I WOULD BE ONE WITH IT.
"ITS POWER WOULD BE MINE... AND MY POWER WOULD BE HIS.
"I TRUSTED HIM... BUT HE TRIED...
"...HE TRIED TO...

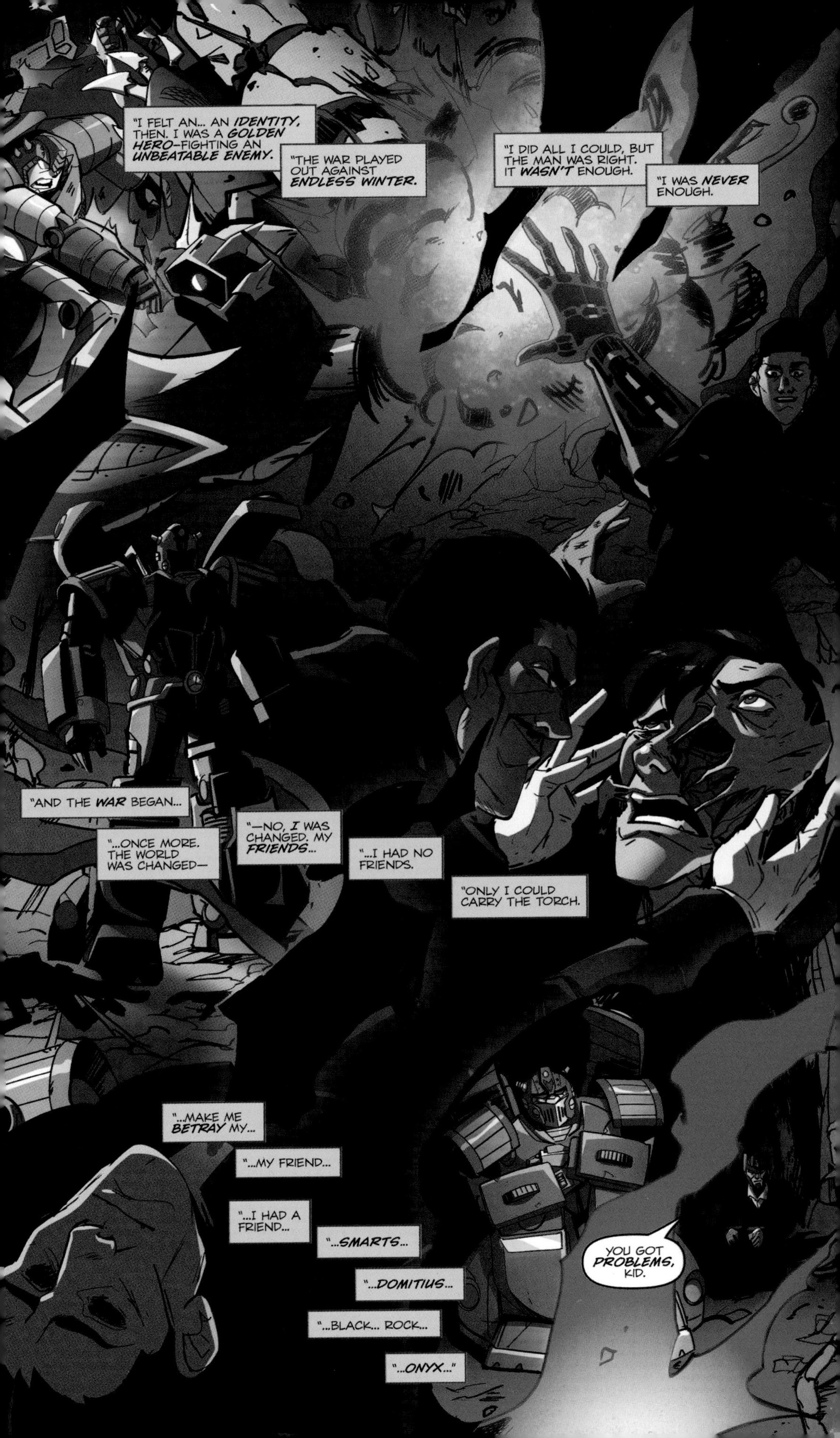
"I FELT AN... AN *IDENTITY,* THEN. I WAS A *GOLDEN HERO*—FIGHTING AN *UNBEATABLE ENEMY.*
"THE WAR PLAYED OUT AGAINST *ENDLESS WINTER.*
"I DID ALL I COULD, BUT THE MAN WAS RIGHT. IT *WASN'T* ENOUGH.
"I WAS *NEVER* ENOUGH.
"AND THE *WAR* BEGAN...
"...ONCE MORE. THE WORLD WAS CHANGED—
"—NO, *I* WAS CHANGED. MY *FRIENDS*...
"...I HAD NO FRIENDS.
"ONLY I COULD CARRY THE TORCH.
"...MAKE ME *BETRAY* MY...
"...MY FRIEND...
"...I HAD A FRIEND...
"...*SMARTS*...
"...*DOMITIUS*...
"...BLACK... ROCK...
"...*ONYX*..."
YOU GOT *PROBLEMS,* KID.

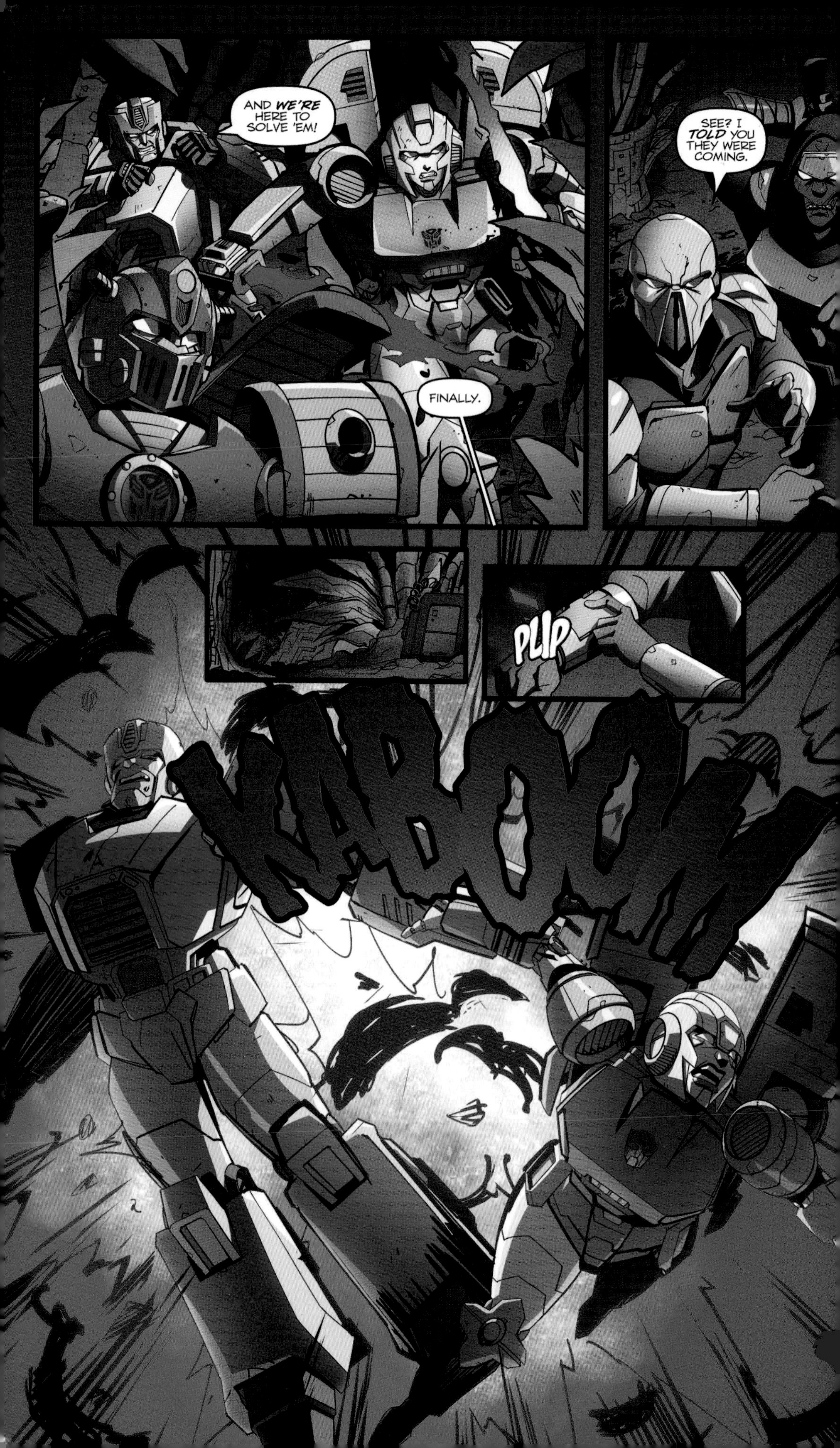
AND WE'RE HERE TO SOLVE 'EM!
FINALLY.
SEE? I TOLD YOU THEY WERE COMING.
PLIP
KABOOM

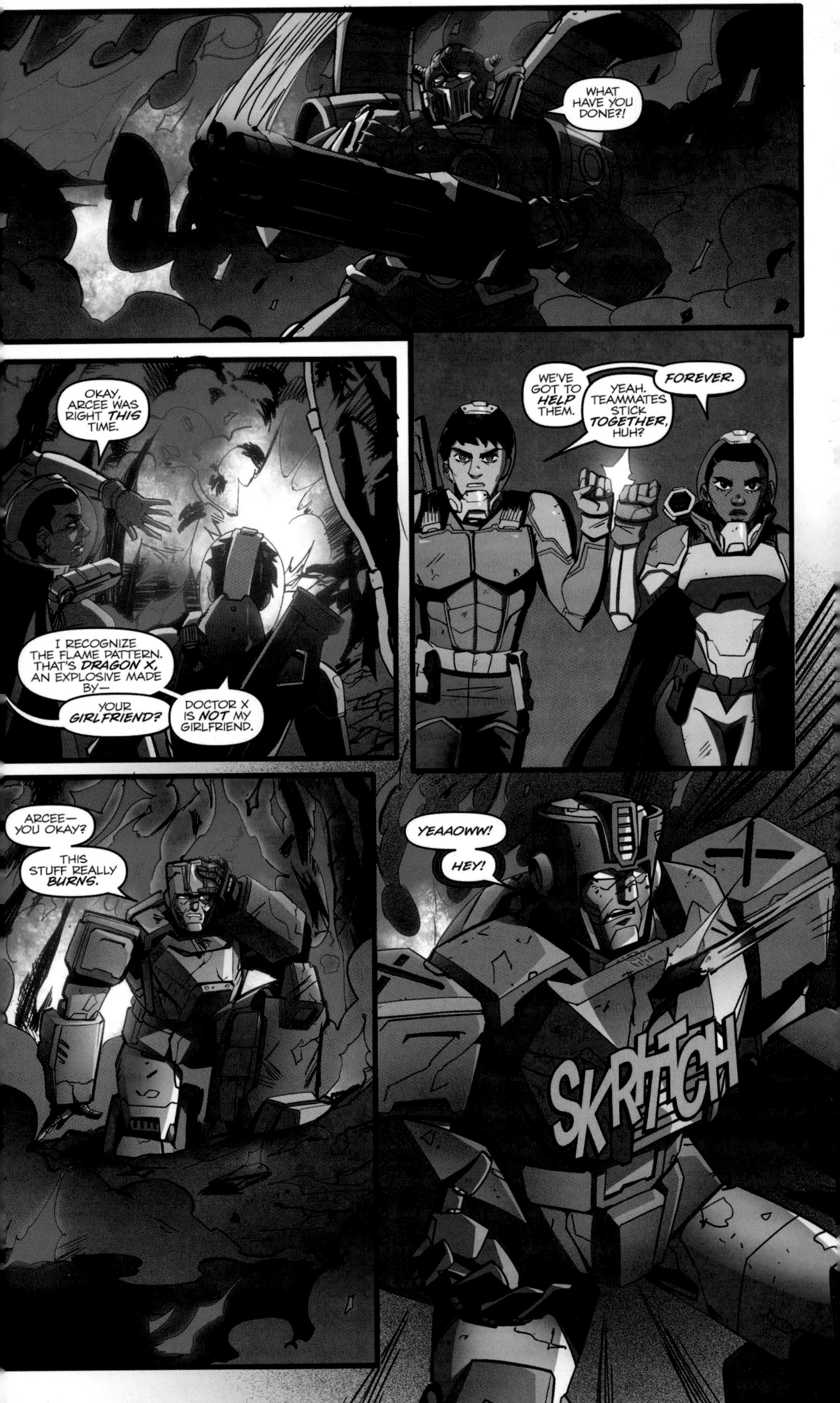
WHAT HAVE YOU DONE?!
OKAY, ARCEE WAS RIGHT THIS TIME.
I RECOGNIZE THE FLAME PATTERN. THAT'S DRAGON X, AN EXPLOSIVE MADE BY—
YOUR GIRLFRIEND?
DOCTOR X IS NOT MY GIRLFRIEND.
WE'VE GOT TO HELP THEM.
YEAH. TEAMMATES STICK TOGETHER, HUH?
FOREVER.
ARCEE— YOU OKAY?
THIS STUFF REALLY BURNS.
YEAAOWW!
HEY!
SKRITCH

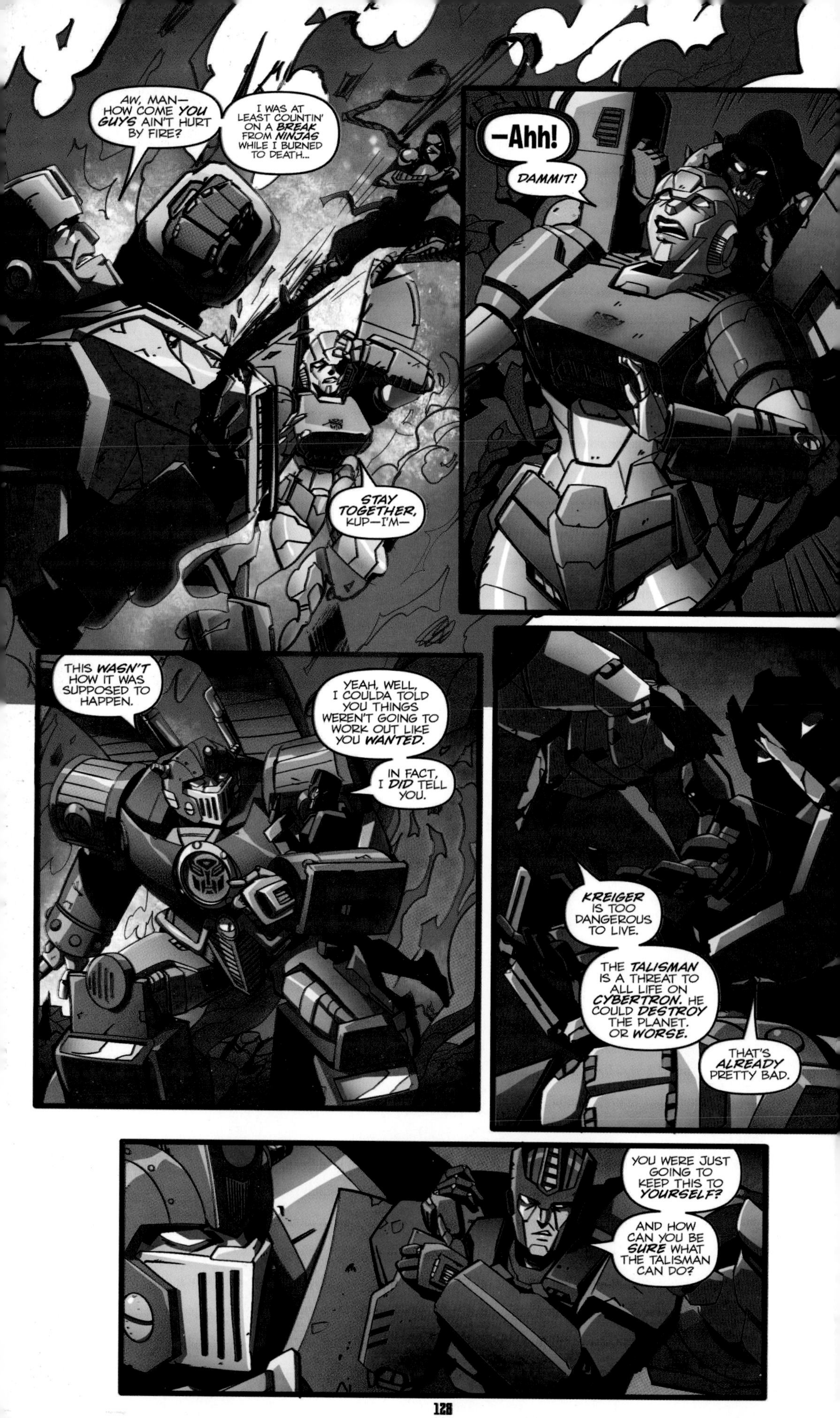
AW, MAN— HOW COME YOU GUYS AIN'T HURT BY FIRE?
I WAS AT LEAST COUNTIN' ON A BREAK FROM NINJAS WHILE I BURNED TO DEATH...
STAY TOGETHER, KUP—I'M—
—Ahh!
DAMMIT!
THIS WASN'T HOW IT WAS SUPPOSED TO HAPPEN.
YEAH, WELL, I COULDA TOLD YOU THINGS WEREN'T GOING TO WORK OUT LIKE YOU WANTED.
IN FACT, I DID TELL YOU.
KREIGER IS TOO DANGEROUS TO LIVE.
THE TALISMAN IS A THREAT TO ALL LIFE ON CYBERTRON. HE COULD DESTROY THE PLANET. OR WORSE.
THAT'S ALREADY PRETTY BAD.
YOU WERE JUST GOING TO KEEP THIS TO YOURSELF?
AND HOW CAN YOU BE SURE WHAT THE TALISMAN CAN DO?

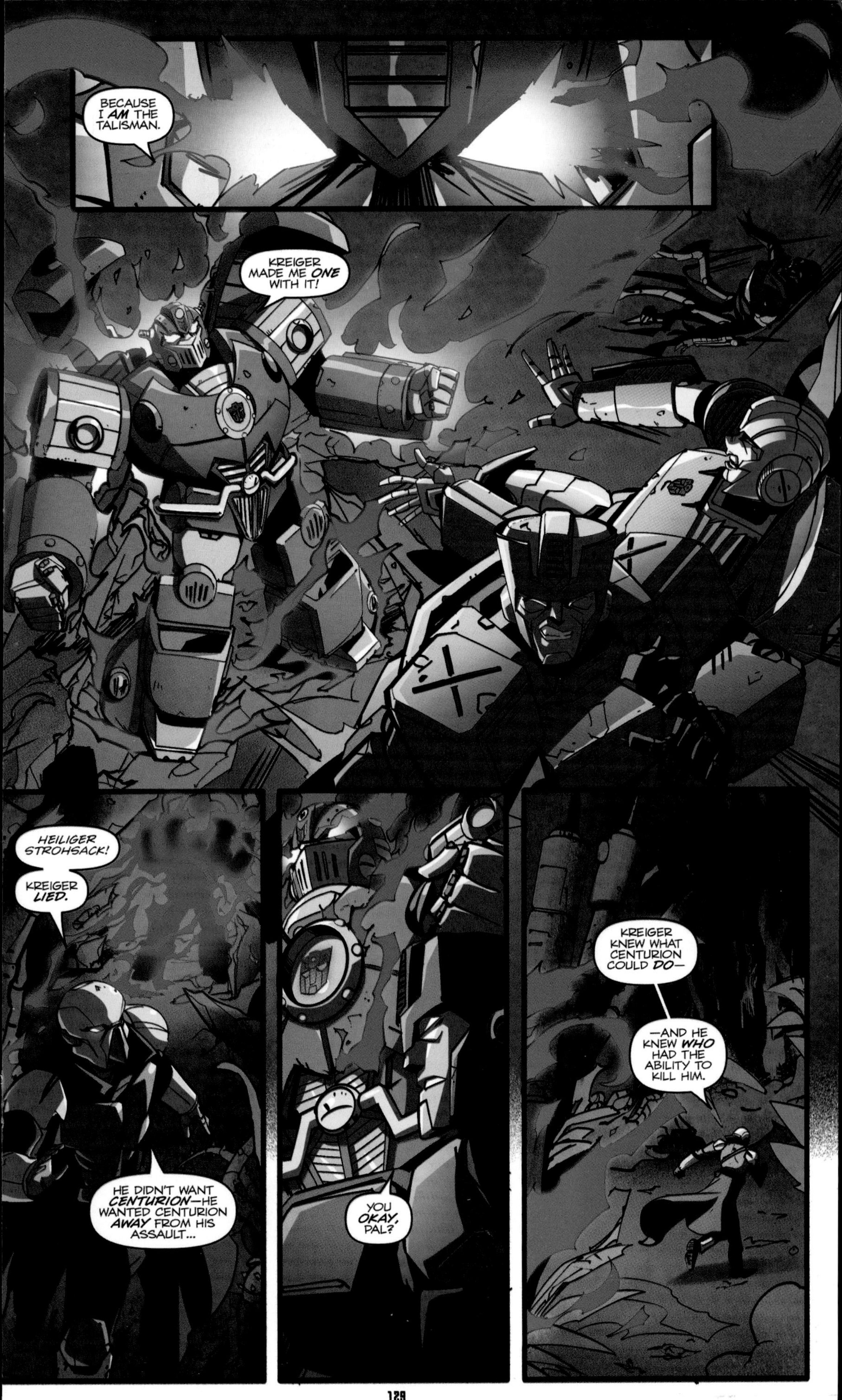
BECAUSE I AM THE TALISMAN.
KREIGER MADE ME ONE WITH IT!
HEILIGER STROHSACK!
KREIGER LIED.
HE DIDN'T WANT CENTURION—HE WANTED CENTURION AWAY FROM HIS ASSAULT...
YOU OKAY, PAL?
KREIGER KNEW WHAT CENTURION COULD DO—
—AND HE KNEW WHO HAD THE ABILITY TO KILL HIM.

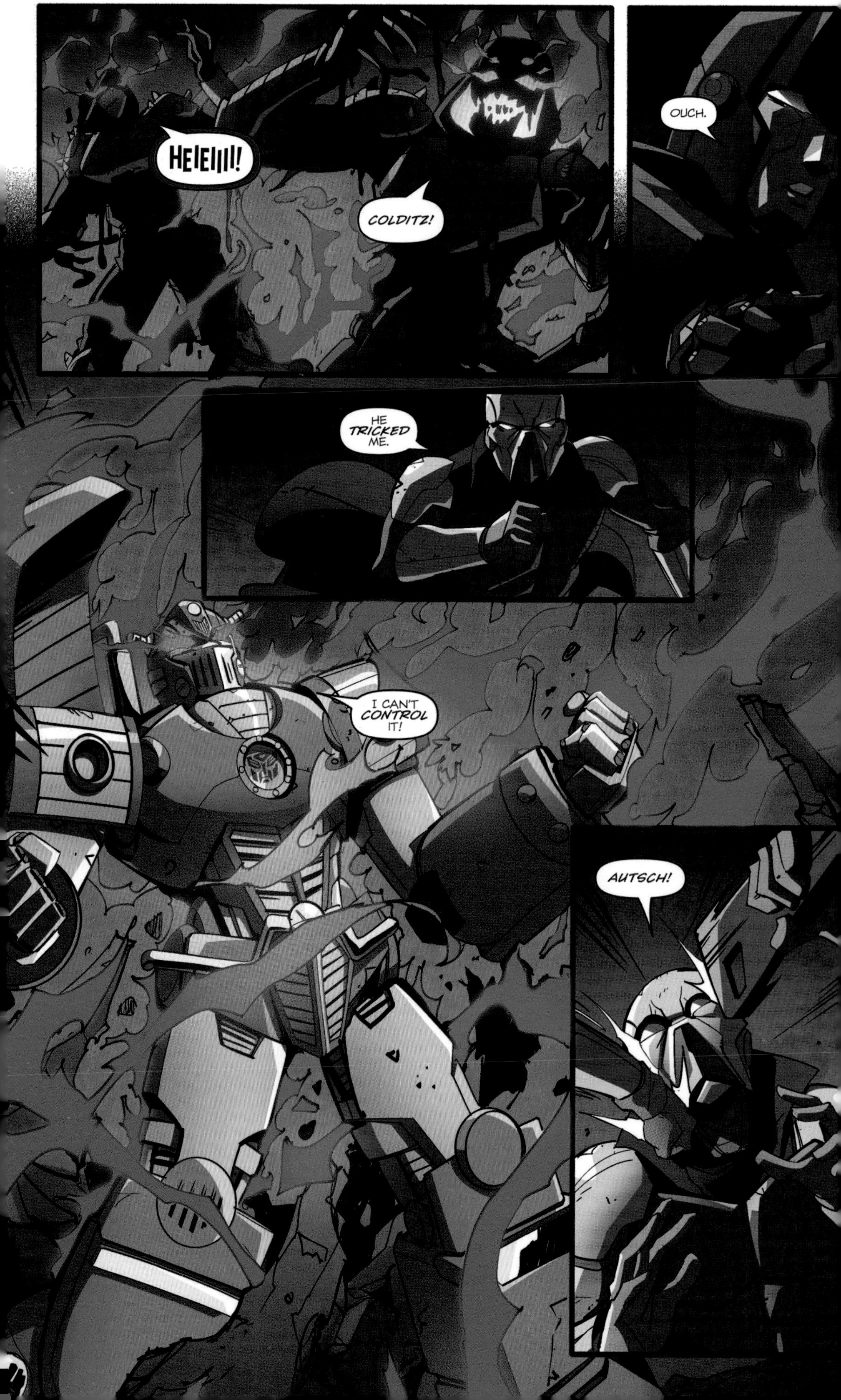
HEIEIIIII!
COLDITZ!
OUCH.
HE TRICKED ME.
I CAN'T CONTROL IT!
AUTSCH!

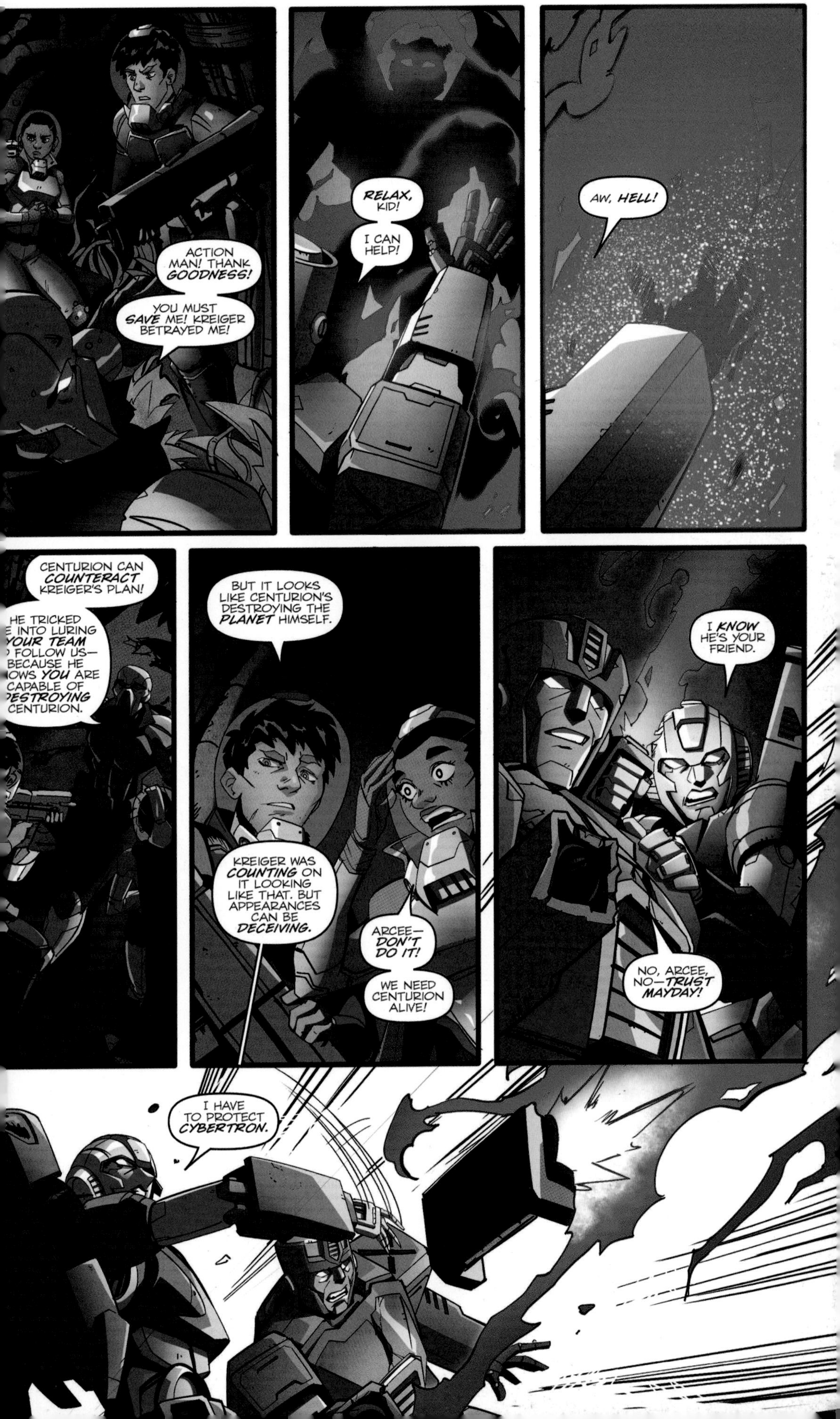
ACTION MAN! THANK GOODNESS!
YOU MUST SAVE ME! KREIGER BETRAYED ME!
RELAX, KID!
I CAN HELP!
AW, HELL!
CENTURION CAN COUNTERACT KREIGER'S PLAN!
HE TRICKED E INTO LURING YOUR TEAM O FOLLOW US— BECAUSE HE OWS YOU ARE CAPABLE OF DESTROYING CENTURION.
BUT IT LOOKS LIKE CENTURION'S DESTROYING THE PLANET HIMSELF.
KREIGER WAS COUNTING ON IT LOOKING LIKE THAT. BUT APPEARANCES CAN BE DECEIVING.
ARCEE— DON'T DO IT!
WE NEED CENTURION ALIVE!
I KNOW HE'S YOUR FRIEND.
NO, ARCEE, NO—TRUST MAYDAY!
I HAVE TO PROTECT CYBERTRON.

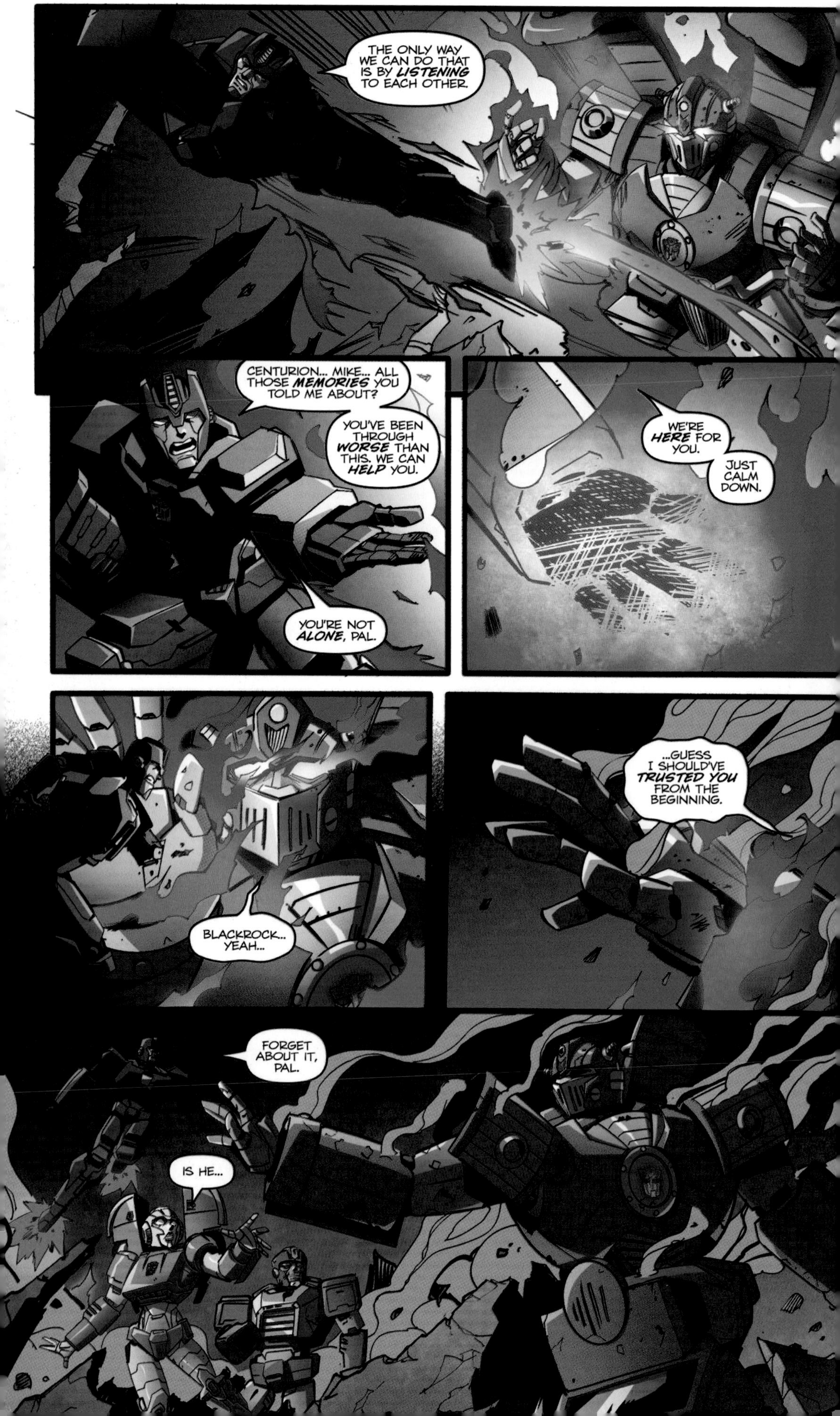
THE ONLY WAY WE CAN DO THAT IS BY LISTENING TO EACH OTHER.
CENTURION... MIKE... ALL THOSE MEMORIES YOU TOLD ME ABOUT?
YOU'VE BEEN THROUGH WORSE THAN THIS. WE CAN HELP YOU.
YOU'RE NOT ALONE, PAL.
WE'RE HERE FOR YOU.
JUST CALM DOWN.
BLACKROCK... YEAH...
...GUESS I SHOULD'VE TRUSTED YOU FROM THE BEGINNING.
FORGET ABOUT IT, PAL.
IS HE...

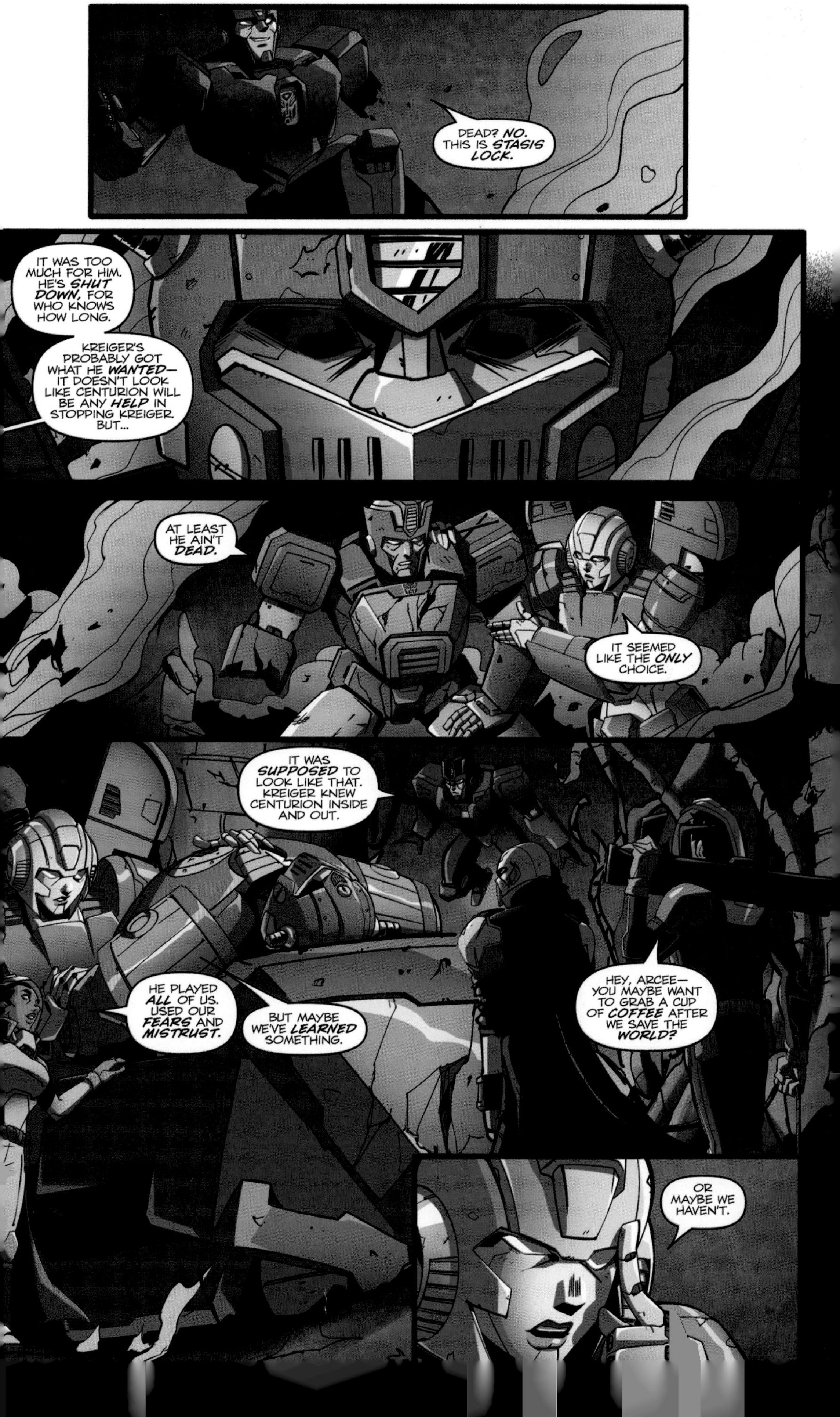
DEAD? NO. THIS IS STASIS LOCK.
IT WAS TOO MUCH FOR HIM. HE'S SHUT DOWN, FOR WHO KNOWS HOW LONG.
KREIGER'S PROBABLY GOT WHAT HE WANTED—IT DOESN'T LOOK LIKE CENTURION WILL BE ANY HELP IN STOPPING KREIGER. BUT...
AT LEAST HE AIN'T DEAD.
IT SEEMED LIKE THE ONLY CHOICE.
IT WAS SUPPOSED TO LOOK LIKE THAT. KREIGER KNEW CENTURION INSIDE AND OUT.
HE PLAYED ALL OF US. USED OUR FEARS AND MISTRUST.
BUT MAYBE WE'VE LEARNED SOMETHING.
HEY, ARCEE—YOU MAYBE WANT TO GRAB A CUP OF COFFEE AFTER WE SAVE THE WORLD?
OR MAYBE WE HAVEN'T.

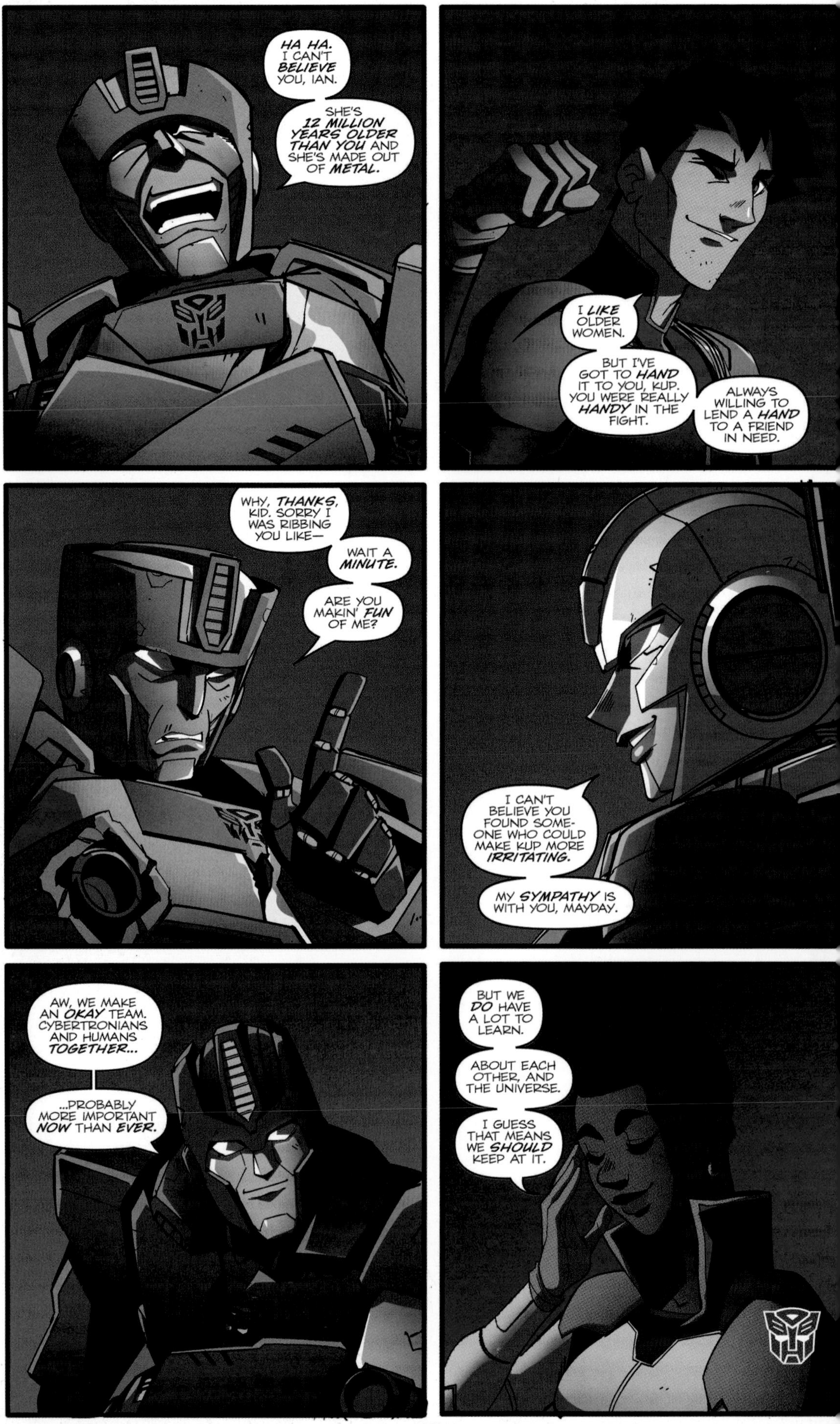
HA HA. I CAN'T BELIEVE YOU, IAN.
SHE'S 12 MILLION YEARS OLDER THAN YOU AND SHE'S MADE OUT OF METAL.
I LIKE OLDER WOMEN.
BUT I'VE GOT TO HAND IT TO YOU, KUP. YOU WERE REALLY HANDY IN THE FIGHT.
ALWAYS WILLING TO LEND A HAND TO A FRIEND IN NEED.
WHY, THANKS, KID. SORRY I WAS RIBBING YOU LIKE—
WAIT A MINUTE.
ARE YOU MAKIN' FUN OF ME?
I CAN'T BELIEVE YOU FOUND SOME-ONE WHO COULD MAKE KUP MORE IRRITATING.
MY SYMPATHY IS WITH YOU, MAYDAY.
AW, WE MAKE AN OKAY TEAM. CYBERTRONIANS AND HUMANS TOGETHER...
...PROBABLY MORE IMPORTANT NOW THAN EVER.
BUT WE DO HAVE A LOT TO LEARN.
ABOUT EACH OTHER, AND THE UNIVERSE.
I GUESS THAT MEANS WE SHOULD KEEP AT IT.

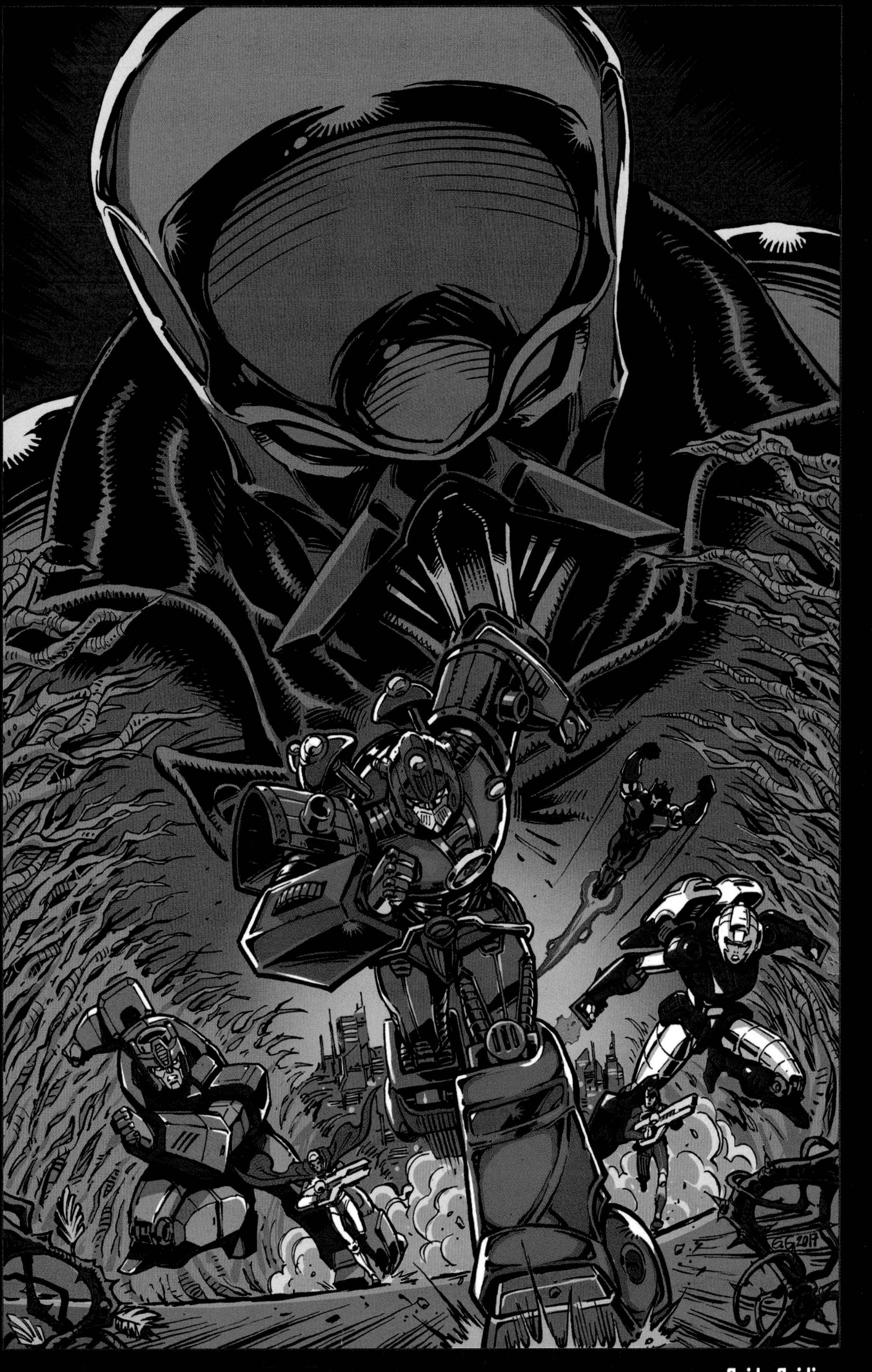

// art by **Guido Guidi**

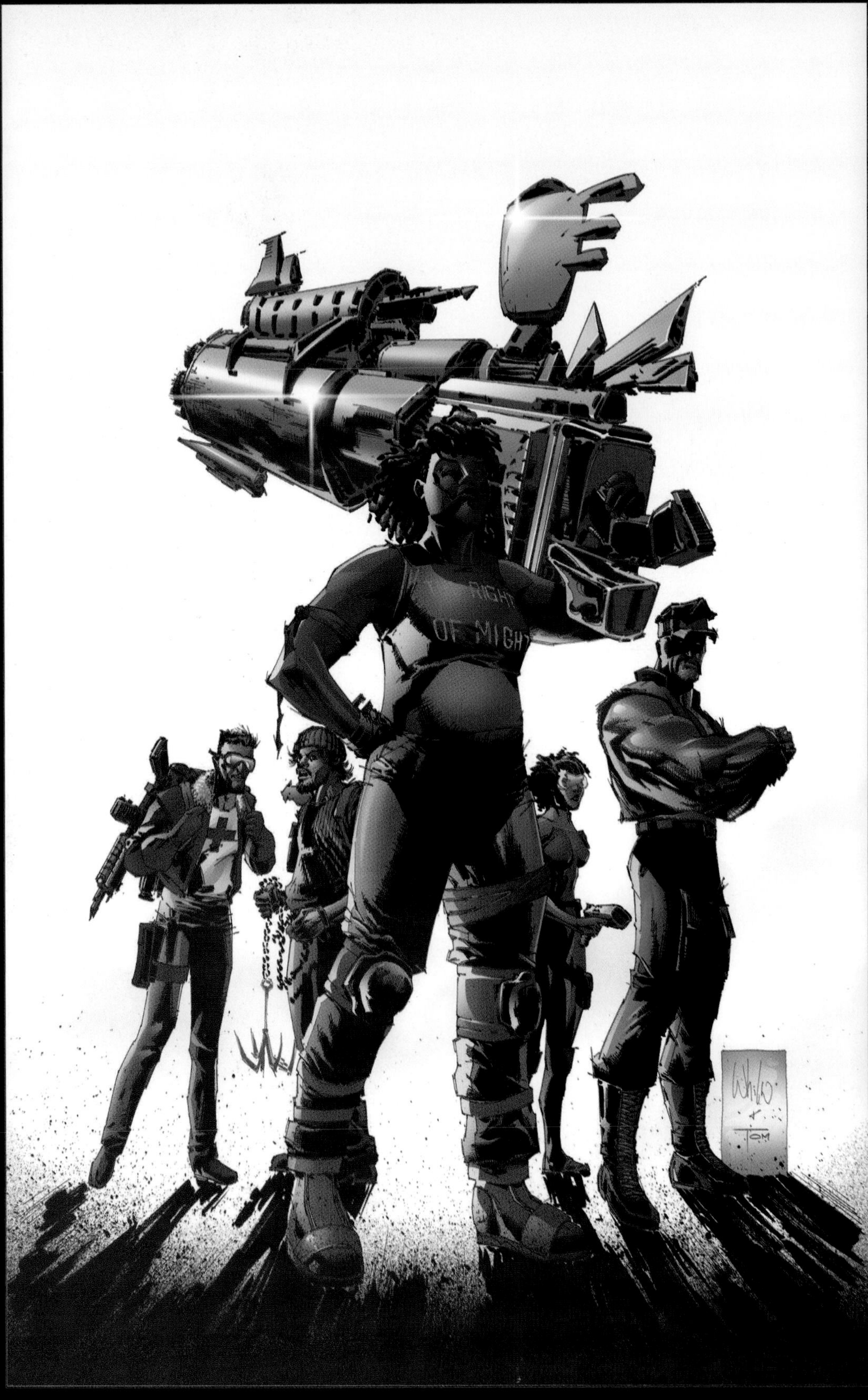
RIGHT
OF MIGHT

// art by **Whilce Portacio**
// colors by **Thomas Deer**

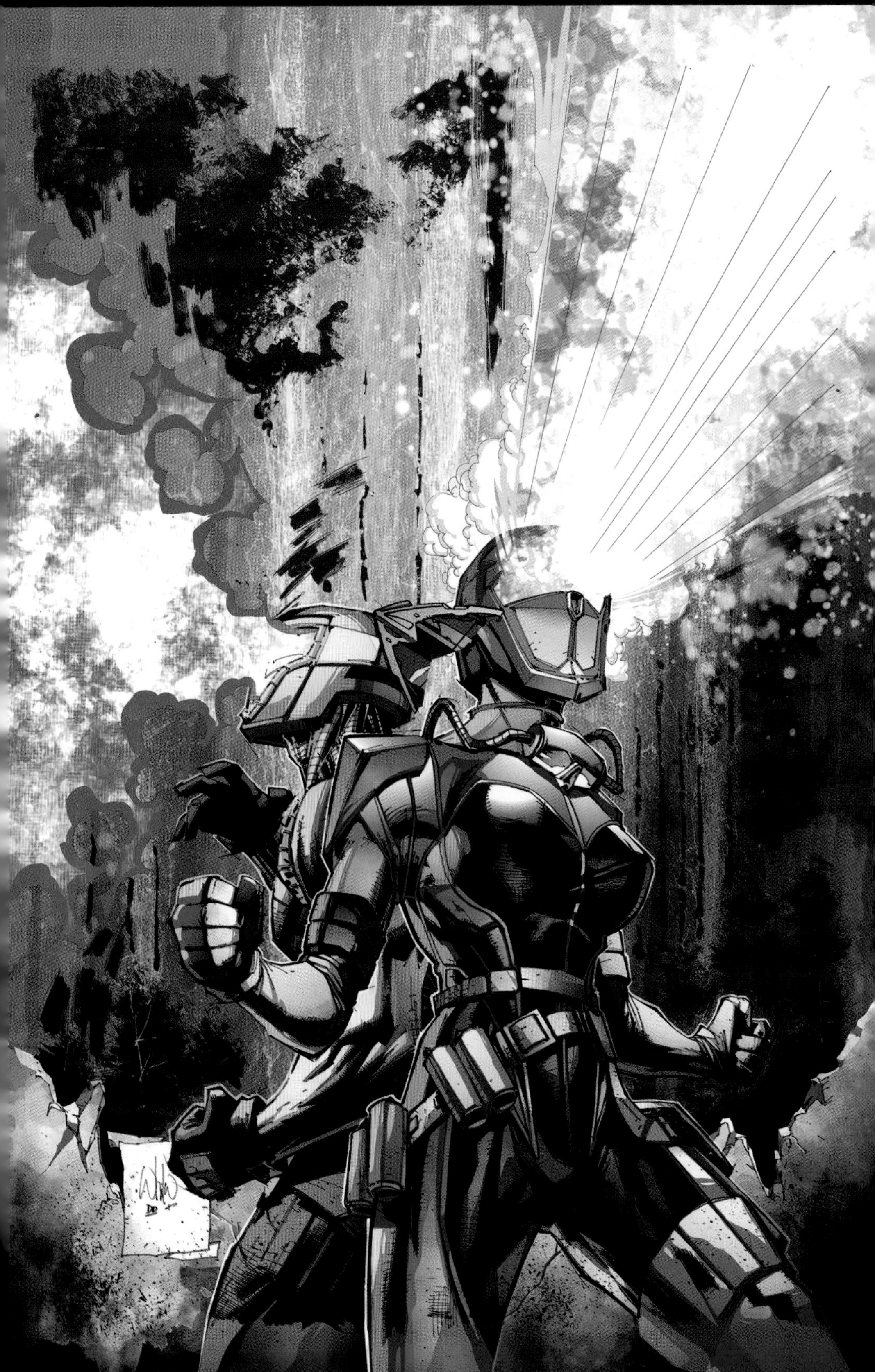

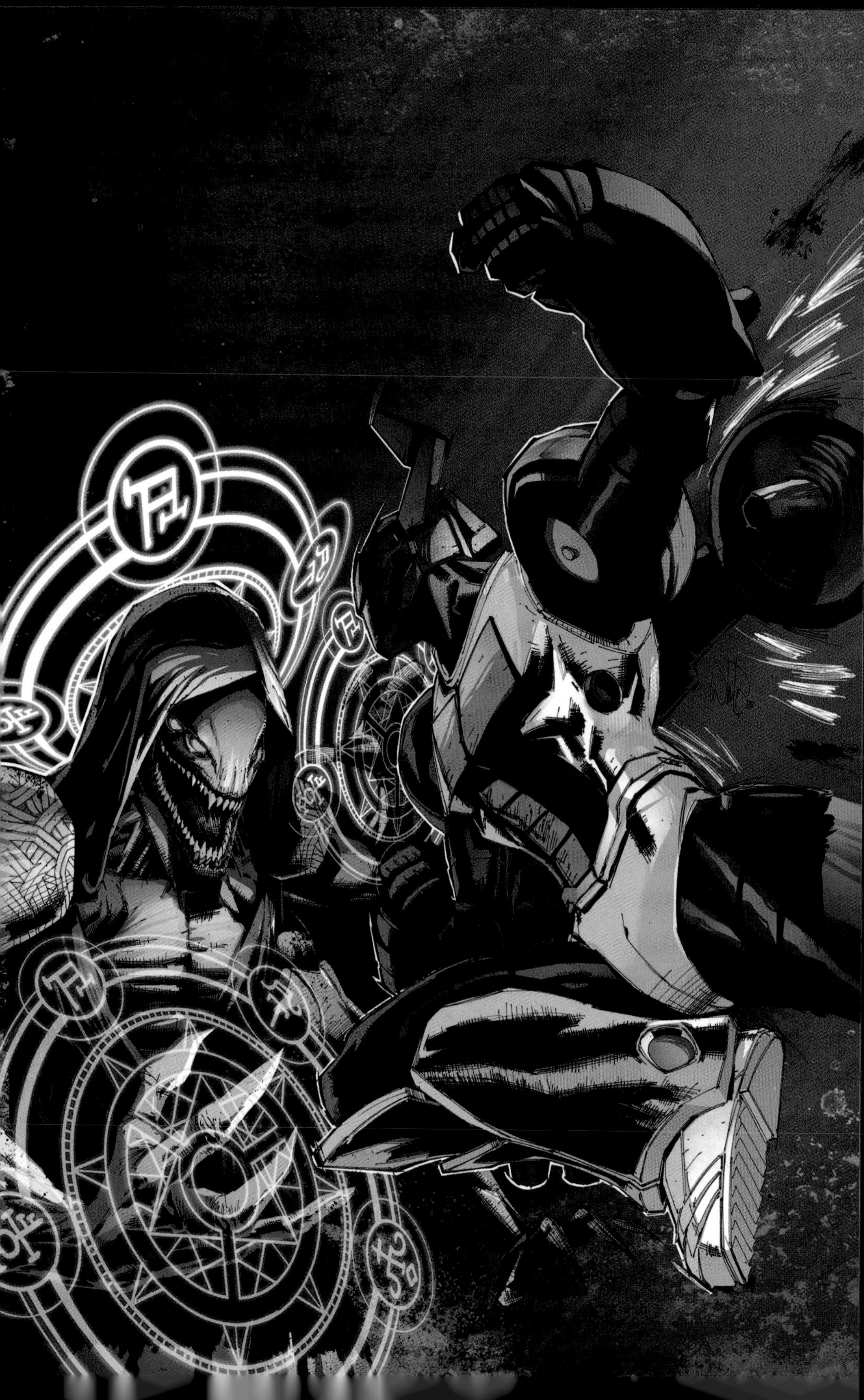

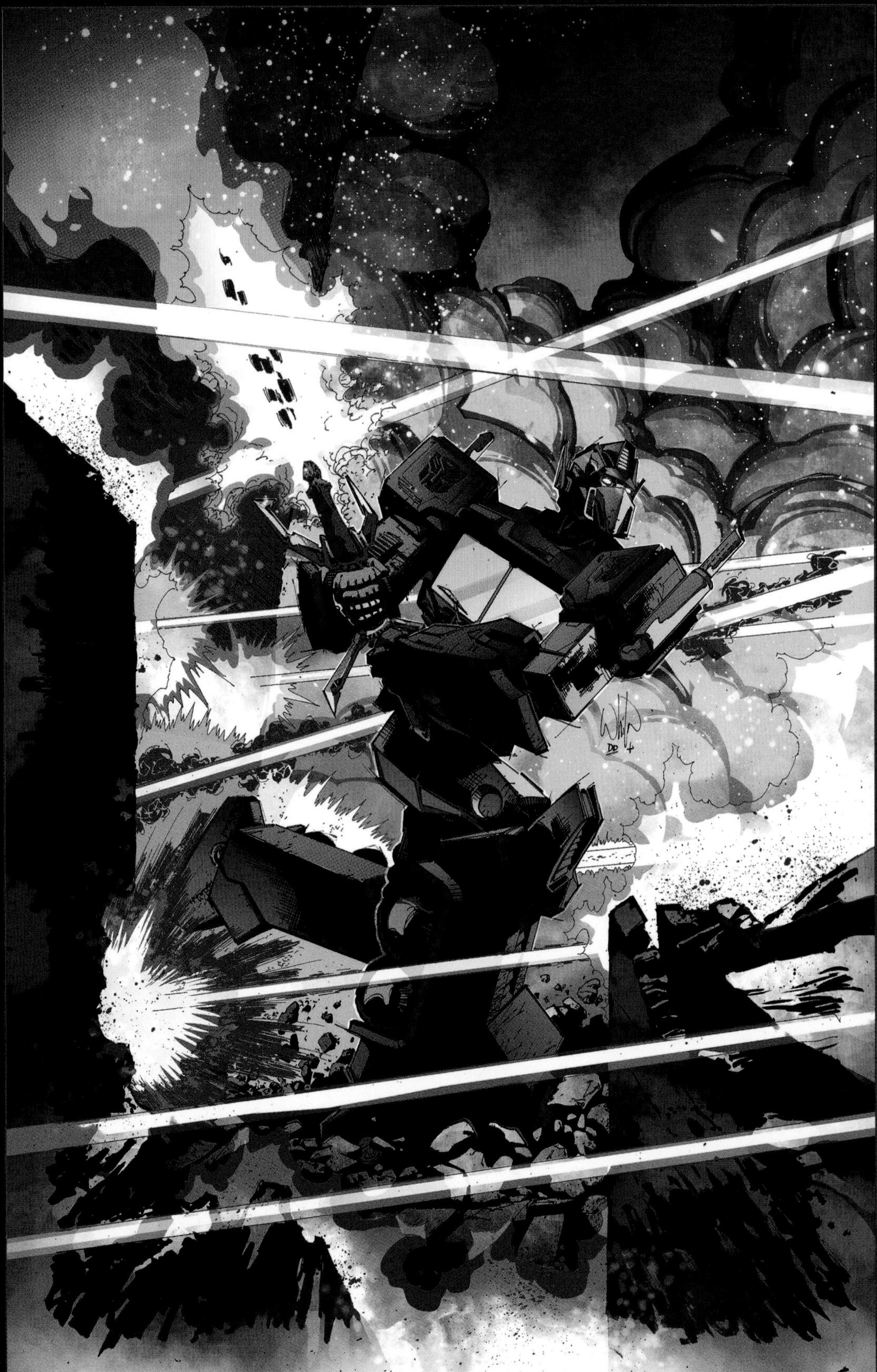

// art by Whilce Portacio
// colors by David Garcia Cruz

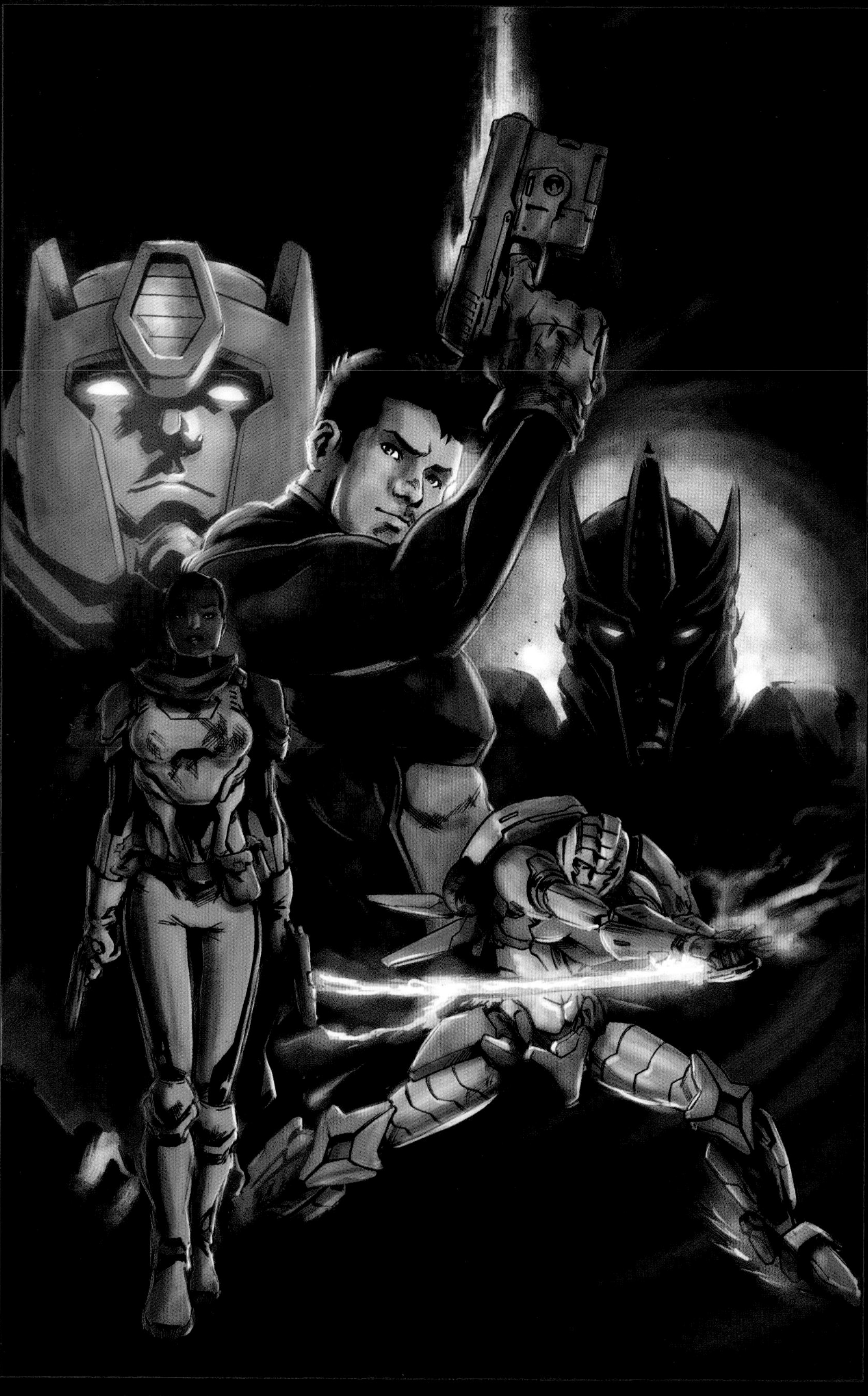

// art by Paolo Villanelli
// colors by John-Paul Bove

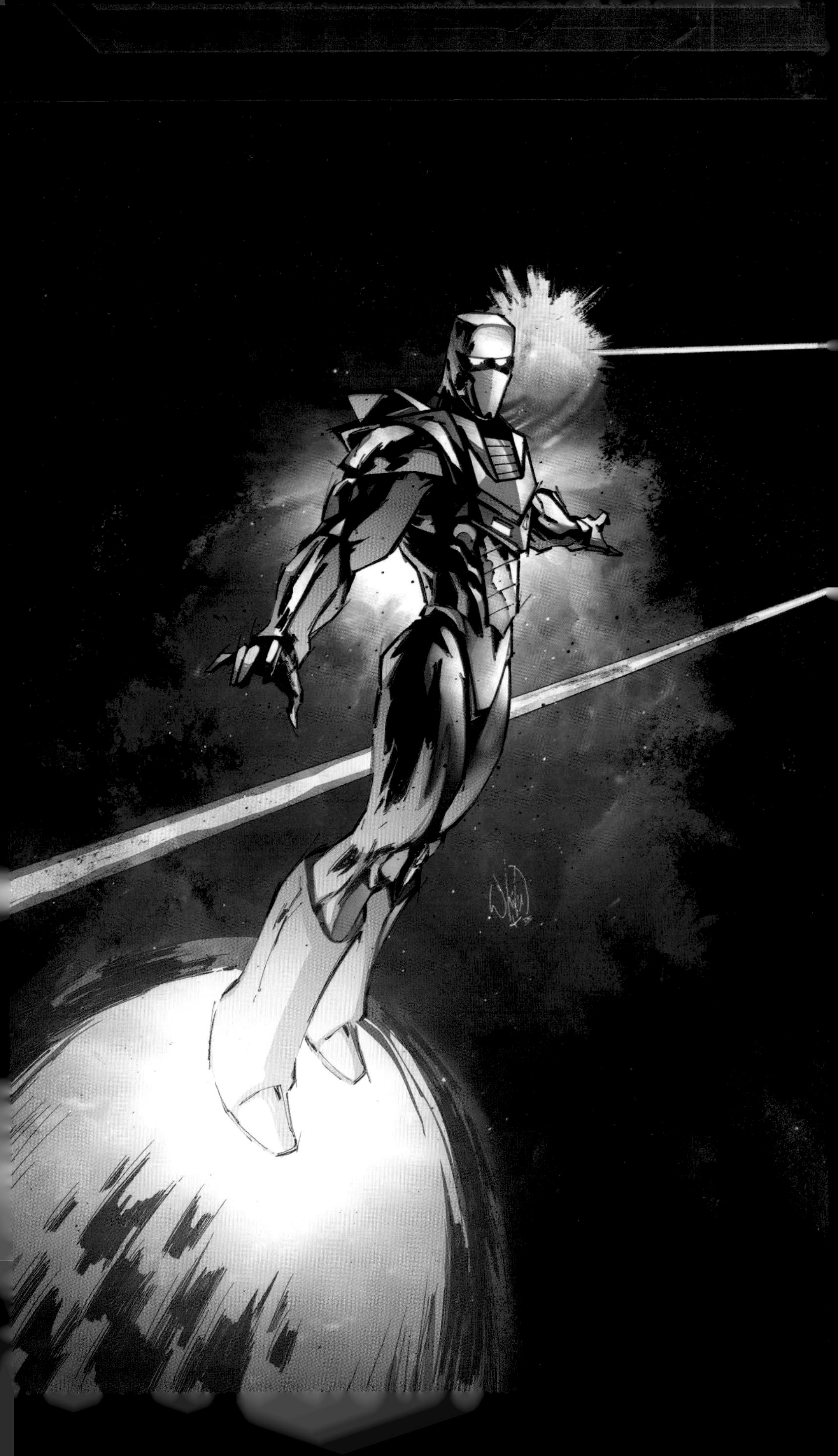

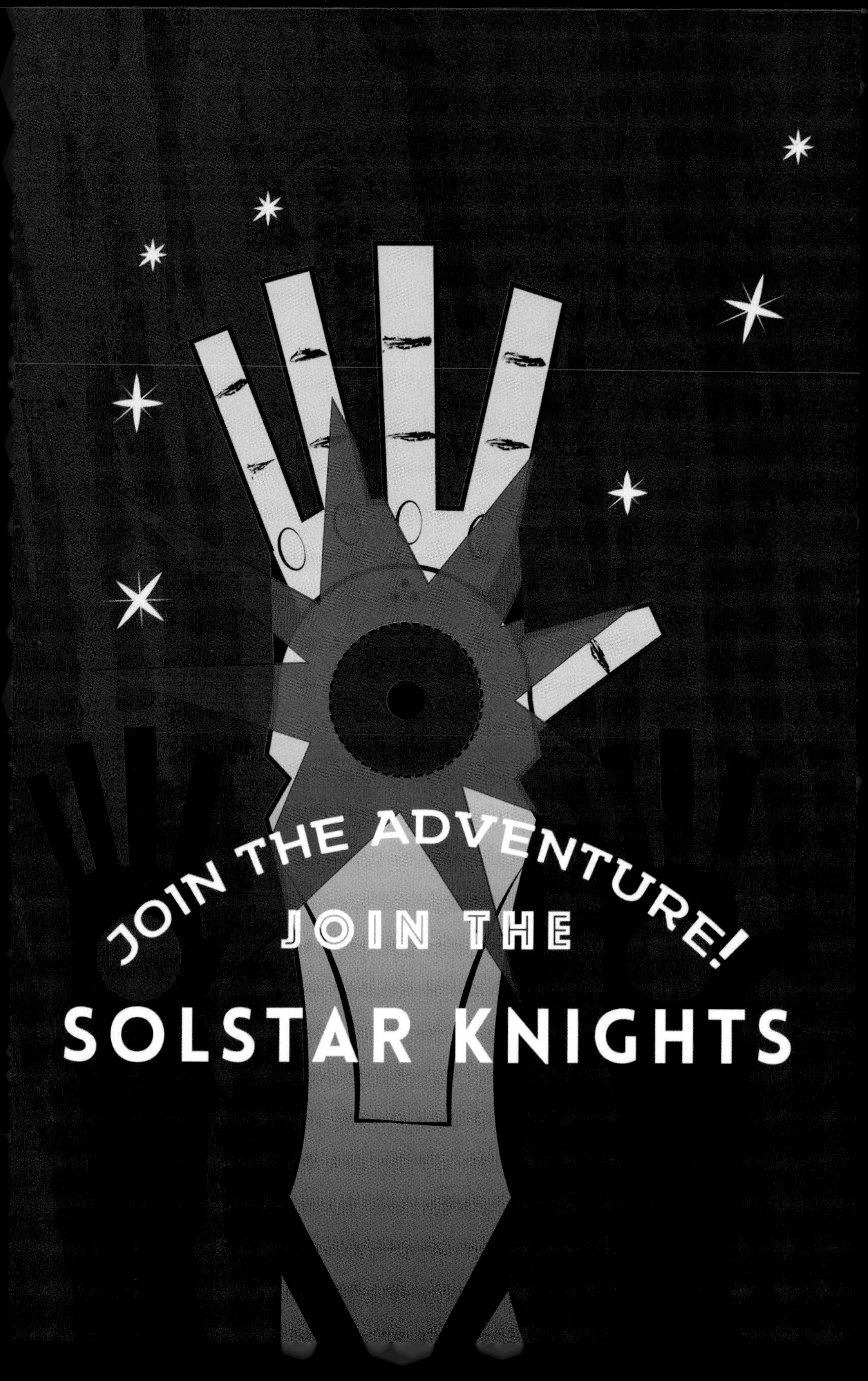
JOIN THE ADVENTURE!
JOIN THE
SOLSTAR KNIGHTS

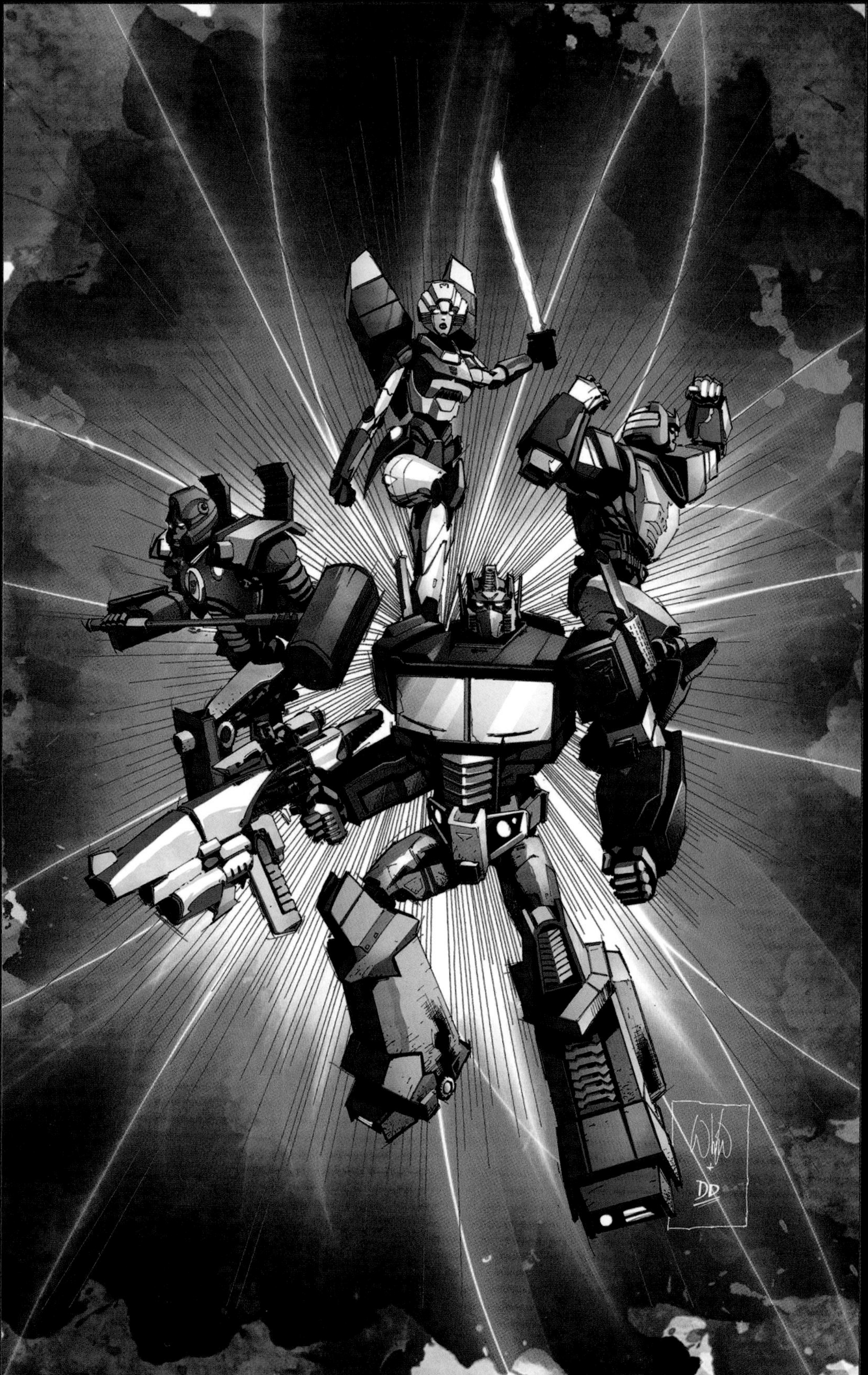

// art by Whilce Portacio
// colors by David Garcia Cruz

TRANSFORMERS G.I. JOE

FIRST STRIKE

CHAMPIONS

G.I. JOE

MASK
MOBILE ARMORED STRIKE KOMMAND

ROM

MICRONAUTS

TRANSFORMERS

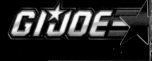

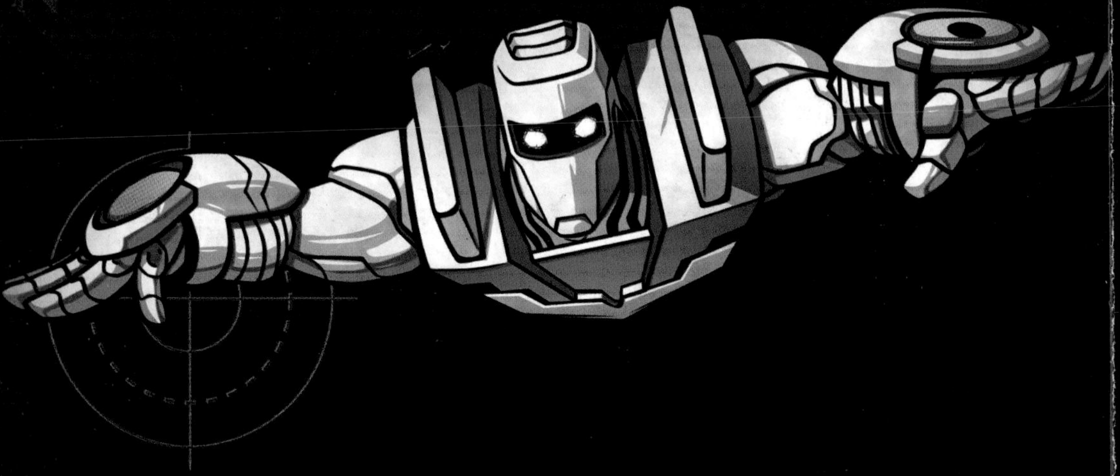

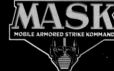